TWO EGGS AND A LEMON
My Four Years In Myanmar

Joanna MacLean

Marrowstone Press   Seattle

Two Eggs and a Lemon by Joanna MacLean© 2016
www.joannamaclean.com

Marrowstone Press© 2016
All rights reserved
www.marrowstonepress.com

Book Design by Marrowstone Press
Text set in Adobe Caslon Pro

ISBN: 978-0-692-53925-5

I would like to thank Wendy Goldman-Rohm and the Chiang Mai writer's group for setting me on the path to write my stories.

To my friends and colleagues who gallantly agreed to read the manuscript in its several versions, namely: Wivina Belmonte, Shari Jean Brown, Maude Fröberg, Lois Haslam, Sylvia Ladame, Christophe Lanord, Michèle Mercier, Uma Narayanan, Lasse Norgaard, Rosemarie North and Brian Smith, as well as Sandy and Kyaw Kyaw from my Myanmar team, many thanks for your useful comments and suggestions.

For the more detailed editorial advice I am indebted to Glenys Bean, Heidi North-Bailey and especially to Leila Magarò for her encouragement, enthusiasm, and support for my writing.

Credit is also due to Heikki Väätämöinen for the use of his photo as the image for '*Chapter Ten* Office Days.'

All other photos used are my own.

For the invaluable assistance in the layout, graphics, editing and technical assistance to nurse this book to publication, I heartily thank Galen Garwood of Marrowstone Press.

Joanna MacLean

*I'd like to dedicate this book to the people of Myanmar
who were always open to my questions and accepting
of my camera lens, and most particularly
to the friends and colleagues who made my years
in their beautiful country so memorable.*

Numbers = Chapters

Table of Contents

Introduction i
Chapter One Dinner at the Strand ~ 1
Chapter Two The First Kiss ~ 9
Chapter Three You'll Get Used To It ~ 19
Chapter Four Accommodating the Boss ~ 27
Chapter Five Crossing the Bridge ~ 35
Chapter Six Health Matters ~ 45
Chapter Seven A Cabbage, a Cyclone ~ 57
Chapter Eight The Glass Factory ~ 67
Chapter Nine At Home ~ 77
Chapter Ten Office Days ~ 87
Chapter Eleven The Tourist Triangle ~ 99
Chapter Twelve Motorbike Manoeuvres ~ 109
Chapter Thirteen Weekend Wandering ~ 119
Chapter Fourteen Riding the River ~ 127
Chapter Fifteen Dust and Ash ~ 133
Chapter Sixteen The Big Splash ~ 151
Chapter Seventeen Farewell Ma Marlar ~ 159
Chapter Eighteen One Hundred Days ~ 169
Chapter Nineteen Playing the Game ~ 175
Chapter Twenty The Fisherman's Son ~ 183
Chapter Twenty-One Cardboard Box Stories ~ 189
Chapter Twenty-Two Golden Rock ~ 197
Chapter Twenty-Three I Moved the Flowers ~ 209
Chapter Twenty-Four Marionettes and Collaint ~ 223
Chapter Twenty-Five Naga New Year ~ 233
Chapter Twenty-Six Down in the Delta ~ 243
Chapter Twenty-Seven The Kidnap ~ 253
Chapter Twenty-Eight The Wicker Basket ~ 263
Epilogue ~ 269

INTRODUCTION

It has been universally acknowledged that bad news makes better press. Stories of death and destruction, oppression, conflict and disaster, and ensuing miraculous recoveries with heroic actions are immediately and continuously beamed across the world via photos and video while *good* news stories more often end up relegated to the back pages or reported only on a slow news day.

Yet everyday, everywhere in this difficult world, there are people, often nameless, who venture beyond the boundaries of courage to make the lives of others more bearable. They intervene in life and death situations, in wars, natural disasters and in political and personal turmoil, driven by faith, by compassion, or simply by the awareness of what must be done. Sometimes they act alone, sometimes within the framework of an organisation, charged with duties and responsibilities that call for dedication and action.

And for these individuals and communities who struggle to care for those in need, to improve lives by providing clean water and health care, to fight against stigma and racism, bigotry and poverty, but who are seldom given credit or accolades, their stories deserve to be told.

In the course of my three decades of work with the International Red Cross and Red Crescent Movement, I have had the privilege of meeting and admiring many such unsung heroes across the world—men and women who put their lives on the line daily, facing imminent danger, and who stand strong in their beliefs and actions when everything and everyone is against them. I have listened to them. I've read their stories, often told with humility and humour. I am in awe of their courage and dedication.

I must clarify that I am not, in any shape or form, one of them. My own career-path has been much more sedate, though perhaps no less interesting. Within this great organisation, I've had the opportunity to work with young volunteers, to assist them in developing health and disaster response programmes, to advise presidents and staff of national Red Cross and Red Crescent Societies on everything from policies to accounting, from humanitarian law to communications. I've designed training courses on the ethics of humanitarian work and the necessary discipline of disaster operations; I've masterminded global campaigns and events. Throughout it all, I have been privileged to work alongside some truly great and dedicated people from all walks of life.

And perhaps, because of the inspiring actions of others, I chose for the final chapter of my Red Cross Red Crescent life, to once again work 'in the field.'

So in 2002, when Myanmar was offered to me as a posting, I did not hesitate. I jumped at the chance to work and live in that most mysterious, closed, and notorious country of South East Asia; it was a last mission before my retirement. Quite fittingly, it would not only be a wonderful opportunity but also my last challenge...or so I thought.

At the time, there was only a small team of the International Federation of Red Cross and Red Crescent Societies in Yangon. Their function was that of working with the leadership and staff of Myanmar Red Cross Society to assist in the development of health and social programmes and in the field of disaster response. There were few funds available to pursue anything more than basic programmes and part of my brief was to bring new donors and support to this country.

My adventure in Myanmar thus began mid 2002 and would last nearly four years.

As the months then years passed, I gradually learnt more and more about this country, a complex nation full of contradictions: beauty and honour with dark secrets in abundance. I came to appreciate and love its people who treasure their history and their traditions, yet who strive to improve and build for their future against almost overwhelming odds. I found among them heroes and heroines, mostly unknown to the outside world; they guard their country's heritage and care for those most in need. I found, as well, examples of corruption and violence toward ethnic minorities and toward those who dared to speak out against the ruling party.

At the time, the press coverage and available documentation about Myanmar was largely negative, focussing on the atrocities, on refugees fleeing for their lives across the borders, and the insane demands and measures of the army. We learned of triads involved in drug and sex trafficking into neighbouring countries. Illicit funds further fuelled the decades long armed struggles of minority groups for their autonomy.

It was more difficult to find in depth information about important social and cultural aspects or even the routines of everyday life; or indeed to find anyone from the 'outside' world, beyond rare Myanmar expats or specialized anthropologists, who were at all interested in the positive aspects.

More recently, the country is opening up. There is now a great influx of capital and tourism. We see a resurgence of businessmen, politicians and advisers of all hues. Press coverage and access to information have been revolutionized.

Today's stories tell of tourist opportunities, hotels springing up everywhere, of traffic jams on previously uncrowded, tree-lined avenues, of trendy bars and the renovation of old buildings, of new fashion icons and dozens of new magazines and journals. There is talk of progress, of the fledgling democracy after the landslide election victory of the National League for Democracy (NLD) in 2015, more freedom of the press, the opening up of new ventures in telecommunications, manufacturing, and all types of industry, while the hotels crawl with men in suits making deals.

Adversely, because of this loosening of the military stranglehold on the different and divergent ethnic and political groups, one also hears of reemerging, age-old conflicts and animosities. New social and environmental issues are also appearing on the horizon. The conflict in the far north Kachin State, the longest running conflict in the world, is unresolved; the Muslim 'Rohingya' people in the Rakhine State are once again uprooted. Previously unrecorded heights of religious conflict are in the news almost daily. Corruption and the rapid increase in tourism is putting pressure on delicate ecological landscapes. And, as elsewhere, the rich are getting richer while the poor are trapped in circumstances from which they struggle to free themselves.

With my insight into the country, I could write about the still relentlessly strong hand of the military, albeit a little more disguised, or about the appalling conditions in the slums. I could write about the 'buying up of large tracts of the cities and country by the Chinese, or about the dilapidated infrastructure and the sorry state of the education system. But many journalists, academics, and politicians are already focussing on these aspects. Articles and reports from humanitarian groups abound as well as pressure groups for all ethnic struggles. According to the 'globalised' tourist industry trend, tourist information is now widely available, touting the best hotels and restaurants and the sexiest travel guides.

What is still lacking today in journals and literature is the voice of the people of Myanmar, their life stories beyond the cities, beyond the thin surface layer of globalization, accounts of their complicated history and culture, of the rhythmic pattern of their lives, their hopes and dreams, the very essence of who they are, what makes them 'tick'.

It is these stories I would like to tell. Stories of a country and people I grew to love and respect.

The descriptions, opinions, and experiences in this book are all mine, but I am not its central character. That role belongs to the people of Myanmar. I am merely an observer with as little importance in this country's story as a grain of sand on the edge of a vast ocean.

I write about what I have seen and have taken part in. I write about the spirit of religion and traditions, the humour and sadness in people's lives, the birth of a child, the death of a colleague. I write about the ordination of a boy into the monkhood, about art and superstitions, the evanescence of ancient ways of life, the aftermath of terrible disasters and the relentless scourge of disease and poverty.

Mine is a different story, obtained by delving beyond the negative sensationalism of the press, a story which will add fine detail to a greater picture, rounding out and putting into a more human context the readily available information streaming in from the media.

I choose to write about and for the often forgotten and unacknowledged communities of families and individuals who struggle and stumble and fall...yet who stop to help each other.

What I hope to share are the multiple facets of the lives of people too often neglected by the media. Herein are glimpses of those aspects which are perhaps important only to the few individuals involved, but which, when woven together, reveal a far more complex tapestry. It is a fascinating picture of a beautiful country with its cross-roads of humanity since time immemorial.

Chapter One
Dinner At The Strand

Evening is falling in Yangon. I slowly make my way from my office to the Strand Hotel, savouring the steamy heat, the noise, and even the dubious fragrances of this city I have come to love.

So much is familiar on this stretch of Strand Road – the restaurant where I had lunch on my first work day, the shrine in the shady old tree, the water urn on its rickety wooden stand with two metal cups from which anyone may drink, and my favourite street stall selling noodles, pungent with fish sauce. I pass the red brick façade of the General Post Office, the letter writers plying their trade on the pavement, and the solid white front of the British Embassy where students wait by the side door for evening language class.

I step back as a lorry, belching black exhaust, rumbles past, loaded with huge teak logs precariously secured by metal chains and narrow side struts. Trishaws crawl alongside, carrying their passengers homeward, the riders laboriously straining to keep pace. Dilapidated taxis, green snub-nosed buses, open sided trucks and old cars vie for space on the wide avenue. Clusters of office workers spill out onto the pavement, chattering off to meet friends or returning home to their families. Three young women with matching uniforms and identical lunch tins, hold hands and laugh, braving the traffic to reach their bus stop.

For a moment I imagine how the road would have appeared a century ago under colonial rule, when the Armenian Sarkie brothers established the 'Strand', sister hotel to their already famous 'Raffles' in Singapore. At that time, the Strand overlooked a park that sloped down to the river where passenger and merchant ships docked. Even now, hemmed in by snarled traffic, a disused railway line, dilapidated fences and square warehouses hiding the river, the hotel manages to maintain its dignity as the 'Old Lady of Rangoon'.

Tonight, I've been asked to give a presentation to a group of American tourists freshly arrived from Singapore. I pause by the potted palms under the hotel's colonnaded portico to talk with the postcard touts, a girl of about twelve and her two younger brothers. This is their fiercely protected territory; no one is spared their well-practiced sales pitch. They tell me about their day and I worry for their future, mostly for the girl. She is very pretty and there are those who would profit from these young girls, already world-wise, flashing their smiles and giving cheek to tourists and Burmese alike. But in truth, they are just children, forced to grow up too quickly.

The doorman watches our exchange then greets me warmly, holding the door open. I step into another world – cool, calm, elegant. The black and white tiled lobby's huge fans whirl lazily, wafting a breeze around the graceful pillars, over the luxuriously arranged rattan armchairs and their occupants. A classical guitarist, seated to one side, deftly fingers a complicated melody, shyly glancing over the tourists as they sip their champagne.

At the far end of the lobby, I spot my contact, Ma Phyu Su, talking with a slight young Singaporean she introduces as Derek, the tour leader. He launches into an explanation of the evening's programme, immediately telling me I shouldn't talk for more than thirty minutes as the group is easily bored. As I set up my computer, he loudly voices his own opinions about the country, oblivious to the hotel staff putting final touches to tables around him, their ears certainly not in their pockets.

"How many times have you led a tour in Myanmar?" I ask him.

"This is my first time. But I've read a lot about the country and briefed the group about what to expect," he responds glibly.

Behind his back Ma Phyu Su rolls her eyes and I smile at her.

Over dinner, I join the guests and listen to tales of their travels so far and learn their itinerary for the next few days. It's the standard tour – a day in Yangon, a flight to Heho and on by car to Inle Lake, visits to Mandalay and Bagan, then back to Yangon. As the plates are cleared, with only dessert and coffee to come, Derek introduces me as this evening's speaker, adding, "I've asked her to keep it brief, as we have an early start tomorrow and I know you are all tired."

"I'll try to stick to the time limit," I begin, "however, I do love a challenge, just as I love his country,"

I look at Derek, "so please clock me at thirty minutes. But for anyone interested, I'm free to stay as long as you would like."

That clarified, I continue, "This beautiful hotel was opened in 1901. For the Americans among you, you might know that it was the year President McKinley was assassinated, and who was succeeded by Teddy Roosevelt. In Britain, Queen Victoria died and Edward VII ascended to the throne. Significantly for me and an interesting but tenuous link between my organisation and Myanmar, it was also the year that Henry Dunant, founder of the International Red Cross, was awarded the Nobel Prize for Peace. Exactly ninety years later, in 1991, the Nobel Peace Prize will be awarded to a Burmese woman whom everyone knows as 'The Lady'.

Even in this room, I dare not use her name."

"I trust you understand that while working here for the Red Cross, I can neither talk politics nor answer 'political' questions. I've read the same books and articles as you and I have my own opinions; but it is not appropriate for me to share them. I'd rather talk to you about other aspects of this beautiful country, its rich heritage, the diverse cultural traditions and, most of all, about its people who have lost their common voice to the outside world."

I see many nodding their agreement. I go on to tell them a little about myself and my work here in Myanmar, my last posting for the Red Cross after nearly thirty years, having worked first in my own country of New Zealand and, since 1980, for the International Federation of Red Cross and Red Crescent Societies (IFRC) in Geneva, as well as in Africa, the Caribbean, Central America, and Asia.

I elaborate, "My position here in Myanmar is Head of Delegation for the IFRC. Our job is to support the Myanmar Red Cross (MRCS) in developing its systems, improving disaster response mechanisms and strengthening health and social programmes. We help train staff and volunteers, while also acting as liaison between them and their donors. It's surely the most fascinating but probably also the most frustrating post of my career."

"However," I continue, "I am not here to talk about the Red Cross, but to share with you images and stories of this country that I think will enchant and perhaps surprise you. I recommend you keep an open mind during your trip. See for yourself. Although what you have read is certainly real, often very disturbing, it is only a part of the whole story."

I begin my 'show and tell' – 'Myanmar, Images and Perceptions' with a map and a few facts, beginning at the foot of the Himalayas in the north to the tropical archipelago in the far south with their seasons, wet and hot. Really hot. I touch on there being a population of fifty-two million with five million in Yangon. I explain about the one hundred and thirty-five different ethnic groups with more than one hundred languages. I comment on the average life expectancy of just sixty-one years, that over seventy per cent of the population live in rural areas. I report on the relatively high literacy rate for both men and women, adding that forty per cent do not have access to health services and thirty per cent lack adequate water supplies and sanitation.

I talk about the mighty Ayeyarwady River, navigable for an incredible 1,500 of its 2000 kilometers, about its riverboats, the biggest inland flotilla in the world until all 600 vessels were scuppered by order of the flotilla company to stop the advance of the Japanese Army up the river in the Second World War. I tell them that before the war, Burma, with its fertile delta, was the largest world exporter of high quality rice, adding that almost half the country is still forested with huge stands of teak; jade, rubies, sapphires, as well as other riches of the earth, are still plentiful today.

"I am fortunate," I tell them, "because through my work I have visited most regions, many beyond the reach of tourists. This is a fascinating country, rich in history and art, with a beautiful people who maintain their traditions, their Buddhist beliefs influencing both their philosophy and their everyday lives."

My slide presentation begins with a group of nuns in their pink robes, the wary eyes of a novice monk as his head is shaved, an old woman giving early morning alms to a line of monks, a holy man in white and a hermit in his tall leather hat, a group of girls walking on the platform of the great Shwedagon Pagoda, its vast stupa clad in bamboo scaffolding for re-gilding.

I reflect on the importance of Buddhism in Myanmar, how it runs like a golden thread through daily life. Every special day starts with a visit to the pagoda, children are educated in the monasteries, which become shelters when disaster strikes. The Buddhist concept of nothing being permanent and everything having its time can be comforting.

"Perhaps," I add, "It has allowed people to keep their sanity and sense of humour through decades of military rule."

Stability also comes from strong family bonds, several generations often living together. I show images of fathers with young children proudly perched on their shoulders, mothers preparing children for school, painting their faces with *thanakha*, the ubiquitous paste used as sunscreen and decoration, boys and girls carrying younger siblings on their backs, a grandmother cradling a baby, an elderly husband and wife smiling at each other lovingly.

I scroll through scenes of daily life—farmers with buffalo in their rice fields, potters moulding huge water jars, children playing flutes made from blue plastic water pipes, market scenes, women washing clothes at the riverbank, kids frolicking and playing naked in the shallows alongside, then a glimpse of fishermen casting their nets, teenage girls rolling cheroots, silversmiths engraving temple bowls, men sculpting stone Buddha images, and women bending over their brushwork on richly lacquered boxes.

Showing the typical kerbside teashops with miniature tables and chairs selling tasty snacks and sweetened coffee, I tell them "Young people today class themselves as either 'teashop' or 'disco' youth, the latter just want to enjoy a moment of fun, the former are more serious. They discuss philosophy, political systems and the latest rumours of bureaucratic blunders or dictates."

A guest at the back interjects, "I didn't expect to see so many smiling faces. Life is tough here. We've all read of the harsh conditions under the military junta."

Before I can reply, Derek jumps in, "The people are repressed and sad, anyone can see it. This afternoon I went for a walk and saw for myself that everyone was depressed. I saw it in their eyes. The women in the market hardly had a smile and even the children on the street didn't have much energy."

I respond calmly, though inwardly irritated by someone who presumes to understand a whole nation after walking a few blocks of downtown Yangon. "There is no doubt that people living for decades under this form of rule are living life on the edge, wary even of neighbours, constantly making-do with less than they need in a failing economy, trying to navigate abrupt changes of policy and to tread a safe path through corruption, propaganda and a convoluted bureaucracy, but my experience has shown me that even in the harshest conditions people do find happiness within their families, in sharing meals with friends, receiving a gift, or a prize at school, or perhaps in exchanging a brief moment with a friendly photographer. As human beings we are remarkably resilient."

Turning to Derek, I add, "It's possible that the people you noticed may have been sad for other reasons also—a wife finding out her husband has a younger mistress, a mother hearing her son has not passed an exam, a man worrying about his wife's medical care. Don't you think life is perhaps more complex than one can gauge from a quick walk around the block?"

Derek quickly counters, "But I am Asian too and we understand these things. I could feel their suffering."

I smile and nod politely, giving up, thinking of the yawning gap between the reality of downtown Yangon and his modern, pristine megalopolis of Singapore.

Turning back to the group I murmur, "Now, where were we? Yes, I wanted to talk about education and children's games." I resume with eager school pupils, serious university graduates posing in their robes, having passed their courses by correspondence after most universities closed, the book street with its towering stacks of old books and the much sought after photocopied novels smuggled in from abroad. Groups of men play checkers with bottle caps, youngsters crouch together, intent on a game of rubber-bands, and young footballers run on the shining wet sands of a west coast beach.

With a reference to 'necessity being the mother of invention,' I click through another set of photos subtitled, 'getting from A to B,' which shows the whole gamut of vehicles that move people and products around Myanmar. Bicycles carry enormous loads of firewood, slim canoes slice through the water with multi coloured sails sewn from old strips of cloth. Pony carts in Bagan, the wooden cars of the Chin State and trucks piled impossibly high with people and produce. The old buses whose drivers invite you to step in through a wide door at the back, seat yourself on a wooden bench and lean your elbow on the rim of the open window to view the world at a slow pace.

I tell them, "For reasons no one can explain, each bus has a bunny-eared Playboy style logo painted above the petrol cap. Every time I see a bus, I check. It's always there."

Out of the corner of my eye I notice Derek tapping his watch. The half hour has passed and I should be closing. Obligingly I finish my presentation within the next few minutes after zipping through a selection of stunning landscapes and famous sights of Myanmar followed by a kaleidoscope of portraits—villagers proud in their traditional clothing, road workers veiled against the harsh sun, tattooed men and women, Naga tribesmen with boar's tusks necklaces, elegant dancers and children laughing at me and with me as I photograph their antics.

I thank the group for their attention, turning to Derek,

"I managed pretty well didn't I? That was just forty-three minutes. As I mentioned, I'll be glad to answer any questions and speak with anyone who would like to stay a little longer."

"I'm not sure that's a good idea as we do have an early start tomorrow," he responds, turning to the group, but is politely contradicted as several hands shoot up.

Some guests comment on the photos, others have questions about the identity and culture of certain ethnic groups, places I've mentioned or Buddhism. A few more ask questions on the international sanctions and their effect on the government and the population. For some thirty minutes I respond as briefly and as best I can, ultimately concluding that there is no simple solution for the complex social and political situation in Myanmar, but that, by their being here, they will have a chance to judge for themselves and form their own opinions.

"All I can tell you," I finish, "is that the longer I stay here and the more I learn about this country, the more complicated it appears. I have found generosity and humour, despair and hope, cunning and ingenuity, friendship and suspicion. Just as we realize as we age that nothing in life is simply true or false, right or wrong, black and white, so, here too, almost everything is in subtle shades, tinged with cultural meaning and history. Perspectives are layered one on another, in a complex web of fact and fiction, politics and power, compassion and coercion. Everywhere one sees the good and bad, the beautiful and the ugly."

I thank them again for their interest, and wish them a wonderful journey. "I wish I could meet you again at the end of your trip," I say, "because I'm willing to bet the images that will capture you, the people you'll meet and the discoveries you'll make, will have considerably changed your views on this country."

I close my computer and step down, smiling, "Welcome to Myanmar and *Bon Voyage!*"

Chapter Two
The First Kiss

My own journey in Myanmar begins in 2002, the year 2545 of the Buddhist era. Landing late afternoon at Yangon Airport, I recall a friend's parting words, "This is going to be a new chapter in your life. When you arrive, do something positive, get down on all fours, kiss the ground and let the country embrace you." As I step down on to the runway, this suggestion appears rather too dramatic and neither easy nor graceful, encumbered as I am by my bags. Anyway, it's raining, and the staff hurry us on board the airport bus.

As we chug across the tarmac, the humid, tropical air wafts sluggishly through the jammed-open window with that seductive but not entirely pleasant airport smell of wet vegetation, damp runway, and aviation fuel. Inside the old bus, returning locals shift heavy packages from shoulder to shoulder, smarten up their hair and clothing, and relax after hectic days in Bangkok, with their shopping and medical adventures in that so-close, yet so-distant city over. Tourists with many-pocketed pants and vests look around apprehensively, clutching well-thumbed guidebooks, their backpacks held firmly between sandaled feet. Interspersed are a few somewhat jaded, nonchalant UN-types, dressed casually, carrying their Bangkok Post and briefcase. Local officials and possibly army personnel, judging from their posture and haircuts, appear hot and constricted in business suits or in brand new jeans and athletic shoes.

Gazing out, my eyes trace the outline of the airport terminal, impressed by the grandeur of the golden pillars, ornamental gables and high-pitched roof. But we trundle past that glorious, unlit edifice and come to a lurching stop outside a shabby, low concrete building. Inside the vast neon-lit immigration hall, long queues of passengers wait at passport control. On the right, people cluster behind a glass wall waiting to catch a glimpse of returning families and friends, many waving, with stories to tell and questions on their lips.

The immigration officers are mostly delicately featured women, smartly dressed in white shirts and navy skirts, hair slicked back into ponytails or netted buns, slides or colourful bands affirming their individuality. With a mere lift of their eyebrows, they solemnly indicate who is to come forward. The supervisor moves from desk to desk checking for problems or eyeing dubious visa stamps. I notice her footwear—high-heeled navy pumps with ankle-high navy socks, typical of women's army uniforms in the Second World War—and wonder if the style has been reintroduced or is a leftover from colonial days. I check discretely to see if others are similarly shod. They are.

Beyond them, people hold up signs and I spy the familiar emblem of the International Federation, the Red Cross and Red Crescent, comforting and solid on its white background. Behind the sign, friendly faces smile, mouthing, "Welcome Joanna MacLean."

All my new small team has come to meet me —Chul, the earnest young delegate from Japan and Yousung his slim, elegant wife; Marlar, the well-spoken, rather plump administrator; Sandy, the shy book-keep-er standing just behind her; and the two eager drivers, Ko Zaw and Ko Thet Oo. With efficiency, I'm whisked up and smoothly maneuvered through the maze of luggage collection, customs officials, and beckoning porters. I step outside into the humid evening air. After jostling our way through the crowd, I climb into a white land cruiser, my luggage stowed in the back. My seat is up front with the driver, Ko Zaw, to better view the sights of this new world.

As dusk descends, we speed along the highway under tall dripping trees, a huge painted archway rising up to greet me at the first intersection—WELCOME TO THE GOLDEN LAND.

"Are you tired?" Ma Marlar asks rather formally. "We thought you might like to have dinner with us. There's a good restaurant on the way to town. It's our pleasure to invite you."

"I'd like that. It'll be my first taste of Myanmar," I assent, equally courteously, curious to spend time with my team and try the food.

We're led into a private dining room and within minutes steaming plates of food are brought to us. At my side, Marlar takes charge.

"Do you like fish? This recipe is a local specialty," she explains, spooning morsels of herb-covered baked fish onto my plate beside a generous mound of steamed rice; deliciously fresh aromas hit my nose as the dish passes in front. "I'm sure you'll love this chicken. It's in a sweet and sour sauce...and you must try the deep fried pork...just a few bites," she adds, placing a large spoonful of each next to the rice. Holding the last dish before me—a shiny, dark green leafy vegetable with creamy nobs of garlic—she asks, "Do you know this? It's stir-fried morning glory. Try it!"

"I know the flowers" I respond, "They're blue and only last a day, but I've never seen the leaves cooked before." I wind several rather stringy leaves around my fork and put it cautiously in my mouth. All eyes are on me. Salt, garlic and a slightly bitter flavour hit my palate, and my eyes water. "Hmmmm." I smile. The team watches nervously as I try each portion, taking small bites, savouring the new tastes and textures, the crunch of the pork and the spicy palate-tickling fish. "It's delicious," I assure them and they smile, relaxing.

We talk as we eat, and I fill quiet moments with questions about the food, my trip, their families, the office. I am the new one, still a guest, but also the boss, and they look to me to take the lead. Our meal finished, Marlar signals for the bill. I notice an unusually large wad of notes being passed over.

Watching me eyeing the deft counting of the notes, our bookkeeper Sandy explains, "These are Myanmar Kyat. The biggest note is one thousand Kyat, worth about a dollar. I hope you have a large wallet."

We drive into town, swerving round potholes, passing heavy, noisy trucks, converted vans with men hanging off the back, old white taxis, and open-sided jeeps, their passengers braving the rain. Streetlights reflect on the wet road.

As we approach a slight rise, coming up to a corner, Marlar says, "Now you will see our Shwedagon Pagoda, one of the most famous and sacred places in Myanmar."

No introduction could have prepared me for the sheer majesty of the great golden Shwedagon, floodlit from all sides and rising above all other buildings of the city. It shines and it beckons.

"I must visit it this weekend," I exclaim.

The team deliver me to my temporary accommodation, an imposing new apartment block in the centre of town, the Grand Mee Ya Hta. It's quiet and dark in the lobby as I check in and get my key. Coming out of the lift onto the ninth floor I have a fleeting impression of being in prison. The high central atrium is surrounded by a walkway on each floor, dark apartment doors opening off it at intervals. Huge ceramic water pots squat outside each door under the dim lighting. I wonder who sits or sleeps behind those doors as no sound escapes from any of them.

Opening my door, I enter a large newly decorated apartment painted in sunny yellow with a small kitchen, a bedroom with bathroom and a living room with a television, sofa and small table, its French windows opening onto a circular balcony. A large bouquet of flowers and a bowl of fruit await my arrival. I peel a small, juicy mandarin, sucking its sweet flavour as I walk through the rooms relaxing and thinking about the day. Then I begin to unpack.

At eight the following morning I'm waiting in the lobby, dressed appropriately for the all-important first meeting with the President and Executive Committee of the Myanmar Red Cross Society. They accepted my candidacy for the position of Head of the International Federation's Delegation, based on my qualifications and experience, but have yet to approve of me in person.

"Good morning, Miss Joanna. Did you sleep well?" asks Ko Zaw, opening the car door and holding my elbow as I climb in.

"I did, thank you. Could it have been the beer you dosed me with at dinner?" I respond with a smile. "How are you today, Chul?" I ask my fellow delegate.

"I'm fine, thank you, Joanna. Yousung and I are very happy you've arrived. We really hope you'll enjoy it here," he responds.

I get my first look at Yangon in the light of day. Passing the high rise Sakura Tower and Traders Hotel, we drive towards a golden pagoda smack in the middle of a roundabout, surrounded by small booths selling all and everything—eyeglasses and photocopies, fortune telling and fashion accessories, medicines, and rubber stamps.

Overhead, a web of black electricity and phone wires are weighed down with dozens of fluttering and preening black crows. On the right, I glimpse a white and blue-tiled Mosque with a small minaret and on the left, an imposing Soviet-style, yellow building with a long balustrade. It faces an open square and a park, beyond which rises the tall steeple of a white and shiny metal-roofed church.

I peer at my map, anxious to identify my surroundings. "That must be the Sule Pagoda, but what about that mosque? And what's that big building over there?"

"This is Sule Pagoda Road and that's City Hall with Maha Bandoola Park opposite," explains Ko Zaw. "That's a Sunni Mosque and that is the Immanuel Baptist Cathedral."

I repeat the names to memorize them, "Maha Bandoola," the words roll easily off my tongue. "What a great name, I love the sound. If I ever have a cat, that's what I'll call it."

I watch the people crossing the road and walking along the pavement—school children in green skirts or shorts with spotless white shirts and older ones in green longyis. The women and most men wear *longyis*, Burmese sarongs, patterns and flowers for the women and checks for the men. Women and children have bold traces of white paste on their cheeks and some babies' faces are completely white, their brown eyes wide open, shining out. I am cropping scenes with a photographer's eye and anticipating the weekend when I will be free to wander and click while everything is still fresh and undiscovered, each image a potential masterpiece to treasure and share.

We turn onto the waterfront road, the river only partially visible, masked by high fences, a railway track, and warehouses. We stop in front of a grey, square building with a pillared portico capped with the words "Myanmar Red Cross" in red.

"So here I am," I say quietly. I walk through a large lobby with scuffed yellow tiles and peeling green paint. A few people sit chatting idly, one man sleeps, an arm flung across his face. The guard, seated behind his small table with an open ledger, is hunched over a crackling radio, listening intently but raises his head long enough to smile and greet us, "Mingalar ba".

A door to the right is blocked by a tangle of black bicycles. Another, to the left, opens into a gloomy storeroom stacked with bulging sacks. Directly in front is the lift, the old cage type which, experience tells me, invariably grinds upwards more slowly than you could have walked, always jerking to a stop a bit above or below the intended floor.

I choose the stairs, but at the first corner I stop, appalled. Great gobs of red stain the walls and floor and I can only wonder at the strength of whoever was so badly wounded that they could make it to the Red Cross in safety and then this far up the stairs. I imagine an accident, a fight, a machete cutting into a limb instead of a coconut husk.

"My God!" I exclaim, "What happened here?" Is my aversion to the sight of blood, a joke amongst my Red Cross friends, already an issue? What have I let myself in for? Will I be able to cope?

Chul laughs at my shock and explains, "Don't worry, it's not blood, it's spit, betel spit. Chewing betel wads produces a lot of saliva, so they have to spit, a lot and often."

I notice then, in a dim corner of the stairs, a wooden box filled with sand, stained a dark red, but no more so than the walls and floor around it. Someone has made an attempt to keep the place clean, but clearly aim is an issue.

Luckily, on the second floor, a totally different atmosphere prevails. I am greeted with smiles and polite enquiries about my apartment, my sleep and my impressions so far. My choice of clothes—navy slacks, white top, red jacket—is also commented upon and approved and I am advised that the Committee will meet with me at eleven.

"Let me show you to your office, then you can look around" says Marlar, leading me through a lobby decorated with posters of the Red Cross Principles I had designed in a previous job. We continue on through a meeting room with an imposing table large enough to seat a dozen, then into a connecting room...my office.

It is huge and dreary. To my right are heavy floor-to-ceiling wooden shelves. Piles of documents and files stagger across them, begging to be dusted, sorted, and arranged. A grey metal desk stands squarely in front of the shelves, an equally grey chair behind. On the desk sits a sagging, plastic filing tray and a stack of correspondence, a lacquer cup with ruler and pens, a calendar with the logo of Myanmar Airways, and a DHL package, still in its plastic wrapper. A large, heavy brown leather sofa and two armchairs are stiffly grouped around a glass-top coffee table.

"A rather masculine room," I remark to Marlar, "I might make some small changes. Would that be all right?"

Not knowing quite what to do next, I pull out my computer, looking around for a socket. I thought I should prepare for the meeting with the Executive Committee, make notes of what I want to say and to ask, but the team has other plans.

Marlar smiles, "Come and look at how we're organised and who does what," she says, motioning me to follow.

I meet again with each of the staff and am introduced to a shy young woman, Snow White, our cleaner, whose name I can easily remember by association with her tasks. I'm shown our eight offices, four of which are

15

empty, but all in severe disrepair, filled with boxes of files, papers, old furniture and, I suspect, vermin.

The team members explain their functions, responsibilities and experience and elaborate on their relationships with previous delegates. I learn about the office and its procedures, and even more about each of my staff, their style, humour, motivation, and working methods. I listen, nod and ask questions.

At eleven sharp, I am summoned to the meeting room, as are Chul and Marlar. The five members of the Executive Committee of the Myanmar Red Cross sit either side of the President, Dr Kyaw Win, and indicate that I should sit opposite. All are elderly men, each dressed impeccably in a cotton longyi, white shirt and a coloured short jacket—grey, yellow, beige and black.

"Welcome to Myanmar, Miss MacLean," the President begins, "We look forward to working with you. You have much experience I know, but this is your first position in Asia isn't it?"

I nod, but before I can reply, he continues, "Actually, I think you might fit in rather well. I say this because I know you designed the magnificent opening show of the Millennium Conference in Geneva.

We are Buddhist and our delegation was impressed by the way you invoked the powers of nature and of man's striving to better himself and care for others. We think you will suit us here in our country. We're most fortunate not to have as many natural disasters as our neighbours, particularly Bangladesh, but as you know we do have some health and social issues to work on."

I am taken aback by his recollection of both that conference and my part in it, as well as being extremely impressed by his perfect English.

"Thank you, Mr President, for your welcome and complimentary words. I look forward to working closely with you. And yes, it is my first posting in Asia. I have a lot to learn, but I trust that my past experience in the Red Cross will stand me in good stead for what we have to accomplish. I believe, together, we can wisely face the issues before us".

I'm careful to match his formality, picking words and phrases I wouldn't normally use.

The meeting continues with the initial expression of large intentions and hopes, then it downplays on broaching the subjects of new funding, expanded programmes, international meetings, training of volunteers and staff.

It's a necessary first sounding out of what is wanted and what is on offer. The members of the Committee nod at the President's words.

Then, without preface or apparent link, the Honourable Treasurer, interjects, "Miss MacLean, may I compliment you on your outfit? I am impressed that your jacket, watchstrap, belt and sandals all match."

I smile and thank him for his kind words, recognizing that the serious part of the meeting is officially over.

Do they approve of me? Maybe not yet, but at least I've passed muster in the clothing department.

Having lightened the mood, the committee members become more animated as they talk about their country and city, suggesting where I should go over the weekend, the best area of the city for a house. Explaining the intricacies of the Burmese language, they proudly tell me what their names mean—a guiding star, a brave warrior, a handsome leader.

They invite me to a nearby Chinese restaurant for lunch and we walk a couple of blocks in the rain under huge umbrellas, the conversation, advice, and questions continuing.

Then, as I step across some broken paving stones, those smart commented-upon sandals prove no match for the pavement, slick with rain and my foot flies from under me, plumping me down on all fours.

I find myself kneeling on the ground, hands spread, face down, rather too close to the mud and clumps of sodden rubbish.

My friend's words come back to me. I pause, catching my breath, then quickly I touch my forehead to the pavement, not exactly a kiss, but a symbolic embracing of this new country and the beginning of a new life.

"Oh, are you all right? Are you hurt? So sorry for you."

Hands reach out to help me up. A little embarrassed, I come up smiling. "Looks like I have really landed now," I quip, brushing off my hands and knees and, amid relieved laughter and sympathetic comments, we enter the restaurant together.

Chapter Three
You'll Get Used It

I've been here three weeks, getting up to speed on office work and politics, and occasionally managing to play the tourist. On weekends I tour the most famous sights but also enjoy just wandering around downtown, through the parks, and along the lakeshores.

Having lived and travelled in other exotic places, I had anticipated with pleasure the differences in dress, style and architecture, in markets, food, and everyday life typical of a new country. However, for reasons I can't quite understand, Yangon has an appeal for me more than almost anywhere else has.

The narrow back streets are crowded day and night with people going about their business or dozing on bamboo chairs. Men carry heavy loads of water, bolts of cloth, chairs, shouting a passage ahead, children darting around them laughing and playing. Steep stairways lead up into terraced houses with lines of washing hung out on bamboo poles, long strings hang down to the pavement with a basket or a giant bulldog clip to haul up lunch, a letter, or their shopping. And always, the cracked pavements, gaping holes to the drains, noxious smells wafting, rubbish. Telephone tables, wires haphazardly strung to large blue and pink plastic telephones are used to call family or friends for just a few Kyat. No privacy, but a connection. The whirring and clanging of sugar cane juice wheels mingles with the sizzle of the beloved snacks from oil filled woks. Street stalls, blocking half the pavement, offer everything from maps and alphabet posters to old books, medicines, plastic bowls, and clothing, as well as seasonal fruits and flowers.

At every turn, I am confronted with new sights and sounds. I'm offered smiles and questions, along with postcards and fruit wedges; I feel no menace, only their interest in a passing foreigner. The people are naturally beautiful and when I ask with my eyes for permission to take their picture, they invariably agree. In that small question and response, a momentary spark of relationship springs to life. In the photos that manage to capture this brief link, I begin to see the spirit of different cultures and races, the joys and sorrows of the country slowly emerging.

Having read as much as I can about Myanmar, I am confounded by how little updated information is available. During my first week, I read *Burma Days* by George Orwell; it's touted at every corner bookstall. I love the descriptions, but cringe at the blatant arrogance typical of the Colonial past. If I had lived then, would I have been as blind to the humanity of others, as ignorant of the complexity and appropriateness of another culture, so convinced that my way was the only way of doing everything? I wonder, just as I did when I lived in Africa and in the West Indies, what my attitude and actions would have been. Unfortunately, I doubt I'd have been any more enlightened and sympathetic than my contemporaries. We are, after all, a product of our environment, history, education and values—key factors that bind us generationally. I question if, even now, I might appear insensitive, or worse, arrogant. I hope not, but I expect it's inevitable to some extent.

On Monday morning of my second week, I stand in front of the map of Myanmar on my office wall trying to get a sense of the country, wondering why some regions are called 'States,' others 'Divisions.'

Entering with some files, Marlar observes my absorption. She takes her time to explain, "The central part of Myanmar, home to the Burmans who represent the largest ethnic group, is split in seven 'Divisions.' That is where the name Burma comes from. It only dates from Colonial times when the country was part of British India. The British distinguished Upper Burma from Lower Burma and fought the French over Upper Burma because of its natural resources—large teak forests, jade mines and gemstones. The numerous other 'nationalities' including the Kachin, Karen, Shan, Arakan, Wa, Mon, and Chin, many of whom are fighting for their independence, live along the borders of this region in what are called 'States'. There are also seven of these. The 'Divisions' and States' are then divided into sixty-seven 'Districts', each sub-divided into 'Townships,' more than three hundred altogether. These in turn house numerous towns, wards and villages.

It is vital that I learn this and much more if my working methods and proposals are to be relevant and acceptable.

"Sometimes our ways are a little different," my colleagues tell me when something intrigues me. They invariably add with a smile, "you'll get used to it."

That second week, feeling a bit in need of company, I wander over to Traders Hotel, to enjoy their 'Happy Hour' offering free food and music. I seat myself at the bar and order a glass of wine. Immediately a bowl of rice crackers is pushed towards me, the wine, moisture beading on the glass, soon follows. I turn around to check out the lounge. A game of darts is in progress, two teams arguing loudly about the score while a maxi TV screen is showing an English football match. A table is set up in the corner with food warmers and plates. A raised dais has band equipment, and in another corner is a snooker table, coloured balls secure in their triangle.

I strike up a conversation with my neighbour, a consultant for a petroleum company. We begin the light banter typical in such circumstances—life in Yangon, about his job, about mine, and what there is to do in Yangon of a weekend. When the food arrives we join the queue for samosas, mini burgers, crispy fish, and chicken wings.

Tucking into the snacks, I hear the first chords of the band tuning up. When they launch into a spirited version of Bob Marley's 'No Woman, No Cry,' my worlds collide.

Amused, I turn to my new friend, "Wow! That brings back a few memories. During my posting in Jamaica in the nineties I was invited to Bob Marley's fiftieth birthday party, though he was no longer with us, having died way too young of cancer. But his wife Rita and his son Ziggy were there, playing his music. It was a fantastic evening."

Now, as I nod along with the music, sipping my wine, I feel good, happy to be meeting new people, discovering this new country, adding new experiences.

After my third week in Yangon, a rather dapper Burmese man in his late thirties appears in my office, preceded by Marlar.

"Do you remember Alfred?" She asks me, "He took part in one of the regional training courses you facilitated. At the time he worked with Myanmar Red Cross. He remembers you."

We chat a little, recalling the course and participants. His English is excellent and he seems very friendly. So when he suggests we have dinner together, I agree, keen to learn a little more about Myanmar.

We take a taxi to the Karaweik restaurant, a concrete replica of a golden barge, imposingly floodlit, protruding into the Royal 'Kandawgyi' Lake. He escorts me into the open dining area, telling me there'll be some traditional dancing later. From our table the Shwedagon shines from the opposite shore, reflected in the rippled lake. Beautiful.

At the buffet table, Alfred explains each dish and I spoon small helpings of meat, fish and vegetables onto my plate next to the leaf packaged steamed rice. He is a good storyteller and, over dinner, explains a great deal about Myanmar culture. We laugh at some of the stranger aspects of life here, like the official bank exchange rate of five Kyats to the dollar while getting a thousand Kyats from the currency dealers on the street.

He proves to be an interested listener, asking about my previous jobs and where I have travelled. The conversation meanders over different ideas, religions and cultures, unusual places, and situations. I'm relaxed, telling him how much I am enjoying the work so far and I mention I am looking forward to traveling to other parts of the country.

"You probably know by now," he says, leaning a bit closer, "That there will be some places you cannot visit; the 'black' zones are off limits to almost everyone. For the 'brown' zones, permission can be given if the area seems peaceful. Of course many places are 'white' zones. Here you'll be free to go, once you have official permission."

"I already have my official work permit, so what else do I need?" I ask, although I have already heard that permission is needed for field trips outside Yangon.

"You'll need a travel permit for a visit anywhere more than twenty-five miles outside of the city, but since you will be with members of MRCS, your staff will request that. Working for an international organisation, it's important the authorities know where you are doing your work, and what you bring to our country," he adds.

Our conversation is interrupted. It's time for the show. The adjoining room has a raised stage with red velvet curtains and a painted backdrop of a lake and a pagoda on a hill. A small band of musicians is seated cross-legged. Alfred points out their traditional instruments—a wooden xylophone, a curved golden harp, some small drums and bells. The sounds are gentle and tinkling, although a little discordant to my western ear. The musicians wear matching longyis in golden brown checks, beige jackets over white shirts, and silk turbans, tight around the forehead, with a wonderful upright pleat over their right ear.

"I like their headwear," I comment as the lights go down,

"These are gaungbaungs, the traditional Burman headwear, worn by men in the past. We still wear them for special occasions, but mostly buy them ready made now. Pity, really." Alfred shrugs.

We are treated to six dances, some evoking legends, the dancers' crowns or wands marking them as kings, queens or magicians; others enact rituals such as rice harvesting. The last dance is a love affair between a beautiful young woman, wearing a delicately embroidered longyi with a train, and a handsome prince. The woman dances, showing all her feminine charm while the young prince mirrors her moves with a swagger.

"Shall we have dessert? You must try the 'Shwe Yin Aye,' it is one of our favourite Myanmar sweets," Alfred offers, as the dances end. We go back to our table with our small bowls of chilled sweet coconut soup —tapioca balls, red sweet beans, dark green seaweed and ice cubes. It's an interesting mixture of flavours and textures, delicious and refreshing.

"Have you thought of keeping a diary of what you see as you travel around the country?" Alfred asks.

"I might. I find everything fascinating. I'm taking photos, but I try to note facts and figures, and recall some conversations," I respond. "It will help with my reports, especially for the donors. Without reports, few donations; without financial support, no programmes. Part of my job here."

"Would you record things as well?" he asks casually. "A colleague of mine told me about a Russian he met, a UN worker, who showed him a hidden compartment at the bottom of his briefcase with equipment to record conversations up to ten metres away." He laughs, and I join in, slightly puzzled at the rather bizarre turn in the conversation. Only then do I realise I haven't asked him where he works, but decide to let it go for the moment.

"Sounds like a James Bond movie. Maybe I should get one, perhaps red for a lady spy?" I joke a little feebly, trying to quell my rising unease. The conversation returns to everyday matters, he calls for the bill and we leave.

As we ride back, I casually and innocently chat about this and that and he responds, smiling, equally casual. As we stop at some lights my gaze falls on a huge red billboard boldly stating 'The People's Desire:'

Oppose those relying on external elements, acting as stooges, holding negative views.

Oppose those trying to jeopardize the stability of the State and the Nation's progress.

Crush all internal and external destructive elements of the common enemy.

Oppose foreign nations interfering in internal affairs of the State.

"I trust you enjoyed your evening. We must do it again sometime," Alfred says opening the taxi door.

"It's been enlightening for me," I reply. "Thank you very much. I'm sure we will meet again."

I walk slowly to my room re-playing our evening with an uneasy sensation in my stomach growing. Was I being checked out by a set of questions on my beliefs and opinions? Did I say anything controversial? Who does Alfred actually work for?

I can't sleep so I take a drink out onto the balcony, into the balmy late night air. I don't think I said anything that would cast me in the light of a snoop, but now I am sure this is what the evening was all about. Another billboard with the words 'The People's Desire' is visible opposite Traders Hotel; it reinforces this sinister sensation. Am I out of my depth here or do I just have an overactive imagination fuelled by the Myanmar beer?

The next day, I ask Marlar to tell Alfred should he call again, that I am not in. She looks at me a little questioningly, but agrees.

I never see him again.

Chapter Four
Accommodating the Boss

The search is on for a house. Six weeks in Grand Mee Ya Hta have given me a chance to find my way around, concentrate on my new job and experience the limited expat life in the hotels, but I'm beginning to feel a bit cooped up.

"Nothing too big or fancy but in good repair. Lots of light and a small garden," I describe my kind of house. Marlar, accordingly, draws up a list and one afternoon, near the end of my second month, we head out on our mission.

Our first stop is in an established residential area with large houses, enclosed by high walls, set back from tree-lined pavements. Ko Zaw beeps his horn and a uniformed guard appears, hitching up his trousers.

Walking through high grass, past a small lake with lotus flowers, dragonflies zipping above, we reach a rather weather-beaten bungalow with a wide veranda. "Mosquitoes," I think. Shoes off, we enter. Clearly no one has lived here for a while. If the guard's brief was to clean, he has ignored it. A musty smell pervades the house, everything looks dark and dingy, the taps drip and the dampness makes me shiver, even in the afternoon heat.

We quickly head to a new grid-plan housing area, where building is still in progress. Here a few finished mansions flaunt wealth and absence of style in equal proportions. Pillars, balconies, turrets and bow windows adorn the houses that extend to the very corners of the sections, barely leaving enough space for a sliver of garden.

An impressive wrought iron gate set into a thick hedge opens to reveal a large house set at the back of the property. Crazy paving leads us between regimented flowerbeds, past a miniature Dutch windmill and over a bridge spanning a small pond. To the left is a golf putting green with flagged stick, to the right a small gazebo engulfed by flowering hibiscus.

The young woman who greets us explains that this is her parents' house; they are diplomats and are presently abroad.

We sit politely on heavily carved wooden armchairs, flowered tapestry in plastic dustcovers. A maid sets down a tray of water glasses, ice clinking. When asked, I explain, "I'm from New Zealand but working for the International Red Cross. I've lived in many different places, just like your parents."

Formalities over, we are shown this great house, slowly, almost reverently, every feature explained. Alongside two reception rooms crammed with heavy dark furniture, is a prayer room full of shrines and Buddha images, burning incense, rice, flowers, and bananas on elaborately patterned dishes. The dining room, crowded with a massive sideboard topped with a silver urn, and a heavy dark table, opens into a huge kitchen. Upstairs are four bedroom suites. We murmur compliments about the furniture, the curtains, the choice of tiles, but I just can't imagine myself at ease in this opulent house.

Our next visit is in Golden Valley where, according to Marlar, the electricity always works because important people—army chiefs, government officials and diplomats—live here. Passing an Embassy and an International School set within a pristine compound, bougainvillea cascading down its white walls, we cruise through an open gate onto a wide drive, smooth green lawns on either side, leading to an another imposing house. This time, with only a maid showing us around, we can be in and out quickly.

"You'll like this one. A good area, lots of light and a nice garden." Marlar has already decided for me.

The house has the strangest layout I've ever seen. Rising up from the centre of the living room is a grandiose, circular staircase which completely dwarfs the whole room; a few chairs and a dining table are set around the periphery.

"Let's look upstairs," I suggest, without much enthusiasm. I've never really imagined myself gliding down a staircase in a ball gown à la Scarlett O'Hara, but this is what comes to mind as I step onto the broad treads. The upper floor plan is constrained by the well of the staircase, eight small bedrooms off to the sides; only the master bedroom seems big enough.

"I wonder who designed this house," I murmur, "It's a little unusual."

My lack of enthusiasm must not be obvious, because Marlar starts promoting the positives again—nice area, reliable electricity, space for visitors, cleanliness. I interject firmly, "Marlar, I would be lost in this big house, there is not a single cosy corner."

A bit despondent, we head towards the last house on the list near Kandawgyi Lake. We drive past a beautiful but dilapidated old wooden house with a turret and turn into a side street bordered by small apartment houses. Next to a monastery with dark russet robes hanging on bamboo poles outside, we turn again, down a narrow dirt lane, crossing a small wooden bridge to reach an open field with fruit trees, overlooked by a cream-coloured house surrounded by a bougainvillea hedge.

"This is it," says Ko Zaw, "No 7a, Saw Maha Lan." As we drive in, the well proportioned house, surrounded by a small raised lawn, edged with a low brick wall and flowering shrubs, appears inviting.

The terrace opens into a hallway from which a staircase of appropriate size rises to the second floor. To the left through sliding doors is a spacious light-filled room with a long window seat looking out over the garden, the late afternoon sun bathing the room with a golden glow. To the right, through identical sliding doors, a second large room, French windows opening onto the garden, leads to a clean, functional kitchen. Its back door opens into a garage and behind is a small maid's room.

"Oh, look at these beautiful parquet floors. Let's see if upstairs fits the bill."

We find another nice surprise at the top of the stairs. A bright, open space with a large bedroom and bathroom opening off it and, to the left, two more airy bedrooms with en-suite bathrooms. The fittings are not the most modern, the colours perhaps not exactly my taste, but the house feels just right.

I turn to Marlar. "I like it." I say, "This'll do me fine. What do you think?"

Marlar frowns a little, "Well, the guard says the electricity is a bit erratic and you'd be rather isolated up here but," she adds quickly, seeing my face, "if you like it, I'll call the owners. The rent on this property is even lower than the others."

That cinches it. I walk through the rooms again, noting the furniture—two beds, some cupboards, a desk and bookshelves. I pace the rooms, judging their size, and we discuss what is needed.

"Once we sign the lease and pay the deposit, we'll contact two guards who've worked with us before. We'll check for furniture left from previous delegates and make a list of what else you would require. Looks like a bit of shopping this weekend!" summarises Marlar, smiling. "Yes, I think you could probably move in next week."

Saturday morning, list in hand, Ko Zaw and I are ready to shop. We wend our way through the backstreets where each item of furniture or appliance, commodity or building supply has its own designated location. On certain streets, lines of shops vying for customers sell fridges, fans, ovens, and air-conditioning units, each shop offering the same Japanese and Chinese brands. On other streets, stores offer paint or metal furniture, bathroom fixtures or lamps, curtains or plastic utensils of every variety, size, and colour.

Another area houses shop after shop, selling almost identical solid teak furniture, made by craftsmen working on the pavement. The newly sanded wood is beautiful, the grain clearly visible. But the fashion is a high gloss look; under thick coats of yellow-orange varnish the beauty of the wood disappears.

"Would you ask if he could just oil the wood so I can see the grain," I ask Ko Zaw. He looks at me quizzically, but passes on my request, and the man nods willingly.

We methodically check off the items on my list—cupboard and fridge for the kitchen, reclining garden chairs, side table and lamp for my bedroom, electric fan for the living room. Then we add smaller items, kitchen utensils, and household appliances.

In the afternoon, we cross the river to visit the 'The Green Elephant,' an elegant shop offering beautifully crafted bamboo, rattan and lacquer furniture. I fall in love with a rattan chaise longue, imagining myself reclining upstairs languidly after completing some task. I order it, as well as a dining table and chairs, a sofa and armchairs with cream-coloured cushions…everything in beautifully woven rattan. My housing allowance will cover the table and chairs. The chaise longue is my treat to myself.

"The armchairs can be delivered next week, the rest within the month," promises the saleswoman. "And what about some decorative items? Have you seen our museum, for inspiration?" She leads the way into a traditional room with mannequins in beautiful silk *longyis*. The woven wall hangings, mats, carvings, and stools are in various states of disrepair, but the overall impression is one of serenity and style.

I spy a large wooden box on small wheels, its top and sides inlaid in brass with double clasps at the front and a sturdy hinged handle either side. My guide slides her hand proprietarily across its smooth lid and opens it, explaining, "This is a Mandalay Box. They were made for attendants and performers at the Royal Palace. The inside of the top is designed like a stage set, with different kinds of wood inlay. This one has jacaranda around the mirrors. See the lighter colour? The border is sandalwood, used for its sweet smell. The top tray has compartments for jewellery and make-up and the larger space underneath is for clothes.

Some of them have secret compartments and intricate locks that chime when the key is turned, in case someone tries to break in. They are very rare now." I thank my informant for this glimpse into the past, the tradition and romance of these boxes truly intriguing. I would love to find a genuine Mandalay Box for my house.

A few days later I'm ready for the move. I say goodbye to the friendly staff of the Grand Mee Ya Hta and wait for the car, impatient to be on my way. I glance at the anonymous young men lounging in the lobby as though waiting for someone; I'm aware they're the 'minders' for this apartment block and who, for sure, already know the location of my new home. I wonder if I'll have my own 'minder' discretely stationed somewhere close by.

As we drive up Saw Maha Lan, I smile at the kids running beside the car and at their parents inquisitively watching our arrival. News has spread that a foreigner will live in the house up the road and from now on we will be neighbours. On arrival, Ko Zaw toots and I hear the slap of slippered feet running down the driveway.

The gate swings open and I'm greeted by the huge smile of Ko Malay, one of my new guards, in a green longyi with a fresh t-shirt, a little tight over his tummy. His colleague, Maung Taut, stands outside the garage, similarly clad, but slim and solemn. He bows his head then raises his hand to welcome us. These are the two men who will look after me, and the house.

Ko Zaw has already delivered the weekend purchases. When I suggest we sit for a while and agree on Ko Malay and Maung Taut's duties, he assures me they know their business and will sort everything out themselves, only checking with me if there's a problem. They both speak enough English that we can communicate easily.

We take a cup of tea into the garden and I enquire about them, their families and their experience. Malay loves to garden and is known for his prowess at catching and killing snakes. Useful, but scary information. Maung Taut owns a small bicycle repair shop and likes to fix things. Evidently he can improvise and set up any electrical appliance I might need, an equally useful skill.

First acquaintances over, the men offer to help me get organised. In my bedroom, we move the bed, placing the side table and lamp next to it, then my suitcases and the box of bed linen and towels are carried up. The sofa and armchairs are angled towards a future TV in the living room, then we head to the kitchen to unpack, stowing everything away.

Ko Zaw and Maung Taut drive off, leaving Malay for the first evening duty. I take my time making my bed, hanging the towels, lining my toiletries on the bathroom shelf. I place my few books in the bookcase and carefully arrange my clothes on the rack.

Later, while I relax, reading on the window seat, the house slowly grows dark around me. Walking through the rooms I find the light switches and am fascinated by the way the lights go on, dim at first, then brightening, like a candle flame.

In the kitchen I ponder my options for dinner. I decide on bread, while it's still fresh, a nice piece of Australian Brie, and a salad. And a glass of chilled white wine...why not?

Malay comes in from the garage and asks, "Can I help you with anything Mrs Joanna? Do you need that pineapple cut? It's ripe."

I thank him and we stand, side by side, chopping and slicing, hunting for the right plates and bowls, preparing my food.

I eat my meal on the window seat, looking out into the now dark garden, seeing only myself reflected back in the glass, a warm glow from the room behind me. I sip my wine, savouring the food and the solitude.

I'm home.

Chapter Five
Crossing The Bridge

A few months after my arrival, we welcome first one health delegate, Mallu, from Finland, and then a second, Yvonne, from Australia. Mallu stays with me the first few weeks then, after moving into her own apartment, she plays host to Yvonne before she too finds her own place. In this way, we get to know each other quickly. Mallu, with years of experience in Africa and the Middle East and her most recent posting in North Korea, is in charge of health and training programmes, working closely with the MRCS Health Department. Yvonne's work is focused on a new integrated health programme in Kengtung, in the northeast, close to the Chinese border, and she spends several weeks at a time in the field.

Meanwhile, Chul, who has been working tirelessly with our MRCS colleagues on a strategy and questionnaire for the first nationwide Branch Survey, now needs assistance setting it up and also for his work in disaster preparedness. We advertise and select four new staff members: Ma Thuza for branch development, Ko Myo for disaster preparedness, Ko Kyaw Kyaw as Office Manager, and Ko Zarni to sort our IT frustrations. Internet connection is irregular, access impossible to more than a handful of websites and certain emails are blocked. One day, I wonder why a chatty email from my nephew James has been 'denied', concluding, with a stretch of the imagination, that his server 'paradise.nz' had been perceived as a porn site.

While attending a MRCS training course on planning and project design, I realise our rapidly growing delegation might benefit from some team building. As my colleague Uma from Malaysia instructs, charms, and cajoles her groups through the afternoon's programme, I make a note to arrange a team-building workshop for my staff. Over dinner, Uma accepts a facilitator's role, suggesting some possible exercises. I'm taken by the idea and air the proposal at our weekly meeting, evoking as much excitement as if I'd announced a party. Within minutes, calendar and map in front of us, we are plotting dates and location for a week-end 'Staff Retreat'. We'll leave on a Friday morning and drive west, across the Ayeyarwady delta, to Ngwe Saung, a beach resort on the Andaman Coast where the sessions will be held. Kyaw Kyaw is tasked with finding a hotel and suitable transport, Marlar with obtaining the necessary permits while I work on the programme.

I'm ready when the van arrives at six thirty on the appointed morning. The local team is on board but we still have to have to pick up Chul, Mallu, Yvonne, and Uma. There's a stranger too. "Companion of the driver," Kyaw Kyaw tells me with a straight face, but I know he is our 'minder'. Checking 'what foreigners do and say' is a well recognized practice in the small international community. From the strange clicks, the abrupt cut-off of some conversations, I suspect my home phone is monitored, so am mindful of what I say even to family. Likewise, we're sure our office phones and emails are scrutinised. When reporting concerns to my superiors, I send handwritten letters, asking colleagues or friends to hand deliver them to Bangkok. I'm more concerned for my staff than for myself so I keep my head down and antennae up, never mentioning names if discussing anything that could be construed as criticism of the government or administration.

The drive to Ngwe Saung is about seven hours, but we stop for tea, then lunch and to visit a pagoda. The mood is happy, snacks and remarks liberally shared among the group. We pass through villages, driving along dry, dusty roads with rice paddies on either side, with people walking, carrying loads, working the fields, selling produce from colourful stalls. I wonder when this once wealthy region will again be able to raise the living standards for its people.

Arriving at our beach resort by mid afternoon, we are escorted to our bungalows stretched along the seafront, and part, agreeing to meet in a half hour.

The first session, kept brief, begins with a short exercise to relax everyone, reassuring them that this is about team building and cooperation, not competition or hierarchy. On a sheet of paper we write the name of the person sitting on our left and a phrase about them. Folding it over so only the name can be seen, we pass the paper to our right, receiving another paper with another name. We write again and fold the paper, and again, until we see our own name. Reading how others see us results in smiles, chuckles and a few bemused faces. "Does anyone want to share their comments?" Uma asks and several do, laughing but also proud. We've been kind to each other, but over the next days, this may change as we delve into status, problem solving, challenges with the MRCS staff, and with donors.

The session over, we wander outside and relax. It's balmy and the pool looks inviting so I take that swim I've been thinking about, enjoying the cool water against my skin, bliss after the long day. Thuza, Uma and Sandy wander over and dip their toes. "Come in," I urge them. They tell me they can't swim, but I can see they're tempted. "Well then, you must," I say, "Just come in with your clothes on. I dare you." They take the plunge, a new experience, and one by one they walk down the steps until they are standing in a line, waist deep in the water, longyis ballooning around their legs, making us all laugh.

Then, from the far end of the pool, I catch sight of three armed soldiers walking through the lobby. The receptionist points to our group. I see Marlar approaching them, greeting them formally and leading them to the meeting room. There's tenseness among my group that wasn't there before. I swim to the girls, still standing in a line, asking, "What's this about? Everything ok?"

"It's the local command checking on us," Sandy explains quietly. "Marlar will show them our identity papers and travel permits. Don't worry, this is standard procedure." Only when they leave, do we relax, resuming our chat.

Later, after a lantern-lit dinner in a nearby village, we all wander through the small night market. I buy a beautiful conical green shell with an ivory lustre and enjoy the feel of it, smooth in my hand; we walk home companionably along the beach.

Saturday is spent in discussion and group work, Uma holding our interest and challenging us to participate, despite our different roles and responsibilities. It isn't easy for our Myanmar colleagues. Age, status and respect are keystones of their culture and speaking openly with a superior is difficult. Recognizing this, Uma invites us to write any concerns or issues and put them unsigned into her 'problem hat,' a woven rattan one borrowed from a hotel gardener. Uma pulls out the notes one by one. Many refer to personal relationships, others raise practical issues like the extra work hours, some are concerned about who gets what information and why. In this way everyone voices their opinions and ideas, respected by the others.

Our Myanmar colleagues teach us, the outsiders, about their traditions and about respect within the family and community. It's an eye opener for us, just as some of the delegates' stories and ideas are new to them.

Little by little my team opens up. I'm impressed by Uma's skill in adjusting the sessions as they move along, inviting everyone to contribute, summing up beautifully, emphasizing key learning points or issues to be dealt with the following day.

This evening its Sandy's thirtieth birthday celebration. Marlar and Kyaw Kyaw have plotted with the hotel staff and we will dine on the terrace. Flowers decorate the whole length of the table, a pile of presents and cards await while heady aromas of grilled chicken, giant prawns, meat skewers and sizzling fish waft up from the barbeque. We've all dressed for the occasion and there's a newfound camaraderie amongst the group after the closeness of the day's exchanges. Sharing a fruit punch complete with umbrella, we admire a stunning sunset, although a few clouds are building up on the horizon. We eat and drink lavishly, all talking at once, jokes flying across the table.

The festivities come to a climax with the arrival of the cake, a chocolate beauty with thirty candles, carefully carried in by Kyaw Kyaw and Myo. At exactly this moment, the wind changes, announcing the pending storm and we quickly pick up our woven place mats, holding them tightly around the cake so there is just room for Sandy to lean in and blow out the candles, before the wind does it for her. "Make a wish, a wish," we chant then break into 'Happy Birthday to you, dear Sandy', dashing for cover as pelting rain drives us inside.

Sunday morning, another round of discussions, working to confront our strengths and inadequacies. Through lunch we continue, fired up by new insights. Then comes the early afternoon exercise, designed to keep us awake through the 'doze zone'. We are divided into three groups of four, a mix of delegates and local staff, each choosing a comfortable sitting place to tackle the next subject delivered by Uma. The following scenario is presented to us:

DEGREES OF RESPONSIBILITY
Crossing The bridge

A young wife, neglected by her husband because he was too absorbed in his work, allowed herself to be seduced. One day, while her husband was on a trip, she decided to spend the night at her lover's place across the river. Early the next morning, wanting to arrive home before her husband, she made her way back to the bridge, but found a madman standing there who would not let her cross. So she went to find a ferryman, who told her she would have to pay for her passage. She had no money on her, she explained her predicament and begged him to ferry her over anyway. He refused to help without being paid in advance.

The woman then went in search of an unmarried friend who lived on the same side of the river. This man was deeply in love with her, but she had never yielded to his advances. She told him her story, pleading with him to give her the money. But he was disappointed by her behaviour and flatly refused. After one more attempt at convincing the ferryman, she decided to take the bridge, but the mad man killed her.

Group Task (20 minutes)

Discuss and agree upon as a group, which of the following six people is responsible for the woman's death? List them in descending order of responsibility, and explain why.

> the woman
> the husband
> the lover
> the madman
> the ferryman
> the friend

In our group, after reading the exercise, we look at each other. No one speaks.

I decide to start the ball rolling, "Well, what a story! I think the man who loved her is to blame for being so stingy."

"Oh no, not at all, it's the woman's fault because she was unfaithful to her husband," interjects Ko Thet Oo, indignantly.

"Maybe, but what about the ferryman? He could easily have let her pay later," states Marlar, "He knew the crazy man was a danger. He's to blame."

"What about the husband," I throw in, "Couldn't he be responsible in some way? He neglected his wife, caring only about his work and his position."

Never could I have imagined the deluge of opinions, values, righteousness, and argument this exercise would induce. Everyone has something to say and in each group the discussion goes back and forth, voices raised, laughter and anger in equal quantities, right through the coffee break and still no agreement. Uma tells us to try and find some consensus in our groups but we can't, as some maintain their original position, with only a few being swayed by argument; others are seemingly stuck in the story, unable to see past the exercise into real life.

Back in the meeting room, as each group gives their conclusions, there are more arguments and although no one comes to blows, we are close to it.

Uma takes control, listing ideas and summarising points we agree upon, then draws out the reasons why each individual is in fact partly responsible for the woman's death. "As in many of life's choices there are no simple solutions, no one is completely guiltless or wholly responsible. There are many contributing factors," she concludes, adding, "If you were any of these people, what might you have done differently?" thereby starting another raucous interchange amongst the team.

"Time for the group photo," I shout above the din, "I know just the place. Follow me." I walk out, the others struggle behind, still loudly voicing their opinions, to an arched, wooden bridge leading from the hotel to the beach. "Right here, on the bridge, how appropriate," I state firmly, and the arguments end in laughter.

As we gather together for the photo, the camera captures a mixed group of all ages, from different parts of the world, but resoundingly now 'a team' after our weekend efforts.

The following morning, we drive back to Yangon. While waiting for the ferry across to Pathein, we share tea and snacks, at ease and joking. I relax and enjoy the busy dockside atmosphere, indulging in one of my favourite pastimes—people watching. Small, high-sterned boats ply their way across the river, the oarsmen expertly rowing against the current, leaning into the oars, facing forward. Bicycle taxis are lined up ready for customers, a few with flowers tied to the handlebar. A mother and son, cheeks identically painted with thanakha, serve noodles in a spotless stall, a woman sells fried chicken, the enamel bowl on her head stacked with golden thighs one side, breasts on the other. Children are everywhere, running, playing, some carrying baby brothers or sisters.

A handsome, muscled young man sits by the riverbank in a white, sleeveless T-shirt and checked longyi, his conical rattan hat slanted low over his eyes, hands clasped around a raised knee, an unlit cigarette drooping from his fingers. He's completely still but intent on something. I follow his gaze to a young woman sitting at a food stall, her flowered longyi artfully draped over her crossed legs, the brim of her hat all but hiding her downcast eyes. Her matching stillness and her slightly pouting full red lips are the only indication that she's fully aware of her admirer. She is also interested. I wonder if this is a new romance blossoming or just a casual flirtation to pass the time. I'll never know

We board the old metal ferry and lean on the railing, commenting on other travellers as we head upstream for several hundred metres to the deep docking place. A lone passenger dressed neatly with a suit and tie stands steadying his bicycle with one hand, holding up an umbrella in the other, very formal and serious…perhaps a village official on urgent business. From a muddy spit of land, a line of people laden with packages wade out to a boat; a young girl carries a small wooden table on her head, the food on top covered with a blue cloth, a man rolls a car tyre, everyone hitching up their longyis as they reach deeper water.

At one point on our long drive back, we slow down where the road is being levelled and laid with gravel. More than thirty young men and women are digging, carrying baskets of gravel, raking out the stones. They wear dust caked clothes under wide rattan hats. Its hard, hot, backbreaking, tedious work for little, or more likely, no pay, a job expected of many as 'required service' to their community. Further along, billows of steam rise from huge dented drums of boiling bitumen, poured manually across the gravel-surfaced road. This crew is made up of young men, their foot protection black rubber boots or, in some cases, just rubber slippers. Sweat pours off their faces. Glancing at my colleagues, I can see I'm not the only one appalled. An uneasy silence falls.

As we continue driving uphill, two massive elephants, ridden by their mahouts, appear suddenly round a blind corner and the van swerves, narrowly avoiding a collision. The elephants continue plodding on down the hill. One of the team remarks, "Well, that gives a whole new meaning to heavy traffic" and we laugh a little shakily, the tension easing.

We return to Yangon a more cohesive team. Our discussions and decisions have established reference points, allowing us to work together better, aware and respectful of differing opinions and approaches.

But the one thing that really sticks, and always causes laughter if alluded to, is 'crossing the bridge.' If anyone becomes romantically involved, we wonder if he or she has crossed the bridge yet. When it's time for someone to get serious in their intentions, we suggest they 'cross the bridge.' When, in future meetings, we mention the phrase 'crossing the bridge,' those team-building days at the beach instantly conjure up the smell of sea and sand, Sandy's birthday dinner, and the heated discussions. But most of all we remember it as the time we stopped being colleagues and became 'family'.

Chapter Six
Health Matters

It's October and the pressure is on again. I'm poring over the multitude of papers spread out before me, piecing them together for the Annual Appeal Document and Budget, a consolidated 'wish list' for the National Society and for the delegation. My team members have already spent long hours with their MRCS counterparts, planning and pricing each vital Red Cross programme. My role is to oversee the whole process, write the preface and analysis, ensure the content is clear and consistent and has the approval of the President. The deadline is just ten days from now.

Reviewing the health programmes, I realize I don't have a clear enough understanding of the more recent projects in the hands of the competent health team. Heading to the Health Office, I ask, "Mallu, when and where are you organising the next Community Based First Aid Training? I've been writing about it, but I really need to see how it plays out in reality."

45

"You're in luck. Dr Htut, Aye Aye Thant, and I are going to Sagaing Division next week," she responds after checking her wall calendar. "We leave on Wednesday, back on Sunday. It's quite an active Division with lots of eager, young volunteers."

"That's perfect for me. Is there anything I could do to help?" I ask, anxious to be involved rather than just an observer.

"How about a session on the *Principles*?" she suggests.

On Wednesday, the four of us, laden with bags, teaching materials, and First Aid Satchels for the volunteers, arrive in Mandalay. A local Committee member and two young volunteers, impeccable in their blue longyis and Red Cross T-shirts, greet us warmly and whisk us into a van for the hour-long trip to the city. Driving across the dry, dusty flatlands, then along a river, we pass through small clusters of houses perched on stilts. It's still early and relatively cool but people here are already busy cooking and trading, as temperatures rise steadily through the day and activities all but cease in the afternoon heat.

At the local Red Cross branch, we meet the eighteen course participants, eleven of them young women. Trained first aiders with a good grasp of English, they are excited to have been chosen to qualify as local trainers.

The course will take place in a monastery in a village beyond Sagaing, a ninety-minute drive from Mandalay. As well as attending lectures, the volunteers will run practical exercises with school pupils and visit a village to pinpoint key health issues.

We wind our way towards the white spire of a stupa on the hill above the village, passing through narrow streets bordered by houses and shops, barking dogs running along, people turning to look at our small convoy of vans with mini MRCS flags flying from the aerials. As we drive closer, other chedis appear, one with a large white concrete elephant, another with an equally large frog at the entrance.

"That's different," remarks Mallu, pointing at the animals, "I thought temples were usually guarded by lions?"

"Yes, that's right," replies one of the volunteers, "though we call them *Chinthe*, the mythical lions of Myanmar. Perhaps none were available, and they used other animals as protectors instead," he smiles.

The monastery is beside the pagoda, a solid concrete structure with an open courtyard, its kitchen built into the rock wall at the back and a big classroom at the side. The dormitories are in separate wooden, leaf-roofed houses, with rows of bamboo beds, a metal trunk at the foot of each with a pillow, sheet and blanket stacked on top, mosquito nets hanging from the rafters.

After refreshments, the volunteers assemble for the first lecture of the afternoon. They are attentive, taking notes while Dr Htut talks about community health issues—sanitation, clean water, mosquito-borne diseases and intestinal problems. Mallu then takes over with a lively anatomy lesson, reiterating the importance of good health, and outlining potential accidents and ailments. Hand-outs are circulated, then it's question time; the animated students are eager to show their knowledge and interest.

Aye Thant talks about the following day's school visit, asking the students what topics they think we should teach the children and how can we best get our messages across. She divides the volunteers into three groups, giving them half an hour to discuss this and present their ideas before dinner.

We circulate, listening, ensuring the groups are working on different ideas. The first group decides to deliver their health messages through songs for the youngest children. The second believes a talk and demonstration on personal hygiene would be useful, and the third plans to show the pupils how to care for their small cuts and scrapes. As each group presents their ideas, there's a buzz of excitement, everyone eager to start preparing their lesson.

Aye Thant asks if they have all the materials they need. "Don't get carried away and stay up too late." she warns, "We have three more days to go and a lot to do, so get some rest tonight."

Thursday morning Mallu and I, clad in red longyis and Red Cross t-shirts, arrive at the school with our MRCS colleagues just before nine and are immediately surrounded by eager, smiling students. News has travelled and villagers are also standing around, waiting expectantly. The school is a two-story wooden building set in a large field with a covered terrace along the front, some water-points and a row of latrines beyond. Older students hang over the upstairs railings and shout out their welcome, leaving reluctantly when called back to their lessons.

Downstairs, the big classroom has rows of wooden desks and benches from the end of which hang the children's colourful woven bags, in greens, reds and blues. At the front is an open area, with a few shelves holding a meagre collection of books and a blackboard on an easel. Windows line one side of the room while hand-made posters decorate the opposite wall—the times tables, a map of Myanmar and the Burmese alphabet. Other posters hang in a bunch from a nail in the beam, the topmost showing the Government's call for national reconciliation, portraying men and women of different ethnic groups. I wonder about how those lessons are conducted and perceived by the children and their parents.

The pupils, aged between six and eight, sit cross-legged on the floor, arms neatly folded, boys on the left, girls on the right. The boys' green and white uniforms are punctuated by the dark red robes of a few novice monks, while on the girls' side, thanakha painted cheeks, flowers tucked behind ears and bright hair ribbons add touches of colour.

Dr Htut introduces everyone, to a chorus of "Mingalar-ba, good morning Dr Htut, Mingalar-ba, good morning Ma Joanna," in that universal singsong chant of school children the world over. He tells them a little about the Red Cross and explains that we are here to talk about their health. He asks questions about their washing habits, how long they sleep at night, what foods they eat, how many have had malaria. They are wide eyed at the strangers, but once a brave boy has answered a question and has been praised, others are eager to speak out and wave their arms vigorously, desperate to show off.

The first group is ready with their lesson, an action song, the words printed on large sheets of paper tacked to the wooden partitions. The children are coached through the melody and words, volunteers performing, children mimicking their actions, laughing as they get things mixed up. When the teacher suggests trying the song outside, the pupils are out the door in an instant, except for a few waylaid by the Doctor who checks on those who look anaemic, are too thin, or coughing a lot.

On the lawn, the children form a circle around the volunteers who remain on the inside, facing out. Two of the children call me to join, putting their small hands in mine and I hum along and perform the actions—washing, eating, brushing, showering, and tucking in the mosquito net. It's fun and the children learn quickly. Between each verse we join hands and sing the chorus, moving in a circle. The children are asked to teach the song to their brothers and sisters and they agree, nodding vigorously, happy with their new knowledge.

Upstairs, other volunteers are beginning their lessons with the older pupils. One team has generously daubed themselves and a few willing pupils with fake blood, others cradling a 'broken arm' or writhing in agony from a bad stomach. With the aid of posters and discussion, diagnoses are made and treatment is agreed upon. The session is lively and all are involved, clustering around to get a closer look or clean a wound, bandage an arm or give oral rehydration salts. The mothers, hanging in at the open windows, beam proudly when their child performs well. One by one, the invalids and casualties are treated, the clear explanations ensuring the messages are getting through, to pupils and mothers alike.

In the adjacent room, the third team has put up posters of latrines, plates of food, flies, washing and collection points on a river. Lined up along the front are buckets of water and saucers with cakes of soap. Their lesson is about the importance of clean hands, safe water and healthy food. Graphic demonstrations about bad stomachs and 'dirty' food cause a lot of merriment, but nodding of heads as well. Each child comes to wash their hands but when the first few just dip and shake, others chorus, "No, do it again. Use the soap."

I watch with interest and ask Mallu, "Aren't these lessons a bit simple? Wouldn't they know already about covering food and washing their hands?"

"Often the most basic messages give the best results. If all the mothers prepare food with clean hands and the family wash their hands after using the latrine and before eating, this alone can cut down the intestinal and gastric problems by as much as fifty per cent," she responds, with the authority of someone who has worked in some of the poorest communities in Africa, Asia, and the Middle East.

We're invited to a meal of rice, beans and vegetables, with a little meat. The pupils are chased away, but the mothers stand around, offering us more and chatting, tots resting on their hips. A baby chews on a corncob. Another sucks a watermelon rind, the juice staining her lips red, dribbles down the front of her dress. The women thank us for teaching their children and say they'll try extra hard to follow our lessons. As we leave, I look back to watch the sea of green and white uniforms and waving hands, the chorus of the 'health' song rising enthusiastically to send us on our way.

The afternoon lesson, back at the monastery, concerns waterborne diseases, including how to make a simple water filter from a clay pot filled with layers of sand and stones. I leave the team and wander down to the village green, or rather dustbowl, which has a well at its centre. I sit by a bright pink and purple bougainvillea bush, in the shade of the huge canopy trees, watching the villagers.

School is out and the kids are kicking balls or skipping rope. Many women and a few men come to the well, buckets slung by lengths of rope at either end of a bamboo pole balanced over one shoulder. They arrive, ambling casually, but turn to walk back home with that particular gait associated with carrying a heavy load, the movement centred in the hips and lower limbs, shoulders set squarely to carry the weight, hands outspread to hold the buckets steady. I wonder how many thousands of times they've done this.

They know who I am, of course. The women smile at me and the children try and draw me into their games or crowd around to chat. I buy a can of coke. It's lukewarm but pleasant to sip until my ride arrives, whisking me off for an evening in Mandalay.

The following day is a village survey. The volunteers pair up, starting at different ends of the village to cover most households. One will ask questions they prepared the evening before, the other will take notes.

Strolling through the village to the Headman's house, I feel as though I am stepping back in time. The narrow, dusty, and long-used road has sunk beneath the level of the bamboo fences and flowering shrubs. We walk as though in a tunnel. Inquisitive villagers smile and greet us, and we stand aside as wooden wheeled buffalo carts creak past. The only other visible means of transport are several old Raleigh bicycles, black and upright. The houses are simple, some on stilts with animals underneath, but most just small wooden, thatched dwellings with packed earth floors. We stop to talk to an old man in a blue turban, checked shirt and *longyi*, leading four white cebu cattle out to graze. A family wanders towards us, their feet white with dust. The young mother, her hair parted in the middle, a bun coiled over each ear, carries a baby and is accompanied by a boy of about nine and two younger sisters, the younger crying but soothed by her mother's hand caressing the back of her neck.

Arriving at the Headman's house we are invited inside. While our Myanmar colleagues discuss the two day programme, Mallu and I are led to a small room, settled into chairs and offered tea. When the headman and our colleagues join us, we are introduced to the Headman's mother, a slight elderly woman in her mid-seventies. She takes my hand and sits by me. She has a little English and I ask about her family and the village. As we talk, another woman comes to offer more tea. I stare a little for she is so like my new friend.

"She's my twin sister," the Headman's mother tells me, smiling. "She lives next door."

They speak the same way and often touch, caressing or linking elbows. Between them they have eleven children and thirty-one grandchildren, they tell me proudly, although they don't specify how many for each, that fact seemingly unimportant. When I ask for their photo, it doesn't surprise me that they stand side by side, heads at exactly the same tilt, arms hanging, the little toe of one touching the foot of the other, for comfort or courage.

As we finish our tea, I try to learn more about them, asking what has changed in their lifetime, for better or worse. They look surprised by my question, then answer in unison, "Nothing."

"But during the war, weren't you in the line of the Japanese invasion?" I push a little.

They look at each other, and one says, "Yes, we moved into the jungle to the north, lived there for a while and afterwards we came back."

But then, just when I feel I can't be too nosy, the Headman's mother looks at her sister, laughs a little, and says to her, "Do you remember when we were young? We only saw birds flying in the sky. Now we see those things our grandchildren tell us are airplanes. So yes, some things have changed," she tells me proudly, happy to have been able to answer my question after all.

Leaving the Headman's house, we walk further into the village and witness a pair of volunteers interviewing a plump woman sitting in her carved wooden doorway, skeins of cotton thread twisted into figures of eight hanging from the lintel above. She has a big smile but no front teeth. She says her health is fine but her eyesight is weak and she would love a pair of glasses so she can sew again and read. When they ask if she has ever been to a clinic, she says, "No. I had all my children at home. I never needed to go to a big clinic, the midwife and health workers always help." Sagaing and Mandalay are only a couple of hours' drive away but in all her life she has never travelled there. "What would I want to go there for? I have everything I want here." she says.

Wandering further, I admire the houses, most with the same pattern of wooden beams and posts, woven bamboo walls, and palm leaf thatched roofs. Outside each house are large pottery water jars with wooden lids, the dipper made of a coconut husk with a wooden handle pushed through it. Some houses have a long pole leaning against the wall with a row of seven plastic bags filled with water and seven filled with sand hung on a bamboo pole between two trees. When I ask what they're for, Aye Thant explains, "In the dry zone, to stop fires getting out of hand, every household has to have, by law, that long pole to pull down burning thatch. The water and sand are to douse small fires. At the driest times of the year, no one is allowed to cook after sunset or before sunrise. In some places, even cigar smoking is forbidden in case people throw them down carelessly."

With all the houses being made of wood and woven bamboo, I can see how easily a fire could destroy a whole village in a matter of minutes, so I am fascinated to hear of these simple, but tried and tested disaster preparedness techniques. As I walk, I check, and indeed most houses comply with the law.

At the next turn of the road four beautiful young women lean over a bamboo fence, greeting us. Their mother calls from the house offering tea. We accept and go inside to sit on a low bench. Behind her are several large raised bamboo beds, nets draped above; beyond is a cooking area, a low shelf holding pots and household items, a few wooden cupboards, and a chest for clothes and bedding. We are offered biscuits and fruit and, with my colleagues' help, I ask a few questions.

"How many children do you have? Any sons as well as these beautiful girls?" I ask. The woman tells me she has four sons and four daughters. The girls help her with the livestock—buffalo, pigs, and chickens—and the boys work in the fields with their father, although one son, she tells me proudly, is in Mandalay training to be a teacher. The eldest daughter will marry a young man from the village this year and, she is sure, the others will soon be well matched too. I pose a more difficult question, but one which interests me, because the family seem so content with their life.

"If you could make a wish and be granted anything you wanted in life, what might that be?"

The mother thinks for a while and then, smiling at her daughters, she answers, "The only thing I can think of right now is to have two more buffalo. I have eight children and only six buffalo so one per child would be better. The extra income would help, especially now as I want my youngest son to be a novice and I can't afford it. Just that, and we would be very happy." I am humbled by her answer and by this close-knit family. Her words impress me, and I wonder how many others in the wider world I know are as contented.

When we leave they go back to their tasks, one cutting fodder for the buffalo with a wooden guillotine, another taking the baskets behind the house to the animals while two stay behind to help their mother spin and weave the colourful woven cotton lengths for longyis and bedcovers to use or sell.

The volunteers are now gathering back at the crossroads, their interviews in the box. We retrace our steps to the vans, the villagers very friendly now and waving, calling out that they look forward to seeing us tomorrow.

In the afternoon, after lunch and a short nap for everyone, I give my lecture. Of course, as Red Cross volunteers, they can recite the *seven Fundamental Principles* word perfect, but how to bring them to life? I talk about storytelling, of messages passed through generations all over the world, then I launch into an illustration of the principle of 'Unity' as told to me by volunteers in Mongolia.

"This story is about the mother of Genghis Khan. Do you know of him?" I ask, and they nod yes.

"His mother was a wise woman and taught her children well, urging them to work together, to look after each other, and to use their collective strength to advantage. To make her point, she took an arrow and gave it to one of her sons, asking him to break it. He broke it easily, as though a twig. Giving an arrow to each of children, she asked them to break it. Puzzled, they did so. She then took a whole quiver of arrows, seven or eight, one for each of her children, and gave it to her firstborn, asking him to break them. As hard as he tried, his face contorted with the effort, he could not. Another brother, proud of his fighting prowess, took the arrows and he too tried but in vain. The eldest daughter, her muscles strong from carrying water and long hours in the fields, also tried, to no avail. Their mother then explained, 'You see, if you act alone, you can be easily tested and defeated, just like that single arrow. But if you stand together and work as one you cannot be broken, you will not be destroyed.'"

"Imagine," I finish, "that is just how we can be in the Red Cross. Singly—one person, one branch, one national society—we can only do a little, but if we work in unison and with purpose, our message and actions can have a huge impact on peoples' health and safety. That is our principle of 'Unity'. Think of stories you could use tomorrow, from history or religion, or perhaps some of your well known proverbs," I encourage them. "Everybody loves a story. If it has a message, even better."

The following morning, we are escorted to the Headman's house by a group of excited village children. Half the volunteers are there, neatly dressed in their Red Cross uniforms, hats and all. The outer room is hung with posters, handmade overnight by the team. Seventy or eighty women and men are seated on woven mats, a few young children clambering on their mothers' laps. Aye Thant tells me, "The Headman says the only other time so many people gather together is for the monthly movie nights."

I stand at the back of the room, leaning against a rough beam and observe the volunteers in action. They have orchestrated their health messages and demonstrations perfectly, each volunteer playing a role, giving information, asking a question, then another taking over with a story or a burst of song. I hear jingles I recognise as does the audience, radio advertisements for soap, matches or paint, but with health messages for the villagers to learn, repeat and remember. Eyes swivel to watch the young health workers point out the health hazards illustrated in their posters and hands go up with questions. There are murmurs of understanding at some points, laughter at others.

When two volunteers lie down pretending to sleep, only one has a mosquito net hung over her. Everyone cranes to see what this is about. Under the net, our young volunteer sleeps peacefully, even adding a realistic snore or two. The other mimes mosquito attacks, all flailing arms and itching and a little later, shivers violently with malaria tremors. The message is clear: night mosquitoes carry malaria, protect your family with mosquito nets.

I leave them to witness the other team's performance. Under a roofed area in front of a shrine, another eighty or ninety villagers are gathered. The volunteers are teaching about cleaning and dressing wounds. One is seated on a chair with a decidedly grisly wound painted all too realistically on his foot, a second volunteer standing beside, reassuring and calming him. A third volunteer tends the wound, explaining what she is doing and why, as she gently cleans the dirt out of the gash. She has thin plastic bags over her hands, perfect substitutes for rubber gloves, thumb and index fingers each pushed into a corner. She covers the wound with a square of gauze and applies the bandage in a neat figure of eight around the foot and ankle. Four willing pairs of villagers are then chosen from the audience, with one as patient, another as nurse, coached through the art of bandaging by the volunteers, their friends vocal in their encouragement or criticism.

In the afternoon, back at the monastery we meet for the evaluation session. I listen to my colleagues debriefing the volunteers, praising them for a job well done and questioning them on how they plan to use their new skills.

Dr Htut and Mallu make their closing remarks and then call me to the front to award the Attendance Certificates. As each volunteer's name is called, they step forward and receive their own First Aid Satchel from Mallu, complete with supplies of basic materials, and then their certificate from me, proud smiles on all our faces.

Our plane back to Yangon on Sunday isn't until midday and we have time to drive up to Mandalay Hill. We admire the views over the river and the city, circling the pagoda platform clockwise, taking time to pay our respect to the Buddha images and at small shrines. I dip a bowl into the fountain and pour water over Garuda, my Sunday-born protector. At his back, the wall is covered with small diamond shaped glass mosaics in which I catch a glimpse of my reflection, somewhat distorted. Above is a carved sign which reads:

Long liveness will be prevailed if you be with Mandalay Hill.

This image stays with me and Monday evening, with the document deadline looming, once again hunched over my desk, I finally put the finishing touches to the conclusion of this year's Annual Appeal.

It's our wish that the services of MRCS will form an ever growing mosaic across the country, and that the response to this new appeal will provide the means to strengthen the existing and emerging health and disaster related programmes and support the staff and volunteers who work tirelessly in their communities to assist the most vulnerable."

As I press 'save,' the slightly quirky phrase comes back to me.

Long liveness will be prevailed. And I wish fervently it will be so for the volunteers and programmes of the Myanmar Red Cross.

Long Liveness indeed!

Chapter Seven
A Cabbage, A Cyclone

When asked, "What motivated you to join the Red Cross?" those expecting to hear about a higher calling are somewhat nonplussed when I respond, "It's because of a cabbage."

At the end of the seventies, after several years in England, I decided to go back to New Zealand and resume my career in teaching. Unfortunately, my return coincided with a fall in school enrolments and the government decreeing that anyone away from teaching in NZ for more than three years must take a twelve-week refresher course at their own expense. As I had been teaching in the UK, I thought this a bit of nonsense. Furthermore, I needed to start earning again.

I searched newspaper ads and asked friends about any job opportunities. Nothing tempted me. One particularly wet and gloomy afternoon, my mother handed me a torn, crumpled piece of newsprint. "I found this in the paper," she said, " it might interest you." The paper had been wrapped around the cabbage for our evening meal. Smoothing out the sheet and reading it while she waited for the food to cook was an endearing habit of hers and she would often regale us over dinner with stories she had gleaned from these pages.

I took the snippet: New Zealand Red Cross seeks Assistant Youth Director to prepare teaching materials and support local youth groups.

"You must be joking," I exclaimed, "The Red Cross is all old ladies and cups of tea!" I'd steered well clear of a Junior Red Cross group at my school. Learning first aid, doing 'good deeds,' and raising money for the needy was just not my thing.

A couple of days later, mostly to please my mother and appear pro-active in my job search, I prepared and sent off an application letter. I was surprised but pleased to be shortlisted, interviewed and finally offered the job to start mid-January 1978.

My first assignment was the creation of teaching modules detailing the work of the Red Cross in war and peace for the lower secondary school Social Studies syllabus. The first of these modules was 'Cyclones in the Bay of Bengal'.

And now, here I am in June 2004, more than a quarter of a century later, standing atop a brick breakwater, looking out over the choppy dull green sea of the Bay of Bengal, ominous thunder clouds in the distance, evenly spaced, like lines on a musical score.

I go back in my mind to that first teaching module I researched—the weather patterns, the low-lying Bangladesh delta at the top of the bay, exotic town names like Cox's Bazaar, Chittagong and Nazir Hat, the huge packed earth pyramids the villagers and their livestock climbed to escape rising flood waters, the maps, the photos, the stories. I had written about it, never imagining I would one day see it for myself, let alone be involved in a cyclone relief operation.

The Rakhine coast of Myanmar is relatively well protected from the Bay of Bengal cyclones. Offshore islands shelter the coastline and the land is higher than that of neighbouring Bangladesh, with mountains rising off the coastal area. This year, however, a tropical cyclone struck the coast near Sittwe, penetrating inland along the course of the Kaladan

River, the shrieking, tearing winds and pounding storm surges destroying thousands of houses, sinking hundreds of fishing boats. More than two hundred people lost their lives, scores more were injured, the children still fearful and fractious. The saltwater and wind damaged the rice crop and the prawn breeding grounds and devastated a number of inland villages. Electricity and phone lines were brought down and many areas were inaccessible for days or weeks after the storm.

A small Headquarters team assisted the Sittwe Branch leaders and volunteers during the first days of the relief operation and in the 'needs assessment' of the affected area. They negotiated with the authorities for the role and responsibilities of Red Cross as auxiliary to the Government Relief Operation to be accepted and respected. After a first distribution to some three hundred and fifty families during the emergency phase, relief supplies from the Sittwe and HQ warehouses are exhausted. More is needed.

The MRCS, supported by our Delegation, launches an emergency appeal through the International Federation for funds to support 25,000 beneficiaries over a four-month period and to institute long term disaster preparedness planning, essential in this high-risk area.

The appeal garners support both from outside and inside the country, new donors and other organizations feeding their assistance through the Red Cross, not having permission to access the region themselves. Dilemmas are faced and solutions agreed upon after much heated discussion, such as the purchase of rice. Should it be the high quality rice set out in our 'standards and procedures', only available in Yangon, or lower-grade rice bought locally to help boost the local economy, costing less, feeding more people and, because it's harder to digest, keeping bellies full for longer? We buy locally.

A month into the operation, a trip is scheduled to monitor a second distribution to a wider area, and to prepare an updated photographic report of the relief operation. Our team consists of U Soe Thein, MRCS Executive Committee Member in charge of Relief, U Kyaw Soe and U Hla Myint, Head and Deputy of Disaster Response and myself from the Delegation. We reach Sittwe after a bumpy flight with a small Yangon

Airways plane and are met by the local Chairman. I participate in the 'welcome-meeting-lunch' routine, though aware I'm here as an observer, photographer, and appeal writer, not an operator.

Then we board a rented launch with colleagues from the MRCS Sittwe Branch. Chugging up-stream, sluggish against the swollen brown waters of the Kaladan River, U Kyaw Soe explains that earlier today the Sittwe team delivered supplies—rice, beans, pulses, salt and oil—to a village school but now await our arrival for the formal distribution.

We pass small villages, children waving and racing along the bank, keeping pace with us until they tire out. The destructive force of the cyclone is visible in the many fallen trees and strangely twisted houses. After nearly two hours, we come ashore and are picked up by an old van. We drive through flatlands, the road elevated, bright green paddy fields on either side, the darkening sky announcing more rain and strengthening winds. The bright plastic rain capes of men driving buffalo through the paddy fields blow wildly, one man leaping dramatically to catch his conical rattan hat as it blows off his head. Beyond them, small villages are almost hidden by trees and, further away, rise bush-covered hills.

The drive takes less than an hour, the deluge starting just as we arrive. The MRCS team run out to greet us at the school gate, holding large umbrellas. The villagers, waiting on the covered veranda stand aside politely as we are escorted into a classroom. The desks have been pushed back against the walls, leaving three rows of wooden benches. A Red Cross flag hangs from the rafters and fifty-kilo rice sacks are stacked at the front of the room. Bottles of oil, packets of beans, pulses and salt are arranged in neat rows on the teacher's desk.

I sit at the end of the front bench to watch the proceedings. After our team has conferred with the local Red Crossers and the registration lists checked, the villagers, mostly women, take their places on the benches. An elderly couple catches my attention. The man has close-cropped white hair and a handsome square-jawed face. The woman is tiny, her grey hair neatly wound into a bun, showing her small gold and ruby earrings, with a soft pink *eingyi* and flowered *longyi*.

He is very protective, his arm on her shoulder or elbow, or their hands lightly touching. Perhaps she feels me watching and turns to me for a moment, a beautiful smile lighting up her face and I catch a glimpse of how she must have looked as a young girl. I wonder how long they've been married, about the pattern of their lives, so different from mine, and smile back, bowing my head a little to acknowledge her silent greeting.

U Soe Thein greets the villagers. From his gestures and the few words I recognize, he is talking about what they can expect in the coming weeks to help them through this difficult time. The group applauds; then, as their names are called, they come to collect their supplies. It's not a lot, but sufficient to provide them with food for another few weeks. Some leave immediately, others hunker down on the veranda, sitting on their rice sacks to wait out the rain or for a family member to help them tote their load homewards.

I gaze out the open doorway across the schoolyard where a crowd has gathered to watch the distribution, unperturbed by the rain, chatting and laughing under bright umbrella canopies. A lone nun approaches, her pink robes and bronze umbrella outlined against the green shrubs and trees along the roadway. She walks sedately, staring straight ahead, passing the gaggle of villagers, neither turning her head, nor slowing her step. I wonder if she is meditating or just very serious and disinterested in village happenings.

My team tells me I'm in for a treat. Today is Friday and as the distribution in Sittwe is planned for Monday, it's been decided that we'll visit one of Myanmar's famous historical sites, Mrauk-U, a few hour's drive away, staying there over the weekend.

It rains through most of the two-hour trip, the van sliding on parts of the road, several pieces of the chassis falling off as we lurch along. First the overhead light drops from the ceiling onto my knee, startling me, then a door handle drops to the floor. A little later, we hear graunching, a rattle and a clunk and, stopping to investigate, the driver holds up, almost gleefully, the now detached back bumper bar. He spends some time, U Hla Myint assisting alongside with an umbrella, and expertly fixes it back on with a twist of rusty wire; at the same time, they tell us proudly, climbing back in, they managed to secure the exhaust pipe which was also in danger of leaving us. At dusk we reach the Nawarat Hotel, the only one in town with the necessary amenities, and settle in.

We share a candlelit dinner as there is no power. I eat what's in front of me, not sure of the ingredients of each dish. The collections of dried frogs, crickets and coils of dubious entrails in the local markets make me a little suspicious. The menu doesn't help, offering pig's ears, duck's beak, offal broth, and stir-fried umbilicus with chilli. I trust my colleagues' choices and wash the food down with slugs of beer. As we chat about the distribution and issues to be faced, I sense my colleagues feel freer than usual to talk, here, in the half-dark, far from Yangon. I admire their ability to 'walk a tightrope' between the different pressures they're under, from their own countrymen and from the donors funding the operation. Though proud of their country and its history, they voice their own opinions carefully.

On Saturday, though it's still raining, the local chairman leads us in a tour of the main sites of Mrauk-U. Our first stop is by a new pagoda, marble steps leading up to a magnificent portico and decorated hall. I'm captivated by a small group of naked boys sliding bare-bottomed from the top of a slanted marble-tiled walkway, brown skin slick with rain, hair plastered to their skulls, beaming as they cavort in this sanctified playground, their antics capturing the essence of childhood. I wonder whether today might be one of those carefree days they will remember as old men.

Mrauk-U is a vast complex. Several hundred chedis and temples—some in total ruin, others semi restored, many still magnificent in their original state—are scattered among trees and high grass, immersed in the rural life flowing around them. Men walk behind their oxen, ploughing furrows in the wet dark earth. Women, knee-deep in rice paddies, tend their crop. Young girls carry buckets of water from the wells to the small houses hidden among the trees and creepers surrounding the tall, dark stone ruins and tiered wooden pagodas. Only a few bright umbrellas and plastic rain capes modernize an otherwise age-old scene.

We approach a huge squat building and, passing under an arched stone portal, enter a long underground tunnel with a vaulted ceiling.

On our right, a thigh-high ledge holds sitting Buddha statues spaced a couple of feet apart, their colours faded but the coiled topknot still black and the robes a dusty brown. On the left are smaller golden Buddha figures, each in its own small niche spaced two and two above, two and two below.

Turning a corner, we reach a section where recent restoration has brought colour and detail back. Beautiful broad, fine-featured faces have been repainted in gold, eyebrows and eyes delicately picked out in black and white, extended earlobes adorned with gold earrings and a few elaborately patterned crowns recreated. Further along, the walls are covered by carved and painted images of battle scenes, horses and chariots, festivals and processions with kings, queens and nobles, decorated elephants and amorous couples, and I wish I knew more about the stories they depict.

At the end of the tunnel, we emerge through an archway dripping with creepers and raindrops, the bright green paddy fields before us dotted with dark stone temples, some with strange bell-shaped structures on their flat roofs.

Having lagged behind with my camera, as usual, I catch up with my colleagues who are now laughing at something. They watch expectantly as I look for the source of their amusement. On a wall of stone carvings, I see a human figure with a buffalo head and splendid horns, a magician in black and white wielding divining tools and a demon-like figure in bright colours, all sharp teeth and claws. Finally, there it is, an amorous couple, naked, the man's arm around the woman's shoulders, his free hand fondling her supremely rounded and nippled breast. Her eyes are downcast, but her hand is outstretched, touching his genitalia. Instead of blushing, I laugh with them, hiding a smile behind my camera as I catch a perfectly angled shot of this wonderfully erotic image of young love.

In the afternoon, while the group is back at the hotel resting, I walk alone through the lanes and fields to explore a high fortress set a little apart. The rain has stopped and a watery sun filters through the clouds, casting a golden glow, bouncing dazzling shards of light off puddles and dripping leaves. The tower, its dark stonewalls punctuated by square holes, rises through the trees ahead, cattle grazing on the lower terraces.

A young shepherd boy sits perched on a high stone rampart, holding a carved catapult, a leather pouch of carefully picked stones beside him. As I approach, he climbs down to greet me, posing for a photo and I ask him to show me his prowess with the catapult. Carefully fitting one of the rounded stones in the heavy black rubber sling, his brings his right hand level with his eye, straightens his left arm to stretch the rubber and lets fly. The pebble hurtles forth and with a 'ping', hits and overturns a can further down the rampart. He must have been passing his time practicing and I am the perfect, appreciative audience.

I take the track up to the building, startling an old doorman dozing at a bare table who sells me a ticket for a thousand Kyat and gestures that I can go where I want. Not here are the seasoned guides or the gawking crowds of tourists. Inside, apart from a few wall paintings, there's nothing much to see, but walking around the outer corridor, punctuated with the square holes I saw from below, I am captured by the magnificent views. The afternoon light bathes the village's two storied woven bamboo houses and their neat, latticed fences, catching the golden tips of the tall wooden pagoda spires visible above the trees and washes over the bright green paddy fields. In the distance, darker green, regularly spaced hillocks, rise from the plain, maybe hiding yet more stupas, the wooden pagodas long gone, decayed beneath the sodden bulk of vegetation.

Walking back, I wave to the boy now shepherding his cattle home. As he comes closer I pull some candies and a small kyat note from my pocket as thanks for the photo and his show of skill and he responds with a beaming smile.

The distribution in Sittwe on this rainy Monday, is in a monastery on the outskirts of town. As sacks of rice are unloaded from the truck by a line of bare-chested men, the recipients arrive and sit in groups at the back of the hall. The women are called one by one, their name checked off the list and a card made for them with three dates, for this and two subsequent distributions. A few sign their names but most dye their thumb on a blue stamp and mark their print on the register. The rations are the same as in the previous village, with the all important hefty sack of rice, but here, oil, salt, beans, and pulses are packed in a multi-purpose plastic bucket. Taking their supplies, the villagers return to the back of the room and continue chatting, puffing on cigars to wait, the rain ceaselessly thrumming, a constant backdrop to the proceedings.

In the street outside, children splash in puddles, lines of bicycle rickshaws ferry people from place to place, a few stopping outside to transport the rice sacks and the women home. I watch them leave, one or two hoisting a huge sack between them on their shoulders and striding off, others by motorbike, perched precariously atop the sack. I snap a photo for the Report – three women under two red umbrellas, their arms around each other, orange buckets with Red Cross stickers swinging from their hands, a trishaw with three white sacks of rice pedalling steadily after them, bright images in the rainy afternoon.

On Tuesday morning, the rain has stopped. I get up early to wander through the streets, the morning market full of colour and vignettes of daily life. Fresh fish is laid out on wooden planks, some already filleted. Baskets of flowers, white daisies, yellow gladioli and purple orchids vie with food stalls offering breakfast. I'm tempted by the steaming soup and rice porridge, but choose fried breadsticks and milky coffee. Savouring my hot food, I walk to the mouth of the river, the stilted houses still covered in blue plastic tarpaulins, courtesy of the Red Cross. The fishermen will all pitch in to reroof them after the rainy season but, for now, they are kept dry.

Reaching the rocky shoreline, I stand on the top of a brick breakwater, looking out over the choppy dull green sea of the Bay of Bengal and watch a new storm approaching, threatening thunderclouds in the distance.

On the flight back to Yangon, my thoughts drift. Earlier in the year I had been invited by New Zealand Red Cross to speak about my experience with the International Red Cross and Myanmar in particular. Presentations in eight different cities in ten days, radio and TV interviews as well as formal meetings with the NZRC leadership and with NZAid, my visit had been busy but rewarding, reaping additional funds for Myanmar.

One of the presentations was in Dunedin, my hometown in the

South Island. After the initial greetings, having checked my computer's connection, the show was ready to go, and I rewarded myself with a cup of tea. As I stood there, flowered china cup and saucer in my hand, greeting the members and audience as they arrived, I had a sudden epiphany. I was now that 'old lady with a cup of tea', whom I had scorned many years ago when my mother had handed me that crumpled, torn newspaper advert from around the cabbage.

Quite by accident, and because of that cabbage, I had found a great organization I fitted into, whose ethics and mandate I could espouse, whose challenges and outreach had given me so much professional and personal satisfaction. And which ultimately had led me here to Myanmar, this fascinating, complicated, beautiful, and frustrating country, and to its generous people.

Chapter Eight
The Glass Factory

I have been looking forward to visiting the glass factory since I first saw some of their creations at a dinner party in a colleague's wonderful old wooden house by the lake. The large reception room looking out across an extensive lawn to the water was filled with beautiful Asian artefacts—lacquer bowls, betel boxes, ethnic silver and brass jewellery and intricate wooden carvings—testifying to the owners many years' life and work in this region. A smoky golden glass vase with enormous, sweet smelling lilies had been placed below a wall hanging, bringing a touch of the outdoors inside. A stack of magazines, photo books and novels with a predominantly Asian theme was topped by more immediate reading matter—medical papers, reports on TB, HIV/AIDS and malaria in SE Asia.

On the long split bamboo dining table, laid for eight, the gold lacquer place mats, the white china and bubbled green glass of the wine goblets glowed in the light filtering from the low centrepiece of bright tropical flowers and candles.

Dinner was served, wine poured, and the conversation flowed easily amongst the group, a mix of nationalities working for international organizations, foreign embassies, or for one of the few multinational companies permitted to operate in Myanmar.

"I love these glasses," I commented to my hostess in a lull in the conversation," enjoying the feel of the heavy goblet in my hand, "Did you bring them with you from a previous posting?"

"No," she replied, smiling, "they're from the Naga Glass Factory here in Yangon."

"You haven't heard of it?" another guest remarked, "then you ought to put it on your 'must do' list." Others chimed in enthusiastically, each with their descriptions of purchases, whetting my interest.

A few Saturdays later, despite threatening clouds heralding the imminent rainy season, I go shopping with Ko Zaw. Apart from household items, we'll check out the animal market for a puppy to keep me company at home. It remains hot and humid as we shop and my mood lowers as the only puppies at the market are rather unattractive terriers, superlative rat catchers but a little aggressive.

Ko Zaw asks. "Where to now? Back home, or is there something else you'd like to do?" Seeing my glum face, he suggests, "What about visiting the glass factory, I know you've been wanting to do that?"

"That's a great idea. Do you know where it is?"

"Not exactly, but I can find out." he replies.

Secretly, I think he just wants an excuse to use one of our recent purchases, a rather large mobile phone, that he pulls out to call his taxi-driver brother for directions.

Out of town, on a small road, we find a sign hanging lopsided from a sagging wood and wire fence, sprouting new greenery:

The Naga Glass Factory, Est. 1953

The wide gate no longer there, we drive in slowly, down a long, rutted track, huge trees on either side, teak and banyan, leafy, outstretched limbs meeting overhead to embrace us in a green tunnel.

We emerge into a clearing with an open-fronted building on our left, its jutting corrugated roof sheltering two low tables and wooden chairs, a shaggy tarpaulin drooping to one side, deserted and silent. I feel I have somehow stepped into another world, all in shades of green and brown. Gloomy, brooding, but teeming full of life forms I cannot see or imagine.

I breathe in the pungent tropical smells of rotting vegetation and fermenting fruit. The brick-edged beaten earth path is bordered by layer upon layer of glass objects—bowls, glasses, vases, figurines. Clear glass mingles with blue and green, brown and yellow, all covered by a thick layer of dust. In some places the mounds are taller than I am, the bottom layers reabsorbed into the earth, thick creepers anchoring them to the ground. Around a bend, some distance away, I glimpse a larger building, partly obscured by the low hanging trees, creepers, and shrubs.

A sudden wind change and the urgent rustle of leaves heralds a breaking storm. Looking up to the glowering sky, I feel the first huge drops of a tropical downpour on my face. Moving quickly we dash into the building and find ourselves in a large room, darkened by the onslaught of the storm.

Along the back wall are massive glass fronted cabinets, the shelves packed tight with glasses of all shapes and sizes, no apparent thought for display. In front of them are three huge wooden tables, partly covered by stacks of newspaper, boxes of all sizes and an assortment of glass products. But most surprising of all are the three women there, each sitting quietly behind a table in the half dark and studiously wrapping objects. They look up as we rush in and smile, but no-one says anything.

Slightly dumbfounded, I manage a "Mingalar-ba". Then, "Good afternoon. Are you open? Can we come in? It's raining." I add rather inanely, my words all but drowned out by the thundering downpour pelting the iron roof. Almost as one, the women rise to their feet and move to greet us formally with a handshake, left hand lightly placed in the crook of the right, outstretched arm. We do the same and I introduce Ko Zaw and myself explaining I have been working for the Red Cross in town for the last few months. Ko Zaw adds a few words in Burmese and they respond, but then, turning to me, they start chatting in clear precise English. We are invited to sit at one of the smaller tables at the front to wait out the rain, and they seem happy for this diversion on a gloomy Saturday afternoon.

In their fifties or older, they all have greying hair pulled back tightly into buns, one has rimless spectacles perched on her nose, and they wear the traditional dark blue or green longyis and white long-sleeved eingyis with elegance. One disappears through a door at the back and reappears minutes later with a tray of small glasses, a rather battered tin teapot and a plate of biscuits. We sip our tea and begin to chat. They tell me they are sisters and, with little encouragement, talk about their family, the glass factory, their parents long deceased and the important people who have visited them, each interrupting the other and carrying on the story in an almost seamless fashion.

"There were nine children in our family, three boys and six girls, but sadly one of our sisters passed away a little while back. Our family came from China, Hong Kong actually, and settled here. Our grandfather started to grow garlic for the market, especially for laphet thote, pickled tealeaf salad, but people told him he needed to be at least a mile away from the village because of the smell, so they moved here. This was a rural area then, but now we're right in the middle of the township. It's grown up around us. Only later did we start the glass making. The first furnace was built in the fifties, just after Independence."

"In 1948", I throw in, proud of my knowledge. "Easy to remember. It's the year I was born."

"Me too", the third of the sisters joins in, smiling. "My name is Soe Soe Win, but everyone calls me Betty. I'm the sixth and the one who keeps the peace around here, because of course we do argue sometimes. We're a big family and we all live in different houses around the compound. Some of the children and now the grandchildren also work with us."

I ask if I can look in their cabinets, explaining that I've admired their glassware at my friends' house. Betty suggests I also look next door, in a small room I hadn't noticed. It has finally stopped raining and pale sunbeams filter in through the windows, glinting off the angles and curves of the glass. The centre of the room is taken up by a large table crowded with glassware and the shelves lining the walls teeter slightly downwards under the weight of the many bottles, vases, goblets, and glass animals. Everything is covered with a thin coating of dust and, on the only bare wall, a calendar hangs open at March, three years ago.

"Would you like to see the furnaces? They're working today. Our brother can show you around and tell you a bit more. He's the clever one." I hadn't noticed an older, sprightly man step into the room, and am introduced to U Myat Kywe, the number two brother. He greets me politely but before he can speak his sisters boast proudly that he has a university degree in physics, chemistry and geology.

"He's always experimenting with things to make them better for the business and tweaking the designs. Sometimes his ideas don't work, but he keeps trying. He's been like that since he was young. He invites other scientists to visit and they talk for hours."

With a wry smile, Myat Kywe indicates that we should walk towards the workshop, more eager, I imagine, to get away from his sisters' comments than to show me the furnaces. Away from the others, he becomes rather talkative himself and, pointing out the flowers and trees along the way, explains they keep everything growing wild everywhere for a reason.

"We haven't felled any trees or cleared creepers for a long time because it is much healthier for the workers and the family. They help offset the heat and absorb or filter the chemicals, like the sulphur from the furnace. Some years ago a Yugoslav doctor studied our factory and did health tests on the workers. He said they were much healthier than glassworkers in his country, and it was because of the trees," he adds as we walk.

The path is wet, several puddles to be negotiated, but the top layers of glassware have been washed clean by the rain and the colours glint alluringly as we pass.

The workshop is a vast wooden building, its open front punctuated by heavy wooden pillars. Huge beams criss-cross the upper levels, holding up several layers of roof, each with a wide overhang over the half walls to allow the light in and the smoke out. From the packed earth floor, which follows the contours of the land, rise two huge red mud-brick kilns, patterned with holes. Several bare-chested men are working, highly focused as beams of light slant in from under the eaves, capturing the eddying wafts of smoke.

"A furnace only lasts eight months, maybe nine. They become mis-shapen from the intense temperatures although the corrugated iron cover helps dissipate heat. We have two, so if one is out of action we still work. It takes about five days for a kiln to cool enough to repair. Initially, we used coke, then changed to coal. Recently we're using petroleum coke, a derivative of diesel oil. It burns completely with no ash." I nod, lost in the detail. Chemistry was never my strong subject at school.

I watch the artisans, fascinated. One man, with a glob of molten glass attached to the end of a long pipe, blows and turns it continuously, working the glass into an ever larger elongated bulb, his arms in constant motion. Once it's the size he wants, he presses it down on a flat metal plate then quickly plunges it in and out of a bucket of water; the glass sizzles and steams. Detaching it from the pipe with huge secateurs, he uses a curved wire to decapitate it, cutting off about a quarter, leaving the shape of a vase. Then, running a small tool around the top, he rounds the edge, pressing it down to shape a curved lip. Holding another piece of molten glass between two pincers, he twists and elongates it, deftly attaching one end to the lower part of the vase on the opposite side to the lip. Keeping it there for a moment so it melts into the glass, he slowly pulls up the other end, looping it over to attach it further up, forming a solid handle. A water jug takes shape before my eyes.

Seeing my fascination, Myat Kywe asks another glassblower to show me how the animals are made. He does so obligingly, working quickly with small pointed pliers to pull and turn a short length of molten green glass into a gecko – plump tummy, raised head, long tail and outstretched legs, exaggerated toes scored into the glass feet. It's done in a few minutes, with great expertise, all before the glass cools.

I thank the glassworkers, congratulating them on their creations. They pick up their tools again, resuming their orchestrated moves and techniques, unchanged over centuries.

"We used to make just a standard range of glasses, bowls, vases and ornamental pieces, like animals and nativity scenes," Myat Kywe tells me as we walk back," Then we had a few foreigners wanting something more contemporary. That got me thinking and experimenting, and now I'm always looking for inspiration to see what else can we do."

Back at the main room, he shows me a lively glass figure of a man about twenty centimetres high, one leg bent, the other stretched out in front as though he is on the move but looking back over his shoulder. "What do you think of this? I call it 'The Durian'."

I look at him quizzically trying to link the figure with a durian, that smelliest of tropical fruits, with its thick green prickled skin hiding shiny, yellow, gloopy flesh.

"Can you see it?" Myat Kywe prompts. "A man jumping up after sitting down on what he thought was a pile of leaves, and looking back to see what 'bit' him".

I see it, and we laugh together.

He shows me some of his more abstract forms, lovely cascades and whorls of glass, several with more than one colour integrated into the design. I admire another figure, this one sitting on a gnarled tree stump, hunched over, one foot crossed over the opposite knee. "That is from when my son got a thorn in his foot and was trying to dig it out. I happened to glance at him and loved the curve of his back and the angles of his legs and arms. You can really feel his concentration and the pain."

"My father was also a sculptor", I confide in Myat Kywe. "He worked mostly in wood, stone and bronze, but I remember when I was very young he also created ceramics. He modelled his figures first in plasticine, then in clay. Once I had to sit several mornings on the bathmat, holding a towel in my lap, just so. I didn't understand why, but when he showed me the beautiful white china child holding an open-mouthed fish, I was so proud. I think he intended to do a larger version with water coming out of the fish's mouth into a bird bath for our garden, but never got round to it. My sister still has the little figure."

"I like that story! It reminds me of something that might interest you." Holding a small glass design in the palm of his hand, he tells me he sometimes amuses himself by including Burmese sayings into his designs. "This one is just a pretty frog with its mouth open, and I have sold many to tourists, but you might appreciate that in Myanmar a frog with an open mouth symbolizes one who takes too many bribes." I nod, smiling, touched at his confidence.

I consider what to buy and finally decide on paperweights, round and smooth with embedded swirls of colour and, of course, wine goblets, similar to the ones at the dinner party. Then I find a chess set, the board in dark and light turquoise, its pieces brilliant blue and clear glass for the opposing sides. I choose individual figurines for a nativity scene in green glass —Mary, Joseph and the baby, three wise men, a shepherd, and his sheep. Finally, I pick up two small, stoppered bottles, imagining one on a breakfast tray with milk, another perhaps holding a single flower by my bed. I tell them I'll surely be coming back for more.

The sisters offer me an avocado drink, blended with sweetened condensed milk, another delicious Myanmar speciality, and I relax, sipping and chatting while they deftly wrap and pack my purchases.

Glancing around, I notice something I had previously overlooked. Behind a half wall, at the back of the shop, is a very old car, dust-covered like everything else but with a slight sheen of green paintwork peeping through in places. "My goodness, what is that wonderful car doing here?" I exclaim.

"Well, the original house is through that door. This was the garage which we gradually invaded with the glass exhibition cases and packing tables. Come and look." On closer observation, I see complete but tarnished chrome bumpers, running boards and radiator, holes rusted through, a gap in the driver's door where the handle was and the leather of the ceiling in tatters. But the steering wheel, in smooth tan wood, is still intact and the dashboard looks as though it still has most of its knobs and levers. One of the headlamps hangs a little drunkenly, held by rusted wires.

"It was the first car our grandfather bought, already second hand at the time. It's a 1937 Vauxhall 14, his pride and joy. Every Sunday he'd wash and polish it. We'd all pile in and go to the market. It hasn't been driven for more than thirty years, but we like having it here, as part of our family history," Myat Kywe adds, smiling at his sisters.

There is ample evidence that mice, chickens and children have made good use of it since then and I wonder what it would cost to renovate and refit this gem of a vintage car, though I doubt if it will ever again feel the road beneath its wheels.

My boxes are ready, neatly tied with string. Ko Zaw takes them and we thank Betty and her brother and sisters for their hospitality and the beautiful glassware, wishing them well.

As Ko Zaw and I drive slowly back down the shadowy driveway, water drips onto the roof from the leafy canopy above.

We emerge into the brightly sunlit street. Cars and trishaws speed by, lorries roar, while on the bustling pavements teashops do brisk business. We are back in the Yangon of today.

Chapter Nine
At Home

As the weeks and months pass, I become used to Ko Malay and Maung Taut's company, although I still find it strange to leave my house without locking the door or checking if the windows are closed and to have the gate swing open as my car approaches.

Malay, slightly tubby, does everything on the run and with a smile. He's a whizz with a catapult and in the evening I hear the zing of his shots against the metal gate as he practises shooting geckos drawn to the light. He's caught and dispatched several snakes on the property including a very poisonous green one. I love that he's spruced up the garden and sometimes watch him cutting the lawn with an effortless rhythmic sweep of his machete.

Maung Taut is slim and quiet, taking his time to do everything properly. He's fixed my bike and leaking taps, coaxed recalcitrant electrical fittings to work again, and always finds ingenious ways to re-use discarded material. I am delighted one evening to find he's transformed a section of rusty metal guttering into a hanging flower box. He has fixed it to the water pipe, which incidentally leaks a little, providing a perfect irrigation system.

We have converted the garage that opens off the kitchen into a room for them, furnishing it with a table and stools, a wooden deckchair on which they can doze comfortably, and shelves for all the necessary paraphernalia.

During the frequent 'blackouts,' I sit on the front steps to enjoy the warm air and night sounds. Whoever is on duty wanders over to chat and I learn about their families and previous employers, about a foreign ambassador who was bad-tempered and exacting, and a family with three spoiled children. In return I tell them about my family and, after a visit to New Zealand, I bring back a photo book to share with them. When first my nephew, Andy, and then my sister Philippa and brother-in-law John come to stay they are warmly welcomed and given extra special treatment. Other visitors are also treated with respect and kindness, but family is most important.

A few weeks after I move in I decide to install a satellite dish. I love reading, but with television I can switch off and relax, blocking out lingering work concerns. It's illegal to watch international news channels, even to have a satellite dish can be suspect but most expats have one. It's possible to buy a dish and a year's subscription in Yangon and the bigger hotels use this system for their guests.

Ko Zaw tells me the satellite he's chosen is legal and will bring two hundred channels at least. I'm impressed and excited that next week I'll be able to immerse myself in news, soap operas, documentaries and movies.

Sunday morning, a van toots loudly, then drives in, disgorging several people. A stout man, apparently the boss, and two teenage sons who have been roped in to assist, (and look none to happy about it), his own father, clearly to give advice and oversee matters and also his wife, to make sure they're well fed and watered. Two younger children are just along for the ride.

Ko Zaw and Maung Taut take charge, showing the technicians

where the TV is and the best location for the satellite dish. I hover in the living room through the first directions then retire upstairs. We have a training course this week and I need to prepare.

There's lots of noise—holes bored for the cable, hammering, instructions shouted from inside to outside and back, laughter and shrieking from the kids on the lawn playing tag. I block out most sounds, but one becomes increasingly annoying: the screen door opening and closing every few minutes. I lean over the bannister to see who is opening the door with such monotonous regularity and discover the cause. Grandfather is chewing betel, going outside every few minutes to expectorate an arc of red spittle into my flowerbeds. I grit my teeth and return to drafting my presentation, trying to drown out the noise.

A little later, everyone troops upstairs through my office to the balcony. The elder boy climbs onto the roof to position the dish. I hear his footsteps above me, and fear for his safety. His mother, on the lawn below, scolds him for being too casual on the steep roof shouting that he must be careful. I'm not making great headway with my presentation.

More banging and drilling and the dish is fixed in place. Footsteps retrace a path above my head and the boy lands with a thud back onto the balcony. Smiling cheekily at me as he passes my desk he wipes his grimy hands down the sides of his workpants. He joins the rest of the family on the lawn as they take a lunch break and wolf down what smells like delicious biryani rice with chicken. Ko Zaw comes upstairs to explain that they now only have to thread the cable from the dish in through the hole in the wall, attach it to the satellite box, and then tune the TV for the best reception. He says it shouldn't be much longer.

I get myself a sandwich and return to my desk, eating while I continue my notes. The noises from below are different now, bursts of talking and music, what sounds like car chases and a full-scale war interspersed with the high pitched crackling of static. Junior is back on the roof and, following shouted instructions, is manoeuvring the dish to face the required direction. I'm confident I'll soon have the house back to myself. I let my mind stray to what I might have for dinner as I enjoy a captivating programme.

Grandfather's head appears from halfway up the staircase. "Miss," he calls excitedly. "Miss, come and see, we already we have your programme. You are a Christian, no?"

Wondering what that might have to do with my television, I go downstairs, joining the whole family who stand entranced, watching. And there he is, in full colour and sound—a televangelist, hair combed to within an inch of its life, broad smile, arms held wide. All the family turn to look at me, convinced I'll be delighted to watch this channel whenever I want. I am not sure whether to laugh or cry, that all the noise has led to this. Before they leave they tell me proudly that I have three hundred and twenty-four channels to choose from.

In the evening, I click through three hundred plus channels while sipping my wine, for once without a power cut to interrupt my fascinated viewing. I learn I have a selection of every type of programme imaginable in just about every Asian language. Amongst them I find an Indonesia Channel showing a movie, with English subtitles. I watch the last twenty minutes of a detective tracking down and successfully nabbing a suspect, before the channel flicks to an Indonesian soap. No subtitles.

After a month of relentlessly checking for something in English, I give in and ask Ko Zaw to sell this dish and its subscription. I'm now prepared to risk breaking the law, buying a dish and subscription which will pickup Thai broadcasts, including a couple of movie channels as well as both BBC and CNN.

Despite having wanted a dog for company, after the first dispiriting experience I abandoned the idea of a pet. But it's not long before I learn that Ko Zaw had not.

On the eighth of May 2003, we are at a formal ceremony for World Red Cross and Red Crescent Day and our whole team meets our Myanmar Red Cross colleagues at a Secondary School in downtown Yangon. The Minister of Health is the guest speaker so we must be seated well before the ceremony starts. It's baking in the assembly room and we wait and wait. After an hour we're stuck to our plastic chairs, grumpy and in need of refreshment. However, if the volunteers can wait and then perform their plays, demonstrations, and songs with energy and style, then we can also wait calmly.

Afterwards I talk with the Minister and congratulate the MRCS President and some volunteers on their excellent performances before leaving the hall to walk back to the car. I notice Ko Zaw having a word with Sandy and when they both look in my direction, smiling, I detect a hint of conspiracy. Ko Zaw waits until I've talked with some of the MRCS staff, splendid in their uniforms and medals, and then approaches me. "I have a surprise for you in the car," he says.

"I love surprises. Nice ones, that is!"

A colleague taps me on the shoulder and I turn to exchange a few polite words. When I turn back, Ko Zaw is standing behind me with a tiny ginger kitten in the crook of his arm.

"The other drivers and I waited for you in a tea-house down the road," he explains. "And this kitten found us. It wouldn't go away and wouldn't stop mewing so the shop owner said to take it. I told her my boss would like it. It's a female, about five weeks old."

I take the tiny scrap in my arms. She is thin, her fur dirty and matted, her huge ears pricked. She looks at me with green eyes. I scratch the back of her head and she starts to purr. I feel her little body gently vibrate against my arm. I've never had a cat and I'm not sure I would have picked a ginger one but here she is and from that moment on she is mine.

Ko Zaw reminds me, "You could call her Maha Bandoola, although that's the name of a general and might not suit a scrappy little girl." So I call her Ma Zaw, which somehow morphs into 'Snookie,' which suits her better. It's the name I call when I come home tired from work or back from a long field trip. We cut her a cat door in the screen door, covering it with a towelling flap so she can come and go when she pleases, and she does just that.

About a year after she has taken over our household, I mention to Malay that she looks a bit plump and wonder could she be pregnant. Malay protests loudly that she couldn't possibly be because he watches her all the time. Having heard his snores in the evening, I am not too sure about that. I've noticed a black and white tomcat visiting and one evening, sitting outside during a power cut, I enjoy this Romeo's stealthy overtures. In response, Ma Zaw is coy and standoffish but I wonder what goes on when I am not watching. When she produces three kittens, I wonder no more. The first, a female, is mostly black with white and ginger patches. The second, a male, is ginger with a white shirtfront, the perfect little gentleman. The third, the smallest, is another female, a soft blend of the parents' colouring, grey, ginger, black and white. I decide to keep the little one and name her Pao Mu Si, 'little sister' in Malay's Karen language soon shortened to Musi. Ko Zaw takes the boy and Snow White takes the other female and so I get used to having two cats around. But not for long.

Back from a field trip a few months later, Ma Zaw looks pregnant again. Malay protests again. But I'm right and some weeks later a second litter arrives, this time with four kittens—two males and two females. From their colouring, Romeo is clearly the father.

Ma Zaw is not impressed with another brood of demanding kittens and once they've fed, it's Musi who washes and plays with them and sleeps curled around them, acting as the perfect older sister. I find homes for them all. But we have both cats spayed pretty soon after.

With the other delegates in serviced apartments and most local staff living in apartment blocks, my house becomes a meeting place for the team and their families. Every few weeks we organize a movie night with dinner and, after a new delegate Alex arrives from the Philippines with his Karaoke machine, we have musical nights as well. These evenings my lawn becomes an open-air theatre the chosen movie projected via the LCD monitor onto a large screen. 'Finding Nemo' is everyone's favourite and requested often.

My house also serves as an alternative venue for hosting more formal dinners for visitors to the delegation and the MRCS, most visitors appreciating being entertained in a home rather than in a hotel or restaurant. For formal receptions, Malay and Maung Taut are in their element; Malay trims and tweaks everything in the garden and puts out tables and chairs borrowed from our neighbourhood restaurant, sets the long table in the dining room with the food delivered by the restaurant, and serves the drinks while Maung Taut makes magic with several strings of coloured lights, artfully draping the cords around trees, through the hedge and along the fence. Countless extension cords issue forth from just about every room in the house and only occasionally blow the fuses.

As well as visits from my family, I play host to several friends from Europe and New Zealand. I help them plan their trips, but as I have to work, I see them only in the early mornings, at the end of the day and between their visits to other parts of the country.

When my Red Cross colleagues from Geneva, Sylvie, Sabine and Ria come to stay, we visit the Shwedagon Pagoda at dawn. As we circle the vast platform in the early morning, I delight in seeing it through their eyes, rediscovering it. I tell them some of its secrets—where to look for the shrines of their birth days and for the prized Buddha relics, the story behind the decoration of the gold-plated *hti*, the highest decoration of a stupa with thousands of diamonds and precious stones, and that the great bronze Maha Gandha bell on the north-west side of the platform, cast in 1779, weighs twenty-three tons.

Leaving the platform, we slowly descend the stairs from the Eastern Gate marvelling at the relics, souvenirs and religious items on sale in the tightly packed stalls. The brass and silver bowls and boxes, monks' robes, painted silk umbrellas, ceremonial swords, fans, religious books all call out to us while the glass wind chimes stir and tinkle as we pass. Painted velvet hangings and photos of the pagoda are strung alongside shelves of wooden carvings of Buddha and monks and, rather incongruously, garish papier-mâché and plastic dolls and animals. There are practical items as well, sunglasses and tiffin tins, strings of jade and sweet smelling loops of beads, bunches of flowers and candles for offerings. One shop offers gongs and drums and as people try out their different tones, the sounds reverberate within the well of the staircase.

We read the advertising outside the booths of the fortune-tellers who cater to a stream of people every day. Some offer readings of your birth chart, while others decipher your future from the lines on the palm of your hand. A few even read the bumps and shape of your skull, running their hands over it with a knowing look. Yet others use cards or hold your jewellery to see your character and what lies ahead. In Myanmar, as in most of the other Asian countries, nearly everyone—businessmen and women, politicians, parents, young lovers, alike—regularly consults a fortune-teller for that auspicious date on which to marry, make their business more prosperous or to ensure their children's health.

Weekends on my own, I like to invite friends over. One day, when my friend Anne remarks that she loves to visit on my 'at home' days, it reminds me of a favourite story told by my maternal grandmother, Norah.

Newly married to Bernard, a young doctor, Norah was guardian of the housekeeping purse and supported her husband as much as she could. His first practice was in York in England, and in those days it was commonplace for a doctor to have his 'rooms' in his home. The social standing of the doctor was almost as important as his actual knowledge and experience. The patients and the income came with the reputation and a certain 'sympathetic manner'.

They could only afford one maid though, and every week she had a half-day off, Wednesday afternoon. So as not to let down her husband, my resourceful granny stayed at home those afternoons, lurking in the hall with her hat on, and when the doorbell rang, she would open the door, telling the next patient, "Oh, you've caught me just as I was going out! Let me show you into the surgery."

We laugh at the story but then reflect on the similarities between my life and my grandmother's. When I first arrived here, I was far from everything and everyone I knew, just as she was when they later emigrated to Australia, where, adapting to a different environment, she soon made a comfortable home for her family and new friends.

"I suppose I too have to play a role here as Head of Delegation, just as she had a role to play with her hat on in those early days of her marriage," I comment.

"Well, for sure you have her grit, her adaptability and skill at making people feel welcome," responds Anne, "that's easy to see. You've fitted right in here."

Looking about at my garden, enjoying a glass of chilled white wine with a good friend at dusk, I think about my team, the colleagues who have become friends, and the places we've visited, the challenges of working together. I feel the warmth of Snookie curled up beside me and realise it's true. Here, I do feel comfortable, befriended, 'at home'.

Chapter Ten
Office Days

"Nice to meet you. What do you do?" Each time I am asked, I hesitate.

I want to tell them about my job but a succinct response is difficult. Usually I just say I work for the International Red Cross and where I am posted at the time.

"Oh, you're a nurse!" they exclaim, though a few younger or more enlightened might ask if I am a doctor. When I reply that I am neither, but Head of the International Federation Delegation in Myanmar, they either look puzzled or exclaim knowledgably, "Ah, so you are an Administrator!"

"Well not that either, really." I reply.

If they show real interest in the Red Cross by asking further questions, I cheekily ask them if they want the long or the short answer. The short answer is gleaned from the Principle of Humanity[1]...*endeavours to prevent and alleviate human suffering wherever it may be found, to protect life and health, to ensure respect for the human being and to promote mutual understanding, friendship, cooperation and lasting peace amongst all peoples.* The long answer is a five-day training course. Most settle for the short answer.

So what exactly is a 'Head of Delegation for the International Federation of Red Cross and Red Crescent Societies'? Like others who take on this role, I've often puzzled about this, and in trying to define it, have reached the conclusion that it's a bit of everything, 'jack of all trades, and master of none' as the saying goes. There is no exact formula, as the specific functions and needs change from country to country, operation to operation. This is what makes the job so exciting, challenging and satisfying. What it requires in all cases is an understanding of the organization we work for and a commitment to the ethics it espouses, coupled with a willingness to align ourselves with whatever is needed in the country or operation of our assignment, be it a relief operation, a health programme, or a streamlining of management practices. Some Delegation Heads are logisticians, others health professionals, engineers, teachers like me, or journalists. They may also be ex-army personnel, have a background in business, or have worked for other international organisations.

Perhaps I could have been passionate about another organization but I was lucky enough to fall into this one that I can really believe in. I like that it's truly an international organization, every country having a national Red Cross or Red Crescent Society led and staffed entirely by nationals of that country, encouraging people from all walks of life to be volunteers either in the short or long term. I like that it operates independently, often being classed as an NGO (Non-Governmental Organisation), but that each National Society is in fact an 'auxiliary in the humanitarian service of their Governments[2], is established by an act of parliament and an integral part of the social fabric of its own country.

A poster I remember from my early days in the New Zealand Red Cross boasted 'We save the Government millions every year', validating the work of volunteers in health and social programmes, in disaster preparedness and response, and their often under-recognised services in their communities.

So how do I see my work here as the Head of Delegation in Myanmar?

Long term capacity building and programme development of the National Society is particularly important so I play a role in providing advice and training, writing project proposals and budgets, in public relations, fundraising and publications. Leading and providing support for the specialist Delegates in the fields of health, branch development, disaster management, finance and communications and guiding local staff are also key aspects of my job.

Good listening skills and a high degree of sensitivity towards the National Society; not always too impressed with being 'observed' or even 'supervised' by an outsider are also very important. Although the Myanmar Red Cross Society has agreed the Delegation may be present in its country, we are still visitors and only here in an advisory capacity. An exception would be if the scale of an operation were beyond the scope of the MRCS and they asked for assistance, in which case the International Federation would manage the operation.

Having been here a year, I can summarise the major concerns and schedule of my work into three parts: first, managing the Delegation itself, second, partnering the Myanmar Red Cross, and third promoting Myanmar operations and programmes to the wider world.

On a typical 'office day', I arrive around eight thirty, walk through the rooms to say good morning, take a quick look at the day's programme, check emails for new requests and for incoming responses to our queries. I then prepare for the meetings—short ones with staff regarding plans and programmes, then longer meetings with the whole team, Myanmar Red Cross staff, the Executive Committee, or visitors. After lunch, training courses and mentoring sessions, then, between about four and six, a quiet and generally productive time when I gather my thoughts, and prepare proposals and reports.

On a more practical level, one of our first undertakings was a clean up of our offices to have a pleasant working environment. When sorting

---

[1&2] *The Seven Fundamental Principles of the International Red Cross and Red Crescent Movement: Humanity, Impartiality, Neutrality, Independence, Voluntary Service, Unity, and Universality.*

through stacks of documents, I found that reading reports from past operations was a handy way to get acquainted with the job, gleaning a few insights into operational necessities. For example, during the rainy season or in flood operations in this country, one of the most vital emergency items is snake venom antidote as it's not only humans who flee the rising waters.

Other immediate tasks were understanding the different roles of the delegation members, allocating responsibilities, prioritizing tasks and then communicating all this effectively to the team, to my colleagues in the MRCS and my superiors in Bangkok and Geneva.

Gradually, it all falls into place, and the work becomes more routine. New staff and delegates are recruited and briefed and their work monitored. Once individual schedules are prepared and accepted, each delegate follows his or her own work thread of training and workshops, preparing project proposals and budgets, regularly reporting and spending enough time out in the branches to know what the priorities and needs are.

The weekly staff meeting becomes a regular fixture and a way to keep everyone in the loop of the overall workload, particular challenges and the all-important deadlines we face. Meetings start at eleven and go through until one, when we lunch together and chat about the lighter news and topics of the day. I've learnt a lot from these meetings and now and again something rather enlightening emerges over a shared plate of noodles.

One day, waiting for letters from my family, I wonder about the efficiency of the Myanmar Postal Service and learn that it's normal for mail to go astray. "I could understand if there was anything valuable in the letters but they're just news from my family. The ones I receive have been opened and reclosed and since they use such bad glue, the letter usually sticks to the envelope," I laugh, "But why would any get lost?"

"Because they want the envelopes," Marlar explains. "People want to travel abroad, to study or meet family members. To get a passport and be allowed to travel, you need to show a letter of invitation and the envelope it came in. Anyone can forge a letter, but without the stamped and postmarked envelope from the country of origin, the letter doesn't count. New Zealand is a sought after destination, so your mail is valuable." A lucrative trade in used envelopes was one I hadn't come across before.

During another lunch I learn about the late night 'visitors.' I prick up my ears as I am not sure what they are talking about. I ask, "What do you mean 'visitors'?"

"From time to time the authorities carry out a swoop raid in a neighbourhood to check that everyone who's registered for each house is there or to check on anyone who shouldn't be there," one of my staff responds. "It can be tough if anyone is caught out, as explanations are usually considered suspect. Everyone is anxious in the following days wondering why their area was targeted and who might have talked."

"Why has no one told me of this before?" I ask, worried for them and understanding this is yet another way the population is kept in its place.

"There are things we don't tell you even though we trust you, because it is better for you not to know. We are sometimes ashamed of our own country," is the quiet reply.

One day, after a presentation by the Health Team, we discuss the issue of HIV and AIDS for the first time and everyone contributes information about the current situation in Myanmar, even though the Government stance is that HIV does not exist in Myanmar. Over lunch, a few more 'health' stories are bandied round the table and for some reason we discuss a story about someone's mother with hemorrhoids. When one of the female staff offers a comment that she certainly knows how painful they are, another counters laughingly, "How would you know, you haven't had children!"

"But I do, I have a ten-year-old son," she responds.

You could have cut the silence with a knife. We've been working together for more than a year and none of us knew. Afterwards, I ask her gently why she never told us she had a son. She tells me her husband won a scholarship to study at a foreign University and never returned. She feels ashamed to have been abandoned. We talk about attitudes in different countries and I ask about her son. She does so with great solemnity and pride. Weeks later I introduce a discussion about cultural attitudes at a staff lunch giving everyone a chance to tell personal stories and learn from each other, the delegates from the Myanmar staff and vice versa. As each story sheds more light on daily life in Myanmar, my admiration for my staff, all of whom need to make their way through a seeming minefield of complicated rules and regulations just to manage their everyday lives, grows.

After the 2004 Tsunami, which devastated countries across Asia and even touched the shores of Africa, when the relief and reconstruction are still active and funds flowing more readily, we welcome new delegates. They help ensure that the finances, operations and all aspects of the programme, as well as the long-term capacity building and training at the local level are well supported. We are now a truly international team, with Phaphe from Botswana, Mustafa from Jordan, Zamira from Albania, Steven from Denmark, Kaija and Heikki from Finland, Evelyn and Alex from the Philippines. Together with my deputy Patrik from Sweden, as well as myself from New Zealand, we can almost boast to be the most perfectly balanced delegation—five men and five womenm, from all over the world. The combination presents an interesting management challenge and an opportunity to learn from the many different cultural styles.

Our work with the Myanmar Red Cross Society is simplified by the fact that we share the same building, and we all have daily meetings with our MRCS colleagues. The counterparts for the specialist delegates are the Directors and their teams in the different MRCS Departments, while my work involves greater contact with the MRCS President and the members of the Executive Committee.

There are days when relations run smoothly, with a sense of shared purpose as we recruit new staff, complete a workshop or training course, agree on the direction of a programme or send reports and appeals to Geneva. We joke a little over a shared dinner after a particularly good meeting and I enjoy relaxed moments with the President when he elaborates on aspects of Myanmar culture or Buddhist lore or tells stories from his postings as a doctor in more than a dozen different states and divisions across the country.

Other days we argue, misunderstanding each other, and feel slighted or insulted and we need to stand back from the situation and slowly renegotiate our relationships. These arguments are not noisy affairs but quiet, deliberate exchanges with meaningful silences and furtive looks. Words are chosen carefully but when someone in the Executive Committee, all of whom speak excellent English, claims to misinterpret my meaning, I know I'm in trouble, and apologies will have to be made before we can move forward.

Sometimes our differences of approach are amusing, such as the day Mallu, our newly arrived and rather plump Health Delegate is introduced in an Executive Meeting. While she's talking about her experience and her expectations, one of the committee who had thus far contributed nothing, commented to nobody in particular, "She will be fitting for the job, she looks healthy and fat enough herself."

I greatly admire the MRCS staff, who work diligently with little equipment or guidance but who manage programmes and prepare careful reports. Occasionally though, I deliberately challenge them to do something differently, such as at the start of the planning process. I'm instructed from Geneva that the MRCS needs a long-term strategic plan to attract more donors. This can't be done overnight, especially when it's not altogether clear to our Myanmar colleagues what is required. We organise a three-day workshop with the presence of the Executive Committee and the senior staff, as well as the members of the delegation. I open the session with an exercise, something they are not used to, asking each table, a random mix of staff, delegates, and committee members, to choose an animal to describe what the MRCS should resemble in five or perhaps ten years' time.

A member of the committee looks coldly at me, folds his arms and leans back, disassociating himself from this childish nonsense. I notice his gesture but don't remark on it as I circle the tables listening to the discussions. One group is already drawing a *Chinthe*, a mythical lion, on their flipchart and writing characteristics around it—strong and dependable, has a heart and works compassionately with others. Another group is arguing the merits of different animals, an elephant or a rooster, both having characteristics that would be admirable in a humanitarian organization. Another is composing a poem about their 'beast'.

As I circle for the third time, I see the reluctant committee member now leaning forward and addressing his group, entering into the spirit of the exercise. I slow by their table rather nonchalantly and hear him announcing, "Our National Society will be a *Pyinsa Rupa* (a mythical combination of five animals: elephant, bullock, horse, carp, and dragon), as it must have the capacity to react and respond wherever it is needed." I am impressed.

Later, I'm amused that he's the one to proudly present their 'animal,' and commend him on his groups' forward thinking. At tea break he approaches me and says loudly for all to hear, "Well that was an interesting exercise Joanna, but can we get to the business of the meeting now?" But in the subsequent days when we deviate from serious topics and stretch our minds through other whimsical exercises, I am pleased to see that he participates willingly, even with enjoyment.

It's not always easy to influence office procedures, some of which appear to have stagnated, and my first participation in a series of candidate interviews for a new head of department is an eye-opener. No putting the candidate at ease with initial questions about themselves, or drawing them out about what they might bring to the position. For candidate after candidate the procedure is the same.

"What are your qualifications? Show us your certificates," comes the first demand.

"Do you know the seven Fundamental Principles of the Red Cross? Who was Henry Dunant?" questions another. More curt questions come thick and fast, some completely irrelevant for the position for which the candidate is being sought. During the interrogations, tea and snacks are brought in for the panel of the Executive Committee and myself. Much is made of pouring and tasting while the candidate sits nervously with nothing to drink and waits for the next question to be fired randomly from one of the panel. Shortly after this daunting experience, I bring up the subject at a committee meeting suggesting politely that perhaps we could interview in a slightly different way, preparing the session beforehand and asking questions relevant to each particular job. Although a member of the committee comments grumpily that this is how they do it in Myanmar, others are open to the idea and a more balanced approach to interviews emerges over time.

An important part of the MRCS work consists of training, a broad spectrum of subjects from basic First Aid to Instructor's training, from disaster preparedness to logistics, and more. The offices adjacent to ours become training rooms. Protocol dictates that I make a speech at the formal opening and hand out certificates at the equally formal closing ceremony of each course. Usually I also do one session with participants on the International Red Cross, trying make it lively and informative, recognizing that everything has to be interpreted and thus needs to be concise and descriptive, even colourful.

Building this relationship with the MRCS is vital for our work in Myanmar, as without mutual respect and understanding, our suggestions could easily be ignored, our advice and actions deemed unimportant. We need to understand the pressures all levels of the MRCS staff are under. In return, they can use the added capacity and resources we bring, although by working closely together, they can also recognize that we too are under pressure from our donors and our own institutional structures.

Every few weeks we're visited by colleagues from other National Societies or meet with delegations from Aid Agencies of foreign Governments. I'm wary during these visits as what we say is reported back religiously. I need to give as accurate a picture as possible, while underlining the necessity of continuing our work with the MRCS and presenting the daily challenges we face. I find myself being protective of my adopted National Society as visitors often have pre-conceived opinions about this country.

"I understand that the MRCS is very close to the Government," a young man from a Nordic Aid Agency starts in typical fashion one morning. "How do you know that contributions are not being syphoned off down the line? It's public knowledge that corruption is rife in Myanmar," he adds, challenging me with his earnest gaze.

"In the present situation," I respond, "I have to agree that just about everything is close to the government in Myanmar. However, considering that most of what we're doing is training and preparedness and is focused on developing the capacities of the society and those of individual staff members and volunteers, there's not that much to 'siphon off'. In fact," I add, warming to my topic, "the MRCS always invites members of the Military and the Police to attend our training sessions so they understand our work and we illustrate how, in disaster situations for example, we can work together and coordinate our actions."

"But what about an operation after a disaster? For instance, the recent cyclone in Rakhine state. We pledged thousands of dollars to that appeal. How did that work out? Does this government even care what happens to their people?" he goads me.

"I think maybe it's important to make a distinction between the Military and Administrative bodies of the Government," I comment calmly. "Also, there are many within the various Departments we deal with who care hugely about their own people and struggle to find the right way to support them, often putting their own jobs on the line if their actions are not entirely consistent with party directives. Can you imagine the pressure on them to conform? We appreciate this in particular when working with colleagues in the MRCS. They're the best example and are able to guide us on how to manoeuvre through the red tape and ensure that we're getting our relief support to the right people."

I steer the conversation away from this line of questioning and invite the young man to learn more about the on-going Branch Survey and what we have learnt so far, about the training programmes and operations we are currently involved in. But he clearly considers I've not answered all his questions and blurts out, "I want to know how you deal with the corruption…it is one of the reasons we are here to talk with you!"

"Can I make a distinction between corruption and survival?" I respond. "I'm sure your Government has its own ways of assessing corruption but that is not something I can help you with. However, I can tell you that from what I know, every family has to survive, to feed and educate its children and to do that, yes, there are ways of smoothing the way.

Corruption is a loaded word in this context; I would rather call it survival." Then, looking him straight in the eye, I add, "I've thought a lot about this issue and wonder how things could be different without a whole new order emerging. I've never been forced to live my life this way, any more than you have. The two of us grew up in probably the least corrupt countries in the world. We've had everything, education, health, jobs, and a passport. We've never really wanted for anything so how can we judge or criticise? Shouldn't we try and find a way to work and support the MRCS so that it can at least do some good?"

I know I've said more than I should, and the discussion moves on. But over dinner that evening he seeks me out, saying, "You know, I rather appreciated your frank opinions. I learnt a lot today."

Chapter Eleven
The Tourist Triangle

*M*yanmar is a land of mystifying contradictions whose spirited people have withstood centuries of oppression from Kublai Khan to King George VI to the present military regime."

'Should I go?' is a question Lonely Planet believes all prospective travellers to Myanmar must ask, and answer, before setting foot in the country. The Travel boycott—initiated by the Nobel Laureate for Peace, Aung San Suu Kyi, and endorsed by British prime minister, Tony Blair —began in 1996. Since then, much of the travel-and-business related world has been debating the pros and cons of the boycott amid an often heated face-off.

Although Aung San Suu Kyi said that Myanmar wasn't ready for tourism, she also noted that 'tourists' can open up the world to the people of Burma just as the people of Burma can open up the eyes of the tourists to the situation in their own country if they're interested.*

---

* *Lonely Planet Myanmar (Burma) 2005 edition. Published by Lonely Planet.*

For several decades, whether to visit Myanmar has been a point of debate, with a fear that tourist dollars will line the pockets of the government rather than benefitting the population. In 2004, Myanmar still has fewer than a half million visitors while in neighbouring Thailand there are twelve million tourists a year.

This country offers so much—from the mighty Himalayan chain, snow-clad in winter, to the *Myeik* archipelago in the far south, a treasure trove of tropical islands and beaches with a pristine ocean floor. I wonder if a day will come when tourists might be offered skiing in the morning and scuba diving in the afternoon.

From my field trips around the country, I am learning how beautiful and varied this country is, but have yet to experience the more classical tourist sights. When my nephew Andy, a medical student from New Zealand, comes to stay, it's a perfect opportunity to do so. We plan our tour to include a few nights at Inle Lake, then on to Mandalay, followed by a river trip to Bagan, a few days there and back to Yangon, allowing us to experience the so-called 'Tourist Triangle'.

Andy enjoys his few days in Yangon, often exploring on his own, amazed at everything on his first visit to Asia. In the evening he recounts his adventures of dodging bustling traffic and negotiating market stalls with their persistent saleswomen, visiting the dilapidated zoo, seemingly unchanged since the 1950s, just a lick of paint each year, the animals confined and despondent in small cages. He's horrified to recognise untreated medical conditions and physical handicaps in people still going about their daily chores and at the young age of some of the labourers. But, he does admit to being chuffed when a woman on a road crew calls out to him, "Hello Brad Pitt", maybe the only other blond she knows, no doubt from a pirated movie.

Malay and Maung Taut laugh with him as he learns how to tie his *longyi* so he is properly clad when he visits Shwedagon and other pagodas, and introduce him to *Mohinga*, the national noodle dish, originally just eaten for breakfast but more recently eaten at anytime. The noodles and optional duck egg, fish or chicken are bathed in a rich savoury fish broth with the flavours of chilli, ginger, turmeric and garlic filtering through to the palate. Topped with crisp fried onions, fresh coriander and a squeeze of lime, a large bowl can nourish you for an entire day.

Ko Zaw drives him to Bago one day where he is impressed at the well-kept cemetery for allied soldiers killed in World War II. Later he's allowed a glimpse of a famous white elephant, but aware that they have been reason for war between Burma and Thailand in the past, he obeys the order not to take photos. Back in Yangon, an MRCS colleague takes him to a public hospital where he has his eyes opened to a different level of technology and resources than that experienced during his medical training back home.

Thus slightly acclimatised after his first week, Andy and I fly east to Heho on the Shan Plateau from where a car will take us to our first destination, Inle Lake. For some obscure reason, taxis are not allowed into the airport grounds and wait some five hundred metres down a rough road. Undeterred, Andy shoulders his backpack, pulling my little black wheeled bag, and we set off down the road, feeling a little like refugees under the harsh late morning sun, the dust painting our feet a dark rust red.

Leaning against an old Toyota Corolla, a driver holds up a sign with our names. The windows, stuck halfway down, allow us wonderful views of the winding road descending to the lake but also cover us with a lavish coating of dust. After an hour's drive we reach Nyaungshwe at the head of the lake, desperate for a cool drink. While we sip iced fruit juice in a café, our driver seeks our next ride, a long black canoe powered by an outboard motor, 'Golden Island Cottages' along its side.

From the village, we steer carefully into a channel leading to the lake itself, rows of floating gardens radiating out on either side—troughs of intertwined reeds filled with weeds, silt and mud scooped from the lake bed and anchored to the shallow bottom with bamboo poles.

Women cultivate the gardens from their canoes and the abundant moisture ensures market crops year round—tomatoes, eggplants, cucumbers, peas, beans and cabbages. Leaving the gardens behind we pick up speed, heading out into the open lake, fresh breeze on our faces, water sparkling and blue mountains rising in the distance.

Our boatman veers off course to bring us near a canoe, cutting the engine. A fisherman stands, one leg on the bow, the other wrapped around the long wooden paddle, deftly manoeuvring it front to side, propelling the canoe forward. Behind him is a huge conical trap with gill net attached. We rock gently, watching him as he gazes at the surface checking for movement. Choosing a spot, he swiftly pushes the trap to the bottom, catching his fish, then spears them through the top of the trap, pulling them up into the boat.

Reaching the far end of the lake we come to our home for the next two nights, The Golden Cottages, a winding complex with woven rattan walls, high on stilts above the lake. It's comfortable but cold at night and we shiver our way through dinner. The hot-water bottle in my bed is most welcome.

At sunrise, I step out onto the small balcony, still wrapped in my bedcover. Mist shrouds the surrounding buildings, only the rooftops emerging. A network of wooden bridges is reflected in the still silver lake water. Sipping my hot tea, I absorb the soft grey light, the silence and the gentle lapping of water against the long wooden piles.

During the day, we are whisked by canoe from one island or lakeshore to another, from one treat to the next. Young women sit cross legged in front of low circular baskets deftly rolling cigars, strong young men stripped to the waist rhythmically hammer steel on an anvil while an older man keeps the fire burning with hand-held bellows. We enjoy the bright colours of silk and cotton skeins hung out to dry and the skill of weavers, lengths of cloth pouring from their looms, brightened with intricate coloured stripes and patterns. The clacking of looms still in our ears, we learn how dyes are made in the rooms below, the women's hands and forearms permanently stained a deep indigo blue from their trade.

On our way back, in the evening, we stop at a pagoda built on an island and join others sitting on the low walls around the platform observing the evening rituals and games of monks and children, vendors, and courting couples. My attention is caught by a group of models being primped and posed for a fashion photo-shoot, modern dresses and stylish handbags setting them apart. An old man, dressed in black with a bright shawl tied turban-like around his head stares at them and then turns to comment to an elderly monk sitting next to him. I wish I could listen in.

Early the following day, we spend an hour at the famous floating market at Ywama where persistent market ladies, their boats filled with everything from conical hats to bolts of fabric, from betel boxes to Buddha images, brass weights, and carvings, entice us. When we move on, the most tenacious vendors hold onto our canoe, coming along with us, offering better and better bargains until, finally convinced we are not parting with our Kyat, they let go, allowing us to glide freely through the channels back out into the open waters.

"Would it be out of the way to visit the 'leaping cat monastery'?" asks Andy, having studied his 'Lonely Planet Guide'. Our driver nods, turning the canoe dramatically, nearly unseating us.

It's a beautiful old wooden building, the main hall elaborately decorated with Buddha statues and small shrines. A line of windows along the back wall faces more canals, louvered shutters held open with wooden poles. We sit on a bench below, facing the temple hall, and wait until an old monk emerges from a side room to seat himself on the wooden floor in front of us. Silently, one by one, four cats step out of the shadows and sit near by, paws together, watching him with half shut eyes. He takes a hoop from under his robes, opening a small green tin of biscuits with the other hand. He slowly coaxes the cats towards him, then, holding a treat in his left hand, raises the hoop above his head, making a chirping sound through pursed lips. A tabby crouches back on its paws, leaps clean through the hoop and is rewarded with the biscuit, followed by another, then another. The fourth cat is not to be seduced into jumping today, but remains alert, watching the others.

"I might try and teach this to Gus when I get home," Andy jokes, and we laugh at the thought of his elderly ginger tom doing anything remotely athletic.

Flying into Mandalay later that afternoon I'm struck by two things —a large snake winding along the tarmac as we taxi in and the enormous airport building. We follow a line of overhead neon lights to baggage collection, the rest of the vast structure in semi darkness. Built recently with assistance from an Italian-Thai joint venture company, it could, working to capacity, handle forty thousand aircraft movements a year. This seems remarkably optimistic, the present turnover but a tiny fraction.

During our three days in Mandalay, Andy and I act the consummate tourists. We visit the reconstructed Royal Palace, destroyed by fire in 1945 during the fighting between the allied and Japanese forces, set inside a walled and moated area at the heart of the city. I take a photo of Andy beside the wax figures of the last King and Queen, Thibaw and Supayalat, and a guide regales us with gory tales from the beginning of their reign with the execution of some eighty possible rivals to the throne, the idiosyncrasies of the Royal couple and their forced exile to India at the end of the nineteenth century when the British seized the city.

From Mandalay Hill we admire the views over the city, the river and the vast rice fields bordered by small levees and palm trees and beyond them, lines of hills topped with stupas. A group of monks following our path around the pagoda platform ask Andy to take their photo. They produce an old instamatic camera and pose with the universal winning smile of tourists.

Later, we visit Kuthodaw Pagoda at the base of the hill, home to the world's largest book—seven hundred and twenty-nine small white pagodas in a tree filled compound, each containing a part of the entire Tipithaka, the Buddhist scriptures, carved in Pali on marble tablets. Reading from his guidebook, Andy informs me that in 1872, two thousand, four hundred scribes worked for months during the Fifth World Buddhist Synod convened by King Mindon, predecessor of King Thibaw, to achieve this feat.

We wander through the three ancient capitals of Amarapura, Ava and Sagaing, exploring pagoda complexes and markets and admiring bronze gongs and bells, marble statues, silver bowls and gold leaf being crafted in small workshops, then cruise up the river in a small ferryboat to Mingun, home to the world's largest working bell, cast in the eighteenth century, weighing eighty-seven tons. It was to have graced the great Mingun pagoda that was never completed. Only its base is left today, cracked open by a massive earthquake, the upper sections collapsed into the rooms below. Clearly, the Kings of Burma believed in making 'big' statements about their status and their devotion to Buddha.

On our last afternoon we drive south of Amarapura to the impressive mile-long teak U Bein Bridge, spanning Lake Thaungthaman and join villagers and monks walking along the high plank bridge, looking across to pagodas on the far side and boatmen cutting clean lines through the still lake waters.

Andy slows and leans down to give a few Kyat notes to some beggars, two men and a woman, sitting to one side. They bow their thanks to him, but when he turns back, he looks troubled.

"They've no fingers," he tells me, shocked that their raised hands are merely palms with dirty stubs, partly covered in bandages.

"I doubt you've seen this in your training, since leprosy is all but eradicated but it's still a problem here, for small numbers of people," I respond to his concern.

As the sun begins to set, we hurriedly retrace our steps to reach the shore in time to catch that most beautiful of sights, U Bein Bridge at sunset, the dark figures of monks and villagers silhouetted dramatically against the crimson and gold sky.

Tired after our long day out, Andy and I meet in the hotel bar and I order my favourite cocktail, Mandalay Sour, a sublime mix of rum, lime and bitters over ice. A marionette troupe skilfully handles elaborately costumed princes and potentates, fearsome ogres, colourful magicians and the great slithering Naga enacting a convoluted tale. Their antics become increasingly dramatic as we finish our second cocktail and we lose the thread a little.

For the Ayeyarwady River trip from Mandalay to Bagan, we are booked on the MV Pandaw, a beautifully restored riverboat of the old Ayeyarwady Flotilla. Originally a paddle steamer, it has been refurbished and fitted with new outboard propulsion engines. Our cabins have polished teak wood floors, brass portholes, curtains and bedspreads in navy linen. We spend the afternoon on deck filling our eyes with pagodas and villages, public ferries, cargo boats and small canoes, marvelling at the great expanse of the river under the changing light. Andy rather hopes we'll get stuck on a sandbar, as he's noticed a sign in the bar which states: 'stuck for three hours, drinks at half price, stuck for six hours, drinks on the house,' but we sail on smoothly. After chatting with other passengers at dinner, the boat moors mid-stream for the night; we are lulled to sleep by its gentle rocking.

An early morning visit has been arranged for a donation of schoolbooks and sports equipment to a village school. The children cluster around us, showing off a little, posing for the clicking cameras, pleased to be away from their classroom routine. Women gather round to sell colourful woven cotton blankets, a speciality craft of the area, carrying stacks of five or six designs folded on their heads and more on their arms, favourites held open for us to see in the typical orange, red, and purple colours.

Locals accompany us as we walk through the village, interested in our progress, our clothes, cameras and comments. An elderly woman sits comfortably on a wooden bench outside her home puffing on an impressively large cheroot, its corn husk wrapping holding a mixture of tobacco, betel nut and sugar cane. She is clearly enjoying her morning ritual as she watches the tourists pass by through half shut eyes.

As we sail down river, the land becomes progressively drier, sparse vegetation standing out against the pale clay banks and the clear blue sky. Around midday we approach Bagan and the first of the famed temples appears on the skyline, rising from the steep embankment on our left, the vast plain with more than a thousand pagodas spreading beyond it. We hire a pony cart for our two days and enjoy trundling along the tree-lined dusty roads between the pagodas, entering the larger buildings and exploring a few more isolated and derelict ones further afield, some little more than the original mud-brick base.

We join other tourists atop one of the pagodas to watch the sunset blaze over the vast temple dotted plain, the silver river stained by the dying sun. Later, we stop to eat at a little roadside café, the rice and herb covered fish baked in charred banana leaves, delicious with a cold beer. Opposite, at the junction of two dusty roads, a huge poster advertises Vegas cigarettes, a ritzy hotel, an aeroplane and a sports car showing just what marvels await if you buy these cigarettes. A lone bicycle rickshaw driver slowly pedals past and I am struck by this juxtaposition of cultural icons. I wonder what the rickshaw driver thinks as he passes or if he even notices.

We are about to experience a hot-air balloon ride over the pagodas and plain at dawn. Excited and a little nervous, we climb into the solid wicker basket and settle into our places, the huge balloon billowing over our heads. It gently lifts and sways as we part company with the ground, the circle of upturned faces becoming smaller and smaller. Our silent ascent in the crisp morning air is accompanied by spasmodic gushes of flaming gas, inflating the canopy, floating us ever higher. A pearly white mist rising from the great expanse of the Ayeyarwady hangs low over the green trees dotting the red clay plain, slowly burning off as the day dawns. The soft rose tinted, morning light casts long shadows, painting stunning pictures. Rust red bricks of the temples against the copper tones of dry grass, brilliant patches of green and the fuchsia, pink, orange and white of the bougainvillea outlining the pagodas. At times our basket comes almost close enough to reach out and touch the age-worn bricks of the stupas. Wherever we turn are chedis and pagodas, large and small, well preserved or crumbling, yet mystical. It's a perfect, magical way to capture the vastness of the plain and to imagine how it must have been at its peak, hundreds of years ago.

"What a great holiday this has been," Andy tells me over a glass of wine on our last evening together back in Yangon, "I could never have imagined any of it and I'm not sure I will be able to do it justice when I tell friends back home. I'm not even sure I quite believe some of the things I've discovered. I loved listening to the monks, learning more about Buddhism, Inle Lake and the jumping cats, the plain at Bagan, even seeing those lepers…How can I explain all of that?"

I too feel that over the last ten days, with Andy by my side, I have gained a deeper understanding of the country's natural and architectural treasures, discovering yet another of its facets, this time blatantly seduced by its timeless beauty.

And I promise myself that I'll be among the first to ski those mountains in the morning and dive the tropical waters in the afternoon. I am sure the day will come.

Chapter Twelve
Motorbike Manoeuvres

This week I'm visiting a village near Kengtung to monitor a pilot project the MRCS has initiated there using some discretionary funds we've garnered from the Australian Embassy. It's part of a regional health programme supported by Australian Red Cross, and I'm hoping to get some great feedback for the donors.

Our health delegate Yvonne and her local team have been working with the elders of this village on the project for several weeks to establish priorities for improving the community's health and safety. They've surveyed and mapped the area, checked the villagers' health and given lectures on water and sanitation, on illnesses such as malaria and tuberculosis, and the more common complaints of diarrhoea and feverish colds. Now, it's decision time for the villagers as they and the RC team will have to agree on how to best use the offered funds—two thousand Australian dollars.

I flew up with Yvonne yesterday and spent the afternoon with the team, who briefed me, showing me hand drawn charts with their statistics of the region—lists of villages, population, cases of various illnesses, number of latrines, water points or wells per village.

Over an early breakfast at our guesthouse, Yvonne emphasises that an important aspect of this particular mini-project is to encourage and support the village's commitment to improving their own health. "Too often, aid programmes dictate what is on offer," she comments, "Not so for this one."

Before long, the four team members arrive to fetch us on 'rough terrain' motorbikes, three for the six of us, the Federation logo above the headlamps, helmets equally well emblazoned. I'm to ride pillion behind Li Lay, the youngest of the team, a charming young woman with a round smiling face, her plaits tied with red ribbons. Ours is the smallest bike, a blue 150cc model, and though I'm looking forward to the day I'm a little dubious about our bike's ability to tackle the hills.

Kitted out with helmet and backpack, water, snacks and materials for the village, we head north. For a while we follow a newly constructed road, the gravel pinging out under our tyres, winding up through hills blanketed with parched vegetation. On our right lie terraced rice fields, dry and barren after the harvest, on our left, rise steep hills, tracks leading to small hamlets, shaded by tall pine trees.

Li Lay and I, on our small blue bike gradually fall behind until we see the others in the distance on the straight stretches, then not at all. Suddenly, a louder than usual 'ping' of gravel and a tell-tale hiss of air announce our back tyre is punctured. We wobble to a stop. "Do you think they'll notice we're no longer behind them?" I ask.

"Let's wait a bit. They'll be back," she responds with confidence.

As we sit by the side of the road, I ask Li Lay a few questions about her family and her job with the Red Cross. Idly tossing a few stones in a river winding below us, we take off a layer of clothing. Laughter echoes in the distance and a group of youngsters appear around the corner, heading in our direction. Three boys zigzag back and forth across the road running hoops made from bicycle wheels, urging them along with deft flicks of a stick. Others run alongside clamouring for their turn.

A fourth boy canters on a 'hobby horse', clearly his motorbike. He revs his engine in that universal small boy way, his 'vroom, vrooom, vrooooms' getting louder and louder as he draws near. With a final descending throaty roar, he stops, dust sifting up from his feet. We laugh at his antics and he chuckles back. His brown pants are pushed up to the knee and he sports orange flip-flops and a T-shirt with a cartoon of two yellow detectives in trench coats and trilby hats, one with a torch, the other with a magnifying glass à la Sherlock Holmes—the 'Banana Detectives'. His 'motorbike' is a long bamboo pole on which he sits astride, his hands clasping the handlebar, a stick stuck through two-thirds of the way up. The end of the bamboo pole is split to hold a small metal wheel fixed with a metal rod. Dismounting and holding his bike upright, his eyes just below the level of the crossbar, he grins at me before taking off again.

Behind them, a herdsman wanders along, his few cows and calves grazing on the sparse roadside plants. He shoos the children away from us and they straggle off after him, disappearing round the corner. It's quiet again, but just for a moment as we hear the welcome sound of not just one, but two motorbikes. We look at each other, smiling.

"We began to worry when we realized you weren't behind," Yvonne admits stepping off her bike, "but we had to catch the others' attention before turning back. They were way ahead of us. What happened?"

"Just a puncture," I point to it, "but no-one has passed this last half hour to hitch a lift. Lucky you came back, it's way too hot for a hike!"

Three on each bike, the lame bike held alongside, we take our time reaching the next village. The men find a repair shop and fix the puncture quickly, joining us in the café where we wait, drinking chilled coconut juice. Opposite us, a young boy is spreading rice on a woven mat, smoothing it out to dry with a long wooden paddle. In the next shop, brick workers, all women, carry and stack their wares by the roadside. The cafe owner waves away our payment, telling us he knows of Red Cross work and is pleased we're working in the remote villages. Yvonne pulls a new, plastic-wrapped T-shirt with a Red Cross health message on it from her backpack to thank him for his generosity. Taken aback at the unexpected gift, he accepts it with tears in his eyes.

We wind higher up into the hills, the road still good, until, at a junction we turn uphill onto a smaller dirt road, and finally onto a track bordered by low shrubs, then taller trees. The track winds in and out of the bush, crosses a muddy stream and becomes considerably steeper. Our bike makes heavy weather of it, so I jump off, walking behind, sliding on sodden corners, trampling through leaves and snagging my jacket on hanging creepers.

Just as I'm wondering if the noise of the bikes is enough to scare lurking snakes, I hear the bikes shudder to a stop. Looking up, I see the path has widened. One side is lined with waiting villagers, some in Red Cross tunics, including a gaggle of young children and several beautifully clad older women in traditional Akha dress. We file past them slowly, shaking hands, greeting everyone. Led by the excited throng we emerge from the tree-lined path into an open clearing with a wooden church, its corrugated iron roof topped with a small turret and a wooden cross. Alongside, a leaking concrete water tank, green slime indicating the leaks are not new, is linked by a metal drainpipe and in front are pens housing cattle and pigs. More villagers are lined up in front of the church, the children standing to attention. A Red Cross flag hangs from a long bamboo pole and a small boy with a tapering Shan drum slung diagonally over his right shoulder beats out a fast and furious rhythm. We are escorted into the church, doubling as the village hall, for the Red Cross team to deliver their health lectures and settle behind a table facing the villagers, a tray of glasses and orange cordial before us.

While the lecture is presented, the project discussed and questions answered, I observe the older women in their traditional Ahka dress. Their fitted dark cloth hats, coloured bands stitched with rows of silver beads, coins and large rounded silver buttons are striking. Strings of tiny coloured beads, mostly red and white loop down from the top, some hanging beside the ears, a large coin or silver disc on the ends, others fastening under the chin. From either side of the crown hang elaborate circular silver ornaments with scores of dangling silver pendants. I also notice some women have a decorated silver square at the nape, beaded and hung with money, loops of beads hanging down the back.

"What does that extra decoration signify?" I whisper to Yvonne.

"Only married women can wear that," she replies and points out how the girls and babies' caps have fewer decorations and are often casually paired with T-shirts, pants or dresses.

The women's jackets are made of thick dark blue cloth, with green and red embroidered stripes down the front, on the cuffs and around the stand-up collar. Red tabs with large buttons show they can be worn closed, though most hang open, folded back to show the blouses. The back is delicately worked, incorporating elaborate patterns of buttons and coins. Matching dark blue skirts reach just above the knees, and coloured square, flat purses, usually two, hang from the waist. Beautifully decorated leggings stretch from below the knees to the ankles, the top dark blue, the bottom with colourful embroidered bands.

Lecture over, we tour of the village. The houses, each with a garden fenced in woven bamboo, cling either side of the tamped yellowish-red clay high street along the mountain ridge. Beyond, dark green stands of trees, a few covered in beautiful snowy blossoms paint a splendid backdrop. Most buildings are raised on solid posts, a steep ladder leading up to woven bamboo floors and walls, roofs thatched with dry reeds. Yellow, black and red corn husks are hung in bunches to dry under the eaves.

Stopping by a slightly larger house, I stoop to peer underneath, seeing neat stacks of firewood and long trussed bundles of dried reeds stored in the shadows, pigs and chickens snuffling and clucking in their search for food. Behind the house, blackened pots and kettles surround a brick fireplace, with bowls and utensils stacked on sturdy wooden shelves. Clothes hang to dry on bamboo poles along the fence.

The family step out to greet and talk to us. The father, a handsome man with a fur hat over his silver hair, puffs on a cigar. Smiling, he reveals blackened teeth and lips, common in this region and a sign of beauty in certain ethnic groups, such as the 'black' Lahu. His wife speaks some English and seeing several children crowding around her, I ask how many children she has.

"Eleven, but now only five. Six already dead," she says in a very matter of fact way.

Li Lay continues the conversation in the local language, all of the team fluent in several languages besides Burmese and English. "She says three died as babies, one boy was thrown from a horse and broke his neck, two died from fever," she translates for me and we discuss the high birth and infant mortality rates of the region.

Children trail us as we walk. I notice a girl of about eleven, her beaded bonnet coupled with a smart new denim jacket, then my eye is caught by a slightly older boy with traditional Akha jacket, the entire back intricately embroidered, the front adorned with a silver disc on both lapels, looped beads hanging to waist level. He grins cheekily at me over his shoulder.

I ask his father standing near by about his son's future and he confides in me, "I want him to have more than we had. He needs an education if he is to go outside this village."

Cattle lie on the road, chewing their cud gazing at us with mournful eyes. Strutting roosters, pecking chickens and a few mangy dogs sniff at anything remotely resembling a morsel of food.

As I reach a clearing with garden plots and a rubbish pit, I realize I haven't seen any trash in the village. The ubiquitous plastic bag has not yet arrived, but when it does, it will become an issue as we have seen in the more accessible villages. Here, nearly everything is still made from natural materials so the rubbish rots and is assimilated back into the earth. Not so with plastic, though the instinct to throw things out will be the same. Information on how to re-use and deal with refuse will be vital if the village is to stay so clean.

We are invited to sit with the headman and several elders of the village council. The headman's house is the only building in the village with a tin roof besides the church. Climbing a steep wooden ladder, we step onto the woven floor of a large veranda, covered with patterned mats, looking out over the magnificent forested valley.

Dramatically unfurling a large piece of paper, the headman lays it on the floor. It's time to begin the real discussion between the villagers and our team. The question of what our joint project can buy hangs expectantly in everyone's mind. On the paper is a carefully drawn map of the village. Each street and house is shown in detail, the periphery roughly sketched with trees and hills and the rippled blue lines of a river. A line and several crosses are drawn in red, the shape of the water tank by the village square also outlined in red.

The village has decided that their priorities are twofold—a more consistent water supply and electricity. Fingers point and jab at the map, voices rising excitedly as the villagers explain where the river should be dammed, how water will be pumped up to the tank and where the small hydroelectric generator should be planted. "The tank needs to be repaired and we need cement for that," an elder explains, "The red line and crosses mark where the electricity poles will be sunk so that power can be brought to the village."

"Everyone will help build the dam and erect the poles and power lines. Work has started. Each household will pay three hundred Kyat a month for the power and will be responsible for their own light bulbs. We know it can work," the headman tells us proudly.

Knowing the intent of the villagers, Yvonne and her team have checked the price of hydroelectric generators, putting an option on a Japanese model available in Kengtung. This will cost less than two thousand dollars so the remaining funds will cover the electric cables linking each house and the cement to repair the tank. The discussion continues, a time frame is outlined and details of the work schedule established. Our team plans the next visit and asks how to get the generator to the village. Another animated discussion ensues on the best route, agreeing it will be through two villages, accessible by dirt roads, and then up the last winding track by a wooden sled pulled by buffalo.

Once business matters are settled we're offered lunch, bowls of fish soup, vegetables, dark meat curry and a lethal looking chilli sauce. Afterwards, a small glass of the local liquor is pressed upon us. I follow mine quickly with a coffee, to mask the stringent taste. The women will eat later, their more important task, to serve the men and guests, over.

As we sip our coffee the talk continues, tying up loose ends, planning the next visit and deciding what must be done before the generator arrives. Around three, we say our goodbyes and, donning helmets and jackets, sling on our backpacks and leave, not the way we came, but on a wider track leading in a different direction.

"This is the way the team will bring the generator," Yvonne shouts back to me, "The track's wider here."

We descend into a valley, ploughed fields on either side where most of the women working the fields are wearing full Akha dress. I'd assumed the villagers had worn traditional dress for our visit, but now realize that it is actually worn every day. Here, they have not yet been put away, brought out only on ceremonial occasions.

The road climbs again reaching another group of houses, high on a ridge. Our motorbikes alert the villagers and children come to run alongside, shouting and whooping with laughter. A short visit to check on a few patients and hand out t-shirts with health messages to the young volunteers who provide assistance in this village, for cuts, bruises, coughs and colds, and to give health lessons in school.

Two young soldiers, casually shouldering their guns, walk towards the house we're visiting and glance up. One talks quietly into a walkie-talkie, then moves on up the road. I wonder what they're reporting and to whom.

Nearby, an old woman stands in front her house, leaning on a smooth carved stick. Her brown lined face turns towards me but I'm not sure she can see me. One eye is completely clouded by cataract, the other brown iris already circled in blue, but she smiles and I smile back. She wears the short Akha skirt and her exposed knees above the leggings are scarred and puffy from the long hours spent working in the fields and at her family hearth. I'd like to know more about her life in these remote hills, but have no way of talking with her. Time is too short for one of the team to interpret.

We bid farewell to the villagers, and rev up our bikes, the children chasing us for the first fifty metres. Descending from the ridge, we follow the winding track, sometimes balancing along the top of dried paddy field walls, our riders manoeuvring skilfully on the narrow banks, showing off their expertise. At a corner, we meet five women coming back from market. The huge rattan baskets they carry on their backs are held by a woven strap across their forehead, looped through a wooden yoke hefted across their shoulders. After chatting for a while, they turn and trudge on up the track. I watch them walk away under the late afternoon sun. I can see only the silver coins glinting on their hats, and, below their baskets, their steady, strong legs in patterned leggings. As the sun sets and the tropical night suddenly descends, we reach Kengtung. Back at our guesthouse, Yvonne and I sit out on the terrace with a glass of whisky, content to relax, chatting idly.

I voice the thought running in my mind during the drive back, "I'll probably never see that village again after the project is completed. But I can imagine the houses lit at night, the children studying, and maybe a TV for neighbours to gather around. That old lady will peer at a world she will never have a chance to see, but for the young ones, the outside world will be brought ever closer." I swirl the amber liquid in my glass and take another sip, "Will you visit them again?"

"Probably," Yvonne responds. "I'll let you know when the project is done, the water running and the electricity connected. I have a lot of confidence in the resilience of these villagers. It's been great working with them over the last few months."

I nod at her words, musing, "Well, it's certainly progress. Their world view and aspirations will change, but I wonder how else and how fast it will affect the village."

Chapter Thirteen
Weekend Wandering

In a country where most of the population lives below the poverty threshold, it's hard to accept that what I take for granted is out of reach for those I live amongst. Each morning I leave my house, my morning routine of breakfast, shower, and dress complete, and from my air-conditioned land cruiser, I follow another routine: waving 'hello' to the children of my small street as they squat to do their morning business over the roadside drainage ditch. Their waves are no less friendly than mine, their embarrassment non-existent, but every morning I am reminded that in even within this short distance, differences are glaringly obvious.

In my neighbourhood, as is typical in Asia, much of life is lived outside, on the front steps, on the pavement or street corner, in the road itself. Nothing goes unnoticed, no harsh words or family scraps are unheard, no joy or event is left uncelebrated, no child cries untended, no novelty is left undiscovered and nothing is allowed to go to waste. All is there for those who care to look.

Some days I stop at the tea-shop on the corner, little more than a stove, a table and four small stools, where the owner always sets down a plate with a fried bun or a smoky morsel for me to try. One particular morning as I'm sipping my hot tea, a strong, tasty brew loaded with sweetened condensed milk, I notice their cups and smile to myself. They're my used yogurt pots, an Australian brand. After that I never throw anything away without first washing it and asking Malay or Maung Taut if it might be useful.

Another evening I spy a crowd laughing and gesticulating around something on the road. Approaching, I see a large recently killed snake, headless but still moving. The heated discussion is about who will take it home to cook for dinner. I don't join in the bidding.

After the first few weeks, I consider the people of my street as neighbours, not just casual acquaintances. The children's games, the small stores, the Nat-houses, the shrine, women gossiping at their daily washing and food preparation, all call to my curious nature. Little by little, as I settle in, I do get to know them better.

I often pause by the house where two TVs are always glowing in a corner of the dim room, each tuned to a different channel, the sound off. One evening there's high drama on both screens. Curious, I peer in and ask, "What are you watching?" My friendly neighbour tells me they are both Korean soap operas, extremely entertaining and subtitled in Burmese.

"But how can you follow both at the same time?"

She laughs, assuring me it's possible, though admitting she might miss some details.

Sometimes in the early evening, the novices from the monastery on my street invite me to play badminton on the road. We whip the shuttlecock, or a crumpled paper ball, up and over an imaginary net, applauding our best shots.

Occasionally I enjoy the animated faces of a row of small boys lining up for a hair cut. Someone's Dad is known for his skills and it's a monthly ritual. The boys strip to the waist and once done they're led to the water barrel to have their head and shoulders sluiced down. They emerge from the dousing, flicking back their hair, beads of water catching the sun, laughing at the fresh, clean feeling.

I become attuned to the sounds of the street and the everyday cries of itinerant salesmen and women passing from door to door with their wares, tea and buns, flowers, fruit, small meat pastries, baskets and brooms. Others call for scraps of paper or rags, bottles, cans, plastic or cardboard to be recycled and sold on. Each has their distinctive cry, half song, half chant. It reminds me of an old book of my grandfather's, *The Cries of London*, commonplace there centuries ago, the cries still alive in the backstreets of today's Myanmar.

On my free weekends, I wander further afield with my camera, a real attraction, causing wonder and merriment for children and adults alike, as they scramble, lean and push to see themselves on the small camera screen.

My circuit takes me past the Traditional Medicine Hospital with its gardens of herbs and dusty plants of all colours, shapes and smells, some oft-used and carefully tended in rows, others clumped and bushy, left to blossom and wither. Behind its peeling façade are the laboratories with pestles and mortars, glass jars, and phials containing mysterious liquids, treatment and massage tables, piles of small paper, and leaf packages tied with string. People sit outside waiting for friends and relatives to emerge with their remedy safely stowed in their bodice or the waistband of their *longyi*. Bicycle rickshaws are ready for those who need a ride home, the waiting drivers relaxing in the passenger seats, chatting, or sitting apart, reading or chewing betel.

Right opposite is 'Top Star', the barber's shop, a quaint cubicle perched on stilts, roofed and open in front, complete with mirrors all round and beautifully painted illustrations of somewhat outmoded hairstyles. Best of all, is the antique barber's, or maybe dentist's chair, all chrome and red padded leather, notched pedals to move the seat. Here, young boys experience their first snip around the ears, young idols try new stylish haircuts to impress the girls, and well-established gents step in for a regular cut and shave. It's easy to keep clean; the barber just sweeps the hair to the road beneath. It's also the perfect place to catch up on news and politics of the day, the customers adding to the barber's repartee. Passers-by join in with random comments adding to the vibrancy of the debate and I wish I could too, but my lack of Burmese keeps me dumb. Besides, it looks like the men enjoy their own brand of humour and gossip and might not welcome a woman's intrusion. I greet them, smiling, as I walk by, and a chorus of "Mingalar ba" is returned with warmth. I can feel witty observations about me fly behind my back as I walk away.

Further up the road is a temple, a market in front. Novices walk apace practising their English, children follow me to see what that foreigner is doing now. The market ladies, knowing that I am an *apio gyi*, an older unmarried woman, hold out bundles of herbs, a ripe mango, or an ear of corn, at a really cheap price. Young girls shyly offer me flowers while young men stare, sometimes cheekily, often bursting into laughter and punching each other when I smile back or wink at them.

At the next crossroads I reach the monks' shop. With so many thousands, if not millions, of monks in Myanmar, it had never occurred to me to wonder where all the robes, alms bowls and bags, thong sandals, leather in winter, velvet in summer, came from. But here it is, a shop festooned with beautiful dark russet cloth, black enamel bowls, maroon and brown slippers, orange buckets filled with basic foodstuffs, bedrolls and blankets, smaller boxes with soap, toothbrush and toothpaste, woven shoulder bags in various subtle hues, a veritable treasure trove for monastic life.

Returning, I walk along the banks and through the gardens of Kandawgyi Lake. I turn and continue up a side road until there directly opposite my little street is the handsome house that had caught my eye on the first day and whose very presence poses questions. Partly shrouded by trees, its overgrown garden and muddy pond bordered by a fence with flowering creepers, is the big white wooden turreted house, now a museum, once home of the country's independence hero, Colonel Aung San. Only a small plaque notes its significance but his bronze statue, just a few hundred metres away in Kandawgyi Park, draws weekend strollers, young couples and families to have their photo taken in the shadow of his embrace.

Once a year the garden is tidied and trimmed for a visit from an official motorcade, an occasion requiring a rigorous line-up of police and soldiers along the road. On weekends a trickle of interested students and tourists wander through the sparsely furnished rooms with their fly-specked photos in sepia tones, considering the impact of his short life and pondering on the aspirations and situation of his even more famous daughter, 'The Lady' who cannot be named, renowned worldwide for her determination to bring democracy to her country.

Sometimes, at dusk, I walk further up the hill behind the house to gaze at the floodlit dome and spire of the great Shwedagon Pagoda, the streams of circling bats taking their routine evening flight silhouetted against the gold and the darkening sky.

On that same street corner, is the ice-cream seller with his shocking pink cones and his ice cream of probably shockingly unhygienic consistency. It is a treat for the locals, but I've never been brave enough to try. I smile at him but move past, instead buying a slice of watermelon from the wheeled cart further up the road, making sure, as always, that the slice is fresh. I often buy fruit here. When in season, pomelo, similar to grapefruit, is my favourite, each pink or pale yellow segment rich with tear-shaped pearls of juice waiting to explode their bitter sweet taste on my tongue.

One evening, walking up my little street, all is quiet, but I can almost feel the anticipation; tomorrow is the New Year street fair.

I wake early. Our narrow gravel road is closed to cars and everyone is out on the street enjoying themselves. Tea-shop owners and local vendors carry as much as they can in crates hung around their necks, drinks, fluorescent sweets, cigarettes, betel packets, biscuits, dried fish and other traditional specialties. Games are set up along the road, start lines and targets drawn in chalk or paint, several competitions running at once.

"Hello Ma, you want to play?" they call me to join in the fun. I agree, drawing quite a crowd but my attempts at landing a ball in the basket, slinging hoops into a painted circle and launching self-made paper darts to soar longer than anyone else's, only highlight the ineptitude of the foreign lady from up the road. Secretly I had rather harboured the notion they might be impressed, as I am normally no slouch when it comes to sport. Not so, to my chagrin. I join them in their amusement, then opt out, relaxing, to watch men and boys playing the local sport, *chinlon*, expertly kicking a rattan ball over a net, their leaping, twisting high kicks beautiful to watch. I draw the line at competing in the 'lord of the greasy pole' but enjoy watching the wiry warriors. A long, thick bamboo pole, suspended between two trees is heavily greased with oil. Each competitor, armed with a pillow, perches uneasily at either end of the pole, trying to whack the other off. He who lasts longest, takes on the next challenger. The rules are not clear, the cheating rife, but the hilarity after every blow, the shouted advice clearly understandable. Getting into the spirit of it, I join in, egging on the underdog, booing the bully and cheering for the victorious.

As dusk falls I thank everyone, smiling, "Chezu-tinbade, chezu-be," and leave reluctantly.

Back home my serene retreat is pounded by a cacophony of music, new Myanmar versions of old favourites and traditional songs, all cranked up to a gazillion amps. The beat continues to thump up through my pillow until the early hours of the morning.

However, it is just a forerunner to the week of non-stop chanting, a beautiful tradition carried on most years in monasteries and temples across the country. At the risk of seeming insensitive and godless, I never could have imagined something so deeply religious could be so incredibly, mind-blowingly irritating. It isn't the chanting itself, but the fact that to ensure it will enhance the lives of those near-by, the monks have rented enormous speakers setting them permanently at full volume. The static all but overwhelms the solemn chanting and I wonder if I am the only person in the whole neighbourhood in fear for my sanity and hearing.

On the first day of the assault I assume it's a holy day and come nightfall, it will end. I listen without undue comment, knowing that I am in a country steeped in Buddhism and I am the foreigner. At the end of the second day and night, I mention to Malay that I am finding the chanting somewhat irritating while assuring him that I understand the importance of the Buddhist rituals. The third day I decide to go to the gym early in the morning and have breakfast in the office, work longer hours and eat in town. By the end of the week, I am stir crazy but have almost succeeded in tuning it out, so it takes a few minutes before the welcome silence of the eighth day sinks in. Should that ever happen again, a field trip to a distant city will definitely be planned.

A few days after the fair, I download my photos onto my computer, choosing the best ones of my neighbours, print them and head back out into the street.

I stop by to give a set of photos to a family, fun ones of the children and a lovely one of three generations, grandmother, mother and daughter in front of their small stall, selling basic necessities—rice, oil, sugar, onions, and dried fish. They offer me a cup of tea, but I decline, indicating I have to visit other homes. They nod and smile their thanks for the photos.

Later, returning home past their store in the last rays of the evening sun, I hear hurried feet behind me. Thinking it's one of the younger children coming to take my hand to walk with me, I turn and wait. It's a little boy from the store, already dressed in his yellow pyjamas and clutching something carefully in both hands. Reaching me, he looks up with big brown eyes, a solemn smile lighting his face, then slowly opens and holds out his hands offering their gift, two eggs and a lemon.

They rest heavy in my hands, the eggs smooth and a little warm, the lemon's knobbly skin releasing its fresh tang.

I think of the all the weighty reports about Myanmar, a country and people vilified for the poverty, ethnic conflicts, the inadequate health services for the people, the decaying infrastructure, the pervasive presence of the military, and the fear. Yet in my hands, I hold the evidence of another reality and I wonder, why is it that those who apparently have the least, offer the most?

Chapter Fourteen
Riding The River

I love telling people that the road to Mandalay is not actually a road, but a river, the mighty Ayeyarwady River. Born in the foothills of the Himalayas, it winds its way down the whole length of the country, spreading its rich silt before reaching the sea in a broad, fertile delta.

The 'Road to Mandalay' is also the name of a luxury river cruiser plying the river between Mandalay and Bagan from August to April. Occasionally she sails on longer trips to Bhamo in the far north, in Kachin State.

My association with this vessel began in the Gallery Bar of Traders Hotel in Yangon when I stopped by to watch a Rugby World Cup 2003 match. Though not usually a rugby fan, I am a Kiwi and watching the All Blacks seemed a pleasant way to spend my Saturday afternoon. The game had already begun. I nodded hello to a few friends, sliding into a side seat to watch the big screen set up at the far end of the bar. Within minutes, I was barracking the Blacks and enjoying the commentary from more knowledgeable spectators, witty comments, shouted encouragement or disgusted jeers as a scrum collapsed, an opponent's tackle was suspect, or a goal missed from right in front of the posts.

After a while I noticed a woman about my age, in a t-shirt and calf-length pants, beer in one hand, laughing as she urged on the All Blacks, "Not like that, you silly buggers!" I heard her shout, in a broad kiwi accent. Tilting my head discreetly in her direction, I asked my neighbour who she was.

"You don't know Sister Anne?" he responded, surprised, "I thought everyone knew her."

I knew her by name only. A Catholic sister, already here for several years with an order of nuns, sharing their mission in teaching, counselling and working with women's groups and children. In fact, when I first arrived I had been rather taken aback to be occasionally mistaken for her. Like others, I had preconceived ideas of nuns but, as I heard her throw out another good-natured comment, I began to suspect that I might have been very wrong in Sister Anne's case.

That Saturday afternoon, I decided it was time to finally meet. At half-time I moved along the line of chairs to introduce myself. She knew about me too, the international community in Yangon being quite small, and we started talking. I had heard she was a hard-working, compassionate woman, who speaks Burmese and knows a great deal about this country. Her down-to-earth and fun-loving character was evident from just a few minutes of conversation. I quickly realised that her motivation, arising from her faith, and mine, from years of working with a humanitarian organization were not that far apart. We chatted through the break, watching the rest of the match together.

Afterwards she introduced me to John Hinchliffe, the captain of the 'Road to Mandalay'. He asked about our work, interested in the details, then sprang a million-dollar question, "Would either, or perhaps both of you, be interested in doing a trip in return for lecturing to passengers? They would appreciate a deeper insight into the country." Would we? What a great opportunity to cruise on the famous Orient Express's 'Road to Mandalay'.

Built in Germany and launched in the sixties, her first decades were spent cruising the Rhine as the 'Nederland'. She was bought by Orient Express, looking for a dependable shallow-draught vessel for their Ayeyarwady cruise and underwent major refurbishment before reaching Myanmar aboard a specialist transport ship, via the Suez Canal in 1995.

She was unloaded in Yangon, and sailed up the Ayeyarwady to Mandalay where local craftsmen added Myanmar style fittings and decorations, woodcarvings and well chosen antiques so the atmosphere would reflect the land she sailed through. The inaugural cruise to Bagan departed from Mandalay in January of the following year.

The Bhamo cruise is in September, at the end of the rainy season when the river is running high and drier weather can almost be guaranteed. This particular trip is, unfortunately, wetter than expected, mostly under darkening skies, but nonetheless full of fascinating sights, good food and great company.

It takes us eight days to reach Bhamo, struggling against the current but only three for the run back down to Mandalay and on to Bagan.

On the highest navigable section of the river, we watch fascinated as the Captain, from his small foredeck cabin, negotiates the churning brown waters of the upper Ayeyarwady's second defile with great skill in minimal visibility during a downpour. High rocks covered in thick jungle rise up around us, ethereal above the mist. Then, the river opens up in a vast expanse of calmer waters, and the sun appears highlighting the lush greenery of the forested mountains, accented by the golden blossom of tall teak trees.

Each day brings new sights and experiences. Together with the other passengers, I gaze in awe as the raging waters form whirlpools around a wooded island crowned by a magnificent line of golden stupas. Ashore, we travel by pony cart to a school where we talk with pupils working on a science project in a laboratory, an old microscope with a cracked glass plate their only equipment. We offer schoolbooks and sports gear at a special assembly, children wide-eyed, as the boxes are unpacked. At a clinic, we unpack boxes of medicines to restock bare dispensary shelves, evoking smiles of relief from the nurses. We climb to a remote wooden monastery in the hills, where cheeky young novices wait for us, raindrops trickling down their newly shaved heads onto their eyelashes, making them blink.

More sinister signs of the reality of life in Myanmar are also noted, like the hand-painted notice by a village wharf:

> DRUG TRAFFAING IS SERIUS OFFNCE WHICH CAN GET OEATH PENALILTY

In contrast, we are warmly welcomed to a pottery village, and witness huge water pots being fired in the searing temperatures of rounded clay kilns. We watch elephants in the jungle working with gigantic teak logs and being washed by their mahouts, and we ride an old cane-train through fields and forests, over precipitous narrow bridges, and pass clearings with bright green rice paddies.

On board, we relax, reading under the blue canopy on the top deck, lounging by the small, turquoise pool, watching the river or chatting with friends over a cool drink as the world glides by—rare commodities in otherwise busy lives back home. Exotic dinners are offered in the softly lit dining room, its large windows reflecting starched white napkins, monogramed silver tableware, and sparkling glasses. In the gold and black thirties décor of the bar, soft piano music in the background, friendships are born and impressions exchanged with fellow passengers from all over the world, the smiling staff happy to pour an evening nightcap and talk about their beloved Myanmar.

Nearing Mandalay, after days of rain, the grey skies open and a watery sun pierces the clouds, transforming the river and surrounding flooded plains into a molten silver expanse. Small boats with colourful sails fly by, canoes heavy with produce hug the islands and banks where darker palm trees dot the tender green, newly sprouting rice crop, while on the steps of a white washed temple, scores of women lay their washing out to dry, an eye-catching mosaic of colour and pattern.

"It's certainly picturesque," one passenger remarks to me as we lean together on the railing, "but I'll stick with my washer and dryer at home, and thank my stars for them."

For the passengers everything is a discovery in this still closed country. For me it's another lesson in the history and endurance, the culture and traditions of my adopted home.

In my lectures, I try to convey the country's complexities from my perspective as a resident and to offer insights into its history and customs, most gleaned from my Myanmar friends and colleagues. Questions are asked about aspects of Myanmar life that perplex the well-travelled visitors, as most have read extensively about the country. Their comments and queries after the lecture spark lively discussions, often continuing through dinner, about religion and prejudice, health care and education, about sanctions and the appropriateness of international aid. I always hope that my own concerns and observations help them form more balanced opinions because, back home, they will certainly talk to others about their experiences in Myanmar. Feeling protective, I hope a few positive stories will emerge, to offset the prevailing negative view of the country.

After dinner on our last night, I'm relaxing on the top deck, enjoying the soft sounds of murmured conversations, the occasional echoing of steps on the wooden deck, the clinking of glasses muted by the warm darkness of the tropical night, the water lapping and swirling round the sleek white hull. Moored for the night, mid-river, far from the larger villages, stars shine brightly through the darkness and sounds from the shore are rare.

Then a vision gradually takes shape. A few lights glimmer in the distance, then more and more appear. A host of small floating lights slowly come into view, suspended in the darkness. Gliding closer and closer, they part at the bow, surrounding us, then slowly disappear downriver, engulfed by the dark night.

Silence falls as we watch this spectacle created by the staff and a group of willing villagers who have set afloat, from upstream, more than two thousand small leaf and bamboo boats, each carrying a lighted candle to leave us with a perfect lingering memory of our last night on board.

Suddenly, I feel guilty for being here while poverty, fear and want abound in many parts of this country, perhaps even a few miles away. But all around me I hear hushed exclamations and spontaneous clapping and my reverie is broken, the feeling lost, swept away by the beauty of the night, the floating lights, the smiles and pride of the crew and the delight of the guests from all walks of life and different worlds, together in this special place and time.

"It's so beautiful, I just don't want to go home," a fellow guest, Leila, remarks, turning to me. "What an incredible journey. Have you enjoyed it as much as we have?"

"I've loved every moment. It's been fascinating and relaxing but I'm looking forward to going home too," I respond, my thoughts flying to Yangon.

On Monday, I will be back in the office doing all I can to support my Myanmar colleagues with their health and disaster preparedness programmes, helping to strengthen the national society, readying it for the upcoming challenges. I'll see my friends again, my team and their families too, when they join the at-home movie night planned for this weekend.

The cruises are a wonderful experience, but ultimately I know it's my everyday life with my colleagues and friends, doing the job that I love in this fascinating country that brings the richest rewards.

Chapter Fifteen
Dust and Ash

The Federation together with Myanmar Red Cross conducted a nation-wide survey of all 300 plus Red Cross branches, their composition, activities and capacity during 2002-03. Visits and meetings were arranged at several locations in each state and division with RC leaders and volunteers but also with members of the public, army, police, local government and the medical profession. A comprehensive report was prepared early in 2004 and served as a basis for further branch development work and the 5-year Strategic Plan.

I have elected to take part in a branch survey visit to Northern Chin State, in the remote north-west, an area seldom visited by foreigners and certainly off the tourist map. The National Society facilitates the compulsory travel permits and prepares our schedule. Our team consists of MRCS Board Member U Soe Thein, a native of Rakhine State, U Hla Myint, Deputy Head of Disaster Response, with Thuza and myself from the delegation. Thuza, our Branch Development Officer, is a beautiful, reserved young woman with a background in NGO work. I look forward to getting to know her better on this trip.

In Kalemyo, we meet the local Red Cross committee and after an early lunch, load our bags into a waiting van. It's clearly seen better days. The windows are jammed half open, there are numerous dents and the back bumper is held on with twine. It's left-hand drive, normal for most Myanmar vehicles, although the country changed to driving on the right years ago, on the whim of a fortune-teller's advice to the then national leader. It's unnerving, as a passenger, to face the on-coming traffic with no means to brake or swerve and to be responsible for advising the driver when it's safe to overtake.

Our driver is a slight young man who drives nonchalantly, one arm on his open window. He chews betel and spits frequently, firing the red spittle expertly out to the right with a quick twist of the head and a pursing of his lips. His bag of fresh betel wads hangs from the indicator stick and I wonder if he's calculated the number needed for the length of the trip.

Outside the town, the road begins to climb and the potholed tarmac soon gives way to gravel, corrugations on the corners where traffic, rain and wind have left their mark. I gaze over low brown hills, the sound of our tyres on the loose stones taking me back to family holidays, driving in the country.

Winding upwards, we pass trucks laden with produce, people, or both, straining on the hills and spewing black smoke. Others rattle downhill towards us, tilting ominously on the corners. We pass occasional clusters of wooden houses, some with brightly painted doors or windows, a few flowerpots adding colour. The front of my t-shirt is slowly turning grey from the dust sifting in through the windows. My teeth and eyes feel gritty.

"Anybody for a cold drink?" I ask hopefully. We stop at a store doubling as a bus and truck stop. Huge posters outside suggest Grand Royal Whisky and Winbody cigarettes, clearly the favourite brand if you have a large horse and a cowboy hat. We settle for a cold bottle of coke or Fanta, the only soft drinks on offer, taking them outside. Several women sitting on the porch shuffle along on their behinds to make room for me, indicating with smiles and gestures, that I should sit with them. When Thuza joins us, we start a conversation, women to women.

"Where do you come from? Where are you going? Do you like our country? Are you a Christian? Do you have children? Do you like our Myanmar food?" The questions come thick and fast, our short replies bringing forth giggles and humorous backchat and more questions. The men move closer, listening in, but feigning no interest. Thuza interprets for me and I suggest we could begin our survey here, so she throws some questions back at them.

"Do you know about *Kyet Cheni* (Red Cross)? Do you have a group in your town? What do they do? Do they do a good job?" we ask. I'm surprised and heartened they all know about the Red Cross and, by and large, think it a good thing. I would like to stay longer but it will soon be dusk and we have a long way to go.

The road becomes steeper, a few slips cutting into corners and roadsides. I hope the headlights work. On a desolate stretch we come upon two children, perhaps brother and sister, about nine or ten years old, bent over, carrying large woven baskets of firewood on their backs, the weight supported by a thick strap across their forehead.

"Can we give them a ride to their village?" I ask, and the van stops abruptly in a flurry of dust. The driver calls to the children who have stopped in amazement, or perhaps fear, several yards back. Darting looks at each other, they move towards us, wary but a little excited at something out of the ordinary. Hla Myint loads their baskets on top of our luggage at the back as they climb up and sit behind us, eyes wide. I offer them biscuits, but only when Thuza takes them from me, do they hold out their hands. Neither eats their biscuits, they just hold them staring at us. Attempts by my colleagues to talk with them draw out only monosyllabic replies.

A few kilometres up the hill they point to their hamlet, a few wooden houses facing a flat dirt square. We turn in and within minutes a crowd of children surrounds the van. Our two passengers climb down in silence, very solemn, still clutching their biscuits, but within minutes they are transformed. Standing tall and proud, the centre of attention, they smile and chat loudly, gesturing dramatically towards us, re-enacting their great adventure. We unload their firewood and hand out wrapped sweets, others arriving at a run to benefit from this unexpected windfall.

We grind on up dusty hills, skin and clothes progressively grimier and getting hungry. The driver has chewed and spat his way through about half the betel wads. Are we halfway there yet? With evening approaching, the stunted and angled trees paint beautiful black silhouettes against the golden sunset.

As we turn through a sharp corner, light angled across the road, I shout for a photo stop. Coming towards us, at a decent pace, is a strange vehicle, Mum up front driving, bringing home her brood of four, perched atop a stack of firewood. She hangs grimly onto the big black steering wheel as they take the corner, the load of wood and children listing precariously, but breaks into a smile as she sees us, then rumbles past, stones spitting out, kids waving and shouting as they disappear round the next corner.

"Wow, did you see that? The whole thing made of wood, even the wheels." I blurt out, fascinated. "But damn, I missed the photo, she was going too fast. How on earth does she control it on these steep roads?

"We'll see plenty more over the next days", U Soe Thein tells me, "It's a typical 'Chin car'. There's fierce competition here as to who constructs the smartest and fastest. You'll see," he adds with a laugh. Talking about the wooden cars, how every day families push theirs up the hills, do their work for the day then coast home in the evening, takes us into the darkness of nightfall, the headlights picking out the road ahead. The road levels out and we descend into a small valley, a glint of water to our left. There are no lights but the outlines of some houses. The driver slows to a stop by an open doorway, a lantern hanging from the lintel.

Ravenous, we pile out, welcomed into the small family restaurant, each table with its checked cloth, vase of fake roses and the all important plastic holder for the toilet roll to clean the table, cutlery, plates, mouth and hands. We sit in the gloom, walls and raftered ceiling receding into black around us, candlelight no match for the darkness, eating rice with chicken and vegetables, served quickly and as usual, barely warm. Here, temperature doesn't seem to matter much, just the taste and spiciness are crucial, unlike in a colder climate where hot food is more comforting.

Around eleven-thirty, we reach the outskirts of a small town. There are only a few lights and even fewer people around though we do startle some dogs lying in the road, setting off a fearsome chorus of barking. The driver hangs out his window to ask for directions from an old man sitting outside his house, deep into a bottle of whisky. Three streets down the hill and two to the left, we finally arrive, tired, stiff and very grimy, at the 'Moon Guest House'.

A woman in her thirties, a sleeping baby tied on her back, leads us up a flight of steep wooden stairs into a small oval hallway, a solid central pillar holding up roughly hewn wooden struts and a corrugated iron roof. Eight doors lead off it, each daubed with a painted numeral, dribbles adding an artistic touch. I am handed a large key with No 8 and as I open my door, a young boy comes huffing up the stairs with my bag. My room has a bed, a chair and a hook on the wall. An embroidered pillow and two folded blankets sit on a white sheet stretched taught over a thin mattress, next to a curtained window. It's basic, but clean.

Thuza hovers at my door, "Joanna, is this okay for you, will you be able to sleep?" she asks with a slight frown.

I nod and smile, "It's fine with me. It's just a bed I need, and some sleep, but I'd really love to wash off some of this dust. You too, I am sure."

"I've already asked about that. Grab your toilet bag and come with me. Have you got a torch? She leads me onto a narrow terrace, a squat toilet with a half-door off at the far end and a barrel of water midway along the railing. By the light of my torch, we help each other to dust off and pour water, keep the latchless toilet door shut and, holding toothpaste and toilet bags up off the wet boards, manage to wash ourselves.

"This'll be a day to remember," I comment with a smile to Thuza before closing my door. She bursts out laughing and tells me she was so afraid that I would be angry.

"About what?" I ask innocently. "I love an adventure, you know that." I hug her goodnight and she smiles in relief.

I lie awake for a while, listening to the others moving around, their wooden beds creaking, just feet away from mine. My mind meanders and just as I register the first reverberating snores through the walls, the day fades into sleep.

In the morning we are all awake early, calling out hello through the thin walls from our beds. After a quick wash and clean clothes, I head downstairs and out into the fresh morning air, camera in hand. The streets are even steeper than I remember from our drive, the houses rising in tiers on the hillside above the guesthouse. On a high ridge I see the outline of a pagoda with a covered stairway leading to it. I calculate at least three hundred steps for the faithful to climb.

The dogs and neighbourhood children are already on the move, watching out for anything interesting but keep their distance. The houses have small gardens enclosed by neat wooden palings, some with rows of vegetables, others with stone flags or trodden earth, stacks of firewood, hens pecking for dropped grain and insects. A few cheeky urchins with knitted caps and runny noses shadow me. When I take a photo, the shy ones look away, but the bolder strike poses, daring each other to ever more extravagant attitudes, overcome with mirth at their own antics, doubling their efforts to impress when I laugh with them.

The first meeting of the day is at the hospital, a centre serving the whole district. It sits atop a hill and we are greeted by the sight of a beautifully tended garden of red agapanthus, red poppies and red bottlebrush, and a group of nurses clad in matching red *longyis*, fresh white blouses and starched caps. Touring the hospital, we talk to the patients and the family members who tend to their needs. The few nursing staff cope with emergencies, assist the doctors in the basic operating theatre, manage the drug rounds, and change dressings, in addition to dealing with the line of outpatients which, at eight-thirty in the morning, already stretches across the grounds.

We meet the Matron, an impressively organized, well-spoken middle-aged woman who gives us the hospital's statistics and some background on this area's common health problems—intestinal and respiratory diseases, malaria, dengue and tuberculosis—similar to most of the other regions of the country although here, with a cooler, drier climate, malaria and dengue outbreaks tend to be more seasonal.

One of the doctors, the local Red Cross Chairman, has gathered an interesting mixture of RC volunteers, policemen, local officials, an army officer, and some teachers to give us an insight into the activities of and opinions about the Red Cross training and actions in this district. We're introduced and offered tea, then the discussions begin, mostly in Burmese, with a quiet interpretation by Thuza, a few comments in English thrown in for my benefit. I follow as best I can, asking a few questions as the morning progresses towards lunchtime.

And lunchtime doesn't wait. At 12.00 sharp, the meeting is adjourned. At a well-laden table, a glass vase with bright pink bougainvillea at its centre, food is ladled onto my plate in copious quantities.

I smile my thanks, talking with the doctor next to me. But our schedule is tight and we have to leave for Haka, the State's main centre for another meeting. We say goodbye to the people of this friendly little town, and are back on the road again for another afternoon of twisting roads, dust and new sights.

U Soe Thein was right; we do see more classic wooden cars on the road and, on the third sighting, stop. The driver is a shy man, his young son peeping out from behind his shoulders. He's lashed long, freshly milled planks either side of his vehicle and is escorted by two friends on foot. He's building his own house, each day working in the forest, sawing and fashioning planks for its construction with his friends' help, just as he will help them when they're ready to build their own homes. Each evening he brings his finished boards back home, steering carefully and taking it slowly so he can chat with his companions who walk alongside. He estimates it will take him another few months to finish.

I'm fascinated by the car's design, at the passenger seat behind, and the sides high enough to hold the load. The wheels are beautifully rounded cross-sections of a tree trunk, about forty cm in diameter and ten cm thick, the growth rings still visible, the rim covered with thick black rubber, probably cut from a used truck tyre, hammered into place. The driver's seat is a raised wooden block with a padded cushion. I lean down to check out the foot pedal, also in wood, connected to a spring and two metal rods that push rubber pads, the brakes, against each rear wheel.

Back in the van, talking about the car's intricate design, I just have to do it...so, in one long breath, I recite my favourite A.A.Milne poem:

"Let it rain! Who cares? I've a train upstairs, with a brake which I make from a string sort of thing, which works in jerks, 'cos it drops in the spring, which stops with the string, and the wheels all stick so quick that it feels like a thing that you make with a brake, not string...So that's what I make when the day's all wet, it's a good sort of brake but it hasn't worked yet."*

"Where did that come from? Who knew we have a poetry lover amongst us? More please," my astonished colleagues respond, laughing at my outburst.

After this I grow quiet, prompting Thuza to enquire after a while, "Are you okay? You're unusually quiet."

"I'm fine," I tell her, smiling, "Long journeys have this effect on me. Having to sit still, I just let my thoughts wander." I am not unaware of the discomfort of today's trip, the shuddering turns on corrugated corners, the dust filling my nose and eyes, coating my clothes and hair. It's not that I don't notice the endless chewing and spitting of the driver, the chatting of my colleagues or the stops at the military checkpoints while our papers are checked yet again. I just follow my winding train of thought through it all, letting it wash over me.

Arriving in Haka as the afternoon sun glares red through our dust covered windows, we drive up the long main street, and turn into the home of a local administrator where we'll stay the night. Thuza and I climb down rather stiffly from the car. We are black with dust, eyebrows and hair matted. We laugh at the dramatic looks we have assumed with this unwanted makeover. We brush each other down, then turn our attention to the bags, whacking them thoroughly with a straw broom to get the worst off before venturing indoors.

* "The Engineer" from *Now we are Six* by A.A. Milne, 1927

My room is spacious, the bed has a flowered bedspread with a towel and soap placed at the foot. I open my bag, grab a clean sarong, and head for the bathroom. Too late, there's already a queue. Staking my claim for fourth place, I go back to my room, pour myself a glass of water and lie down gingerly on the bed, careful to shed as little dirt as possible. I doze until I hear a discrete knock on the door, "Joanna? Joanna, are you awake? In fifteen minutes we have to meet the local committee. We can't be late, they've already been waiting half the afternoon. We're all ready." Thuza tells me through the door.

Amazing what a bucket of water or three can do in five minutes. The bathroom is small with wooden slats underfoot and a square tub brimming with water. I would love to submerge myself and feel the clean water sluicing away the dirt, but grab the orange plastic bucket and after a hurried dousing, throw on my sarong and dash back to my room. Clean T-shirt and *longyi*, hair combed and dripping deliciously cold down my back, I join the others, all transformed by their speedy ablutions.

We drive to a small village where the local Red Cross Chairman, resplendent in his navy uniform and starched white shirt, peaked cap positioned precisely on his newly dyed head of hair, welcomes us in his office.

When I first arrived in Myanmar, I thought I was onto something, that if I could identify that uniquely Burmese string of DNA that staved off grey hair, I could make a small fortune. Only after weeks of careful observation and discreet questioning did I realize that nearly everyone, men and women alike, regularly dye their hair to a uniform shade of black with glints of red. The appearance of the local chairman confirms that the hair-dying fashion is a nationwide trend, not just confined to the dapper city types.

We talk with the volunteers about their activities and aspirations, lack of resources and, one of the biggest problems for them, uniforms. Although all tidily kitted out with the requisite navy blue skirt or trousers and white shirt, they tell us that many of their friends don't become members because they can't afford to. This bothers me, as offering your services for your community should not cost money.

"We need uniforms for our first aid duties and the parades on public holidays," a young man tells us. "As Red Cross members we want to show who we are when we represent our organization.".

The discussion moves on to training courses and teaching materials, disasters the branch has dealt with and the lack of supplies in the small warehouse. We leave a copy of the Branch Survey questionnaire, asking the chairman if it could be completed by the next day. He looks at his group and they nod solemnly, proud to participate. This is the first visit by Headquarters staff and clearly an event to be noted in the log book. Signing my name, I write out my full title, *Head of Myanmar Delegation, International Federation of Red Cross and Red Crescent Societies*. I wonder who will be the next international visitor to this village.

Driving back to Haka, the chairman with us, we stop at an isolated house. "What's this stop for?" I ask.

"To make a donation. The house caught on fire a couple of weeks ago and the father, a tailor, was badly burned. His hands were damaged fighting the flames and now they shake so much that he can't use his machine," Hla Myint explains.

The family is expecting us. The two girls and three boys are dressed in their best, hair fluffed up or slicked down according to their sex. The father sits in the only chair of the house, one foot on a plastic crate, his right arm lying along the armrest, palm up, covered with blisters and seeping wounds. His wife brings a tray with cordial and a plate of biscuits, indicating with a shy smile that we should sit on stools at a low table. As the men talk amongst themselves, Thuza draws her into conversation about the fire and how they are managing now. One wall and the whole ceiling are scorched black from the fire, although some magazine pages stuck haphazardly on the wall cover the worst. I still smell the smoke and imagine how scared the family must have been.

"It was early evening and I was cooking dinner," she tells us, "As I went to get rice from the shed the draught fanned the burner flames and a cloth caught fire. It spread so quickly. I shouted to the children to get their father. Luckily he was close, working in the vegetable garden. We could only whack at the flames with wet cushions and bedcovers. My husband fought till he put it out. I don't know how he managed, but his poor hands..." Telling the story, the worry and fear resurface in her eyes and the children gather round.

Hla Myint calls out to the driver, who brings in a large cardboard box from the van, placing it carefully on the table. It's a standard family disaster kit with Red Cross stickers all over it. When he opens it, the children are wide-eyed at the unexpected treasures: clothes, cooking pans and utensils, candles, towels, soap, toothpaste and toothbrushes, cooking oil, sugar and salt, canned fish, a few colourful storybooks, and a box of pencils. A second trip from the van produces a plastic bucket, four big blankets and a sack of rice. The mother allows her tears to fall, overwhelmed at what she sees. The children shout with excitement, running about clutching whatever they've grabbed from the box. I wonder how long these provisions will last and how they'll manage through the coming weeks, but for now it's a windfall.

Back in Haka, Thuza and I tell the others we want to explore the town. U Soe Thein reminds us to make sure to be back before dark as we'll be eating with the family and it would be impolite to be late. Pleased to be on our own, we zigzag up the main street, chatting with people. I shoot off photos of the kids, knowing they'll love the attention, but with adults I ask permission with a questioning smile.

I capture a proud young father carrying his shaven headed son, clad in a blue shirt and red gumboots and nothing else and a family craning out an upper story window with light catching on the glass pane and reflecting the shops opposite. Diners at a roadside cafe with an open kitchen behind—clay oven with waist high vents rising behind looking like organ pipes—offer a plate of food, but I shake my head regretfully, thanking them.

When a young boy shoots at me with a stick, I clap my hands to my heart and feign a gunshot wound and intense pain. He looks worried for a moment, but then we laugh, enjoying the play-acting. A solemn boy of about eight feeds his baby sister from an enamel mug, a picture of a red bear on it. They stare at us and I can't coax a single smile but another lad, wearing a filthy t-shirt stating 'I'm utterly adorable' and not one but two over-large baseball caps, a peak on either side, beams us a huge smile.

In her well-stocked shop, a lady pharmacist in a spotless white coat sits on the floor, weaving a length of cloth on a portable loom strung from a beam, tied around her waist. She speaks good English and explains she learnt this skill from her grandmother and it now fills her time while she's waiting for customers. She also sells hand-embroidered pillowcases and I see Thuza eyeing them. I buy her one, 'Love always' embroidered on it, the words entwined with yellow flowers and green leaves, teasing her about whose head she would like to rest next to hers. She blushes.

On the broad steps of the market, an old man is selling knives with carved wooden handles, his brown woollen hat folded artfully, perfectly framing the equally brown and wrinkled skin of his face. He smiles at me with such a twinkle in his eye, I ask for a photo, flirting back a little myself.

Two women are engaged in heavy bargaining over a large, live black rooster. It's difficult to tell who's selling and who's buying as they both hang onto its legs at arm's length, to keep away from the pecking beak.

Through the market I am silently followed by a beautiful round-eyed boy who carries his baby brother in a red woollen shawl, his little sister at his side, arm thrown protectively around her shoulders. "I think I've got a shadow", I comment quietly to Thuza, who frowns, "I didn't think you'd noticed".

"Of course I've noticed. The photos prove it," I say, slanting the back of my camera for her to see, clicking through photos of the children, all shiny eyes in solemn faces.

"Oh, I see," she says, clearly a bit flustered. And then I get it. I do have a shadow, of a slightly more sinister kind, one who reports back on the foreigner's every move.

"Well, he must be wondering what this crazy foreigner is up to, play-acting with kids, buying a romantic pillowcase, talking with market ladies," I joke, to lighten the moment. She's not convinced so I take her arm, "We're not doing anything worth reporting on. Don't worry."

As we leave the market and walk back through the darkening streets, I glance behind, trying to pick out 'my shadow' but cannot spot him, seeing only the colourful pageant of the main street.

After dinner with the family I am offered a glass of local whisky and accept, downing it in a single, eye-watering, pungent gulp. It's rough but good and the men laugh at me. Thuza stares in amazement. It'll help me sleep I think. No so. The family is a large one, and they dribble in, noisily, late into the night.

We breakfast at a roadside coffee shop with mugs of foaming three-in-one coffee heavily laced with sugar and accompanied by fried bread before meeting with the branch chairman to collect the Survey Questionnaire. "We worked on it until late last night," he tells us. When we thank him for his commitment and his leadership of the volunteers, he beams with pride at these words from the men and women of Headquarters in the far-off capital city.

Back in the van, Hla Myint briefs us, "First to Falam, where we meet a group and have lunch, then on to Tiddim where we'll spend the night." I check my map, another long drive today. I read some notes about the region, then focus on the road and the scenes around me. The terrain becomes steeper as we drive north, winding our way along the sides of hills amid steep outcrops of rock and stunted grass. Groups of wooden houses cling on the mountainsides and fields of high corn stalks edge the flatter sections of the road.

Stopping for drinks, I'm intrigued at yet another ingenious example of non-technology—the vacuum packing of dried nuts. By a roadside stall, a teenage girl sits between a cardboard box of assorted nuts, a pile of plastic bags and a stack of printed labels, a candle burning in an old enamel holder in front of her. With a small spoon she shovels nuts into a plastic bag, holds it up to gauge the right amount then leans in to suck the air out of the bag before running its edge above the flame to seal it. Folding a label over the sealed end, she staples it into place, stacks the bag on top of the others, then starts again. I watch, fascinated, for a few moments wondering where these nuts will be sold, reminding myself that even though something might look hygienic, it is not necessarily so.

After meeting the Red Cross members in Falam, I wander down the winding, main street. Most striking are the many churches of various Christian denominations, most I've never encountered before, all with impossibly long names like 'The Brotherhood of the Venerable Order of the Holy Saints' or the 'Mission of the Holy Sisters of God for the Enlightenment of the Soul'. The missionaries have clearly been busy here and I remember reading that in the whole of Chin State there are only a handful of Buddhist temples. By one church, I stop to listen to a choir practising. A young woman with a basket of shopping also stands outside the church, listening intently. Her toddler has a cabbage unwrapped at her feet, chuckling at such a beauty of a plaything as he unpeels the leaves, smells and chews them, throws the pieces up in the air.

Rounding the last corner, I stop, captivated. The road continues down into the valley in a series of sharp turns and switchbacks. As far down as I can see, a perfect line of houses follows its twists and turns, each house anchored by their thresholds onto the road and supported by tall pillars, rising from the ravine at the back. I marvel at this capacity to make a home even in the most inhospitable terrain.

The afternoon drive towards Tiddim is a repeat of the day before—dust sifting in through the windows, betel spit shooting out, desultory chatting in the back of the van. In the distance we see smoke, just wisps at first but then great dark clouds of it. My colleagues explain it's the season for burning off the old harvest, clearing the fields, fertilizing them before sowing the new crop.

We stop in a small village just as the sun is setting, a huge red ball filtering through the clouds of smoke, ash and dust. It has the same wooden houses and 'Chin' cars parked outside. When we show our interest, kids drag them up, starting a small competition, each team shouting for us to look at how fast they go. I notice a boy with a badly repaired harelip. Another, perhaps his brother, leading a pair of buffalo to a water trough, also has a harelip and one of the girls steering her car, with two kids hanging on behind, has the shortened arms and legs of dwarfism. I wonder if these stem from near relatives intermarrying with a resulting higher incidence of genetic disabilities as often occurs in remote areas.

Dinner over, I'm shown to a bathroom. Nearby, a boy and girl of about twelve are working away at a task I just can't make out. A huge pot of something sticky and black sits between them and they are spreading it all over longish, pale pink objects. What the heck? I ask Thuza to look too and she questions the children. Their reply makes me look more closely. They are stripping the hairs off the pigs' trotters, ready for the market. Waxing takes on a whole new meaning.

We wait while the driver buys yet another supply of betel. I can only assume we still have a long way to go.

"The driver says we should be there in three hours," announces Hla Myint and I know it will be longer. Fire on the hills surrounds us as the burn off continues. We pass few cars and house lights become less frequent. It's quiet in the car, everyone lost in their own thoughts, perhaps overawed by the spectre of flames in the dark, ash coating the windscreen, the floating flakes caught like snow in the beam of the headlights.

Finally, below us, we see lights and begin a long descent into the town. We drive up to the hospital entrance on the main street. A few people are sitting on the steps, one with a nasty looking fracture of the arm, waiting for the night shift to come on. It's already eleven. The doctor, our contact in Tiddim arrives minutes later. We make plans for the morning and he directs us to the Hospital Guesthouse, apologizing that after ten there's no electricity.

My bed feels a little like the landscape we've been driving through, all hills and valleys. After tossing and turning for a while, I decide no mattress would be better. By torchlight I tug at the heavy kapok-filled mattress that reluctantly slides to the floor. Taking the blankets off the second bed and laying them underneath, I retuck mine on top and stretch out on my side, a pillow tucked between my knees, another under my head. "Bliss," I think and fall asleep, for a while. I wake to the wondrous crack and rumble of a thunderstorm, wind moaning through the badly sealed windows, a loose corrugated iron sheet whacking rhythmically overhead. I am lulled into sleep again as the storm abates, the thunder losing its menace, rolling away into the distance.

I'm the last to emerge into the beautiful fresh morning, the air sparkling, washed clean of the ash and dust of last night. Enjoying the sun's early warmth, we admire the spectacular view, row after row of mountains, blue on blue, stretching into the distance.

Down in town it's already lively, with children going to school, women carrying firewood and buckets of water, shops opening up to display their wares. Most houses are two storied, the upper rooms living quarters, the ground floor for business. The doors look hand hewn, many carved with flowers and birds. One doorway has two large rattan trays propped either side, the fruit and vegetables for sale set out in a mosaic of colour. In one, circles of purple aubergine, yellow corn, green leeks, red tomatoes and peppers, white flaky garlic are temptingly, artfully arranged, while in the other, polished green and red apples and yellow pears are lined up, begging to be tasted. I buy some apples, a beautiful young girl of the house putting them carefully in a fold of newspaper, taking my Kyat. She hands me the fruit, whispering "Thank you," in English.

We spend the morning at the local high school with the Red Cross Youth Group, led by the Doctor we met last night who's come straight from the hospital. It's a great opportunity to learn more about the motivation and training of young members, their plans for the coming months. The doctor and one of the teachers encourage them to speak out, several offering their comments in English. Afterwards, they ask me to tell them about New Zealand and the International Red Cross, interested in other youth groups around the world.

It's a long journey back to Falam and then to Kalemyo, this time in daylight. I gaze out at the blackened terrain we passed through last night, fires still smouldering, at the villages that had been sleeping, the workers in the fields, the packed buses with people and baggage perched on top. The road is rough and, in many places, jagged edges gape where a section has collapsed in a landslide, leaving scarred paths far down the hillsides.

"It's good we've managed this trip before the rainy season," Hla Myint comments. "Parts of this road disintegrate and villages, even Tiddim can be cut off for weeks at a time. It's unstable so that's why they don't seal the road." The logic eludes me and I don't press for further explanations, but the reality is harsh for these more remote areas of the country.

Back in Kalemyo, at a comfortable hotel, I spend a good ten minutes standing under the shower, delighting in the hot water.

In the morning we drive to the airport. Outside, people are sitting or standing in groups with assorted luggage, striped plastic carriers, worn suitcases and cardboard boxes tied with string.

"What's all this about?" U Hla Myint voices our concern. We learn that no planes are flying today, the burn-off from neighbouring China and India as well as local fires having compounded to produce an impenetrable wall of dust, ash and smoke. The airport has no radar facility so planes can't land.

And so it is for the next two days. Each morning we pack, joining others outside the gates of the airport, waiting to learn if flights have resumed. No one is allowed into the airport so I observe the town going about its early morning business. A line of monks collecting alms walks silently out of the gloom. Elderly schoolmistresses with wide-brimmed hats ride by on up-right black bicycles. Traders peddle cakes, drinks and sticky rice as pony carts and bicycle trishaws transport shoppers and school children.

On the third morning, the sky is a little clearer. Hla Myint queues early, managing to get tickets. We wait at the gate, sitting on our suitcases, surrounded by other hopeful travellers, until the incoming plane lands and they confirm the return flight. My patience is fraying, my mind thinking of home, when suddenly, coming down the road towards us are five boys on horseback dressed as princes for the celebration before they become novice monks. Their ponies are decorated with rosettes and flowers. Family members accompany them, dressed in their finest *longyis*, carrying silver offering bowls, red roses and smoking incense. They hold golden umbrellas over their precious sons' heads.

As we finally soar up over the mountains on the flight back to Yangon, I gaze out over the tall peaks and wide plains spread below me, reflecting on this week's experiences. Images and recollections, a shower of bright sparks, whirl through my mind as I strive to reorder the people and places, the stark contrasts and glaring contradictions of this stunningly beautiful land, with its unrelenting poverty and deep pride.

Chapter Sixteen
The Big Splash

The traditional Myanmar year is based on a twelve-month lunar calendar. Festivals and Buddhist holidays revolve around this lunar year, which begins with Thingyan, the Myanmar New Year in early April. The festival goes on for two or three days. Water is poured from delicate silver vessels, sprayed from water pistols, hurled from buckets, and even blasted from fire hydrants to wash away the old year and welcome the new.'*

'Before breakfast everyone is soaked, but no one changes...and no one escapes ...for the wetting is considered a compliment.'**

For weeks my staff have been reminding me not to make plans during *Thingyan*, the Water Festival in April as they've hired a van and want me to celebrate the holiday with them. I'm looking forward to it but with some trepidation, having heard about their exploits from previous years.

It's so dry and hot that the idea of being doused in cool water is a welcome one. A few intense rain showers, called the 'little rains', a gentle reminder that the monsoon will start soon, have brought out the beautiful yellow blossoms of the Padauk trees, brightening the dusty streets and filling the air with their delicate perfume. Women wear them in their hair, trishaw drivers tie them to their handlebars and I pick some every morning from the tree by my gate. They last merely a day before withering, but each day their blooms announce *Thingyan* is coming.

Another sure sign is the busy construction of *pandals*, wooden platforms, on key roads around the city. With four days of holiday ahead, many organisations, private companies and even government departments build and decorate these perfect vantage points from which to drench passing cars and pedestrians.

Today's the day. I'm ready and waiting, wearing old slacks, a thick T-shirt, a peaked cap and sunglasses, a little protection from the water thrashing I am expecting. The small white van stalls in my driveway, coughs, starts again and finally makes it to my door. Sandy, Zarni, Kyaw Kyaw and Mallu shout out excited greetings, laughing. They grab my hands and pull me into the back of the van. We're off.

A friend is elected driver for the day so Ko Zaw joins us in the back and we sit on narrow benches, three to a side, a big plastic tub between us, water sloshing from side to side, a couple of dippers floating on top.

My first shower is from the kids on my street. As we round the corner by the shrine, they're waiting. A line of boys wielding pump-action water guns catch me on the back then angle in to hit my face, but I duck and it only wets my cap. I flick water back but they run off laughing, then turn to do a little 'neh-neh-neh' dance to show I've missed. The girls, less well equipped, but deadly accurate, fill their ladles from a water barrel and from their low angle, score a direct hit on my face. I wipe it laughing, wondering how long we'll even try to stay dry, as the girls join the boys in their dance.

Driving around Kandawgyi Lake and then down Shwedagon Pagoda

**Insight Guide—Burma / Myanmar*, APA Publications GmbH & Co. 2000
** Shway Yoe, *The Burman, His Life and Notions*, Macmillan & Co. 1882

Road towards town, we are targeted by children and a few adults waiting on corners and kerbs, armed with water guns or buckets and even a few hoses. Other vans, equally well equipped, come alongside and the water flinging starts in earnest.

We turn into Anawrahta Street, heading towards City Hall, joining the weaving, colourful mass of cars and people streaming down the road, high wooden pandals either side, decorated with flowers, ribbons, posters and banners. Most have a predominant colour, neon pink or livid green, orange or yellow, their hosepipes alternating between squirting steady high-arching sprays of water and aiming at those who challenge them, wetting all and anything that passes. Most teams, in matching outfits, have perfected songs and dance routines they perform with great enthusiasm to booming music from huge speakers. Everyone is laughing and wet, hair plastered to the skull, clothing glued to the body.

It's complete chaos. I don't know whether to watch or throw or duck at the blasts from the hoses because as one of the few foreigners I'm a sure target. Sitting behind the cab I have a modicum of protection, but when a group turns a massive fire hose on me, catching me right in the small of my back, its fierce pressure makes me gasp and squirm to ease the pain. But we're moving on and laughing about who and how many we've hit ourselves.

The dousing continues, we're hemmed in on all sides by other vehicles, people darting between cars and sloshing water from the pavements. Water flung from ice-filled water barrels forces sharp intakes of breath and outpourings of strong expletives, but we do our damage as well, our tub replenished more than once from the hosepipes of the more approachable pandals.

We're stuck at a corner. Music blares from a truck holding a dozen gyrating youngsters. They're in jeans and bright sleeveless tops, their hair dyed green, purple and blue, cut into geometric patterns, one with a bright red 'mohawk', a complete contrast to the usual neat Myanmar attire of *longyis*, shirts or blouses. It's a pleasure to see that for at least these few days there is a sense of liberation with standard protocols flaunted, individual craziness accepted.

A little later, caught in the spirit of things, I recklessly fling a dipper of water at a policeman vainly trying to move the traffic along. The moment the water leaves my dipper, I am shocked at my own action. I hold my breath, wondering if this offence to an officer of the law will land us in trouble. Out of the corner of my eye, I see Zarni's face, frozen, watching, until the policeman reaches up to shake my hand. I am pardoned and mightily relieved. Safely round the corner we collapse laughing, reliving the moment, everyone joking at my audacity.

Fun as it is, the morning takes its toll and we are soon ready to take a break, dry off and eat something. We wind through narrow backstreets looking for food stalls and a parking space. Sandy, Mallu, and I clean up as best we can, mopping each other with the now very damp towels. We are more than ready for the fried rice, banana leaf-wrapped fish and sodas the men bring back.

"What's that you're eating?" I ask Ko Zaw, as he crunches dark morsels from a twist of paper with obvious relish. Grinning, he offers me some, "Dried crickets, very tasty, try some." I smile back at him, all eyes on me but demurely decline.

Over lunch we rehash the morning's highlights and stories from other years. I'm surprised the water pressure is strong enough to support the hundreds of hosepipes on the pandals and the endless filling of buckets, barrels and bowls across the city. I learn that in order for sufficient pressure to be built up, parts of the city have had their water rationed over the past ten days. Though *Thingyan* is an important celebration, if your apartment block is one of those deprived of water and you live up steep stairs, carrying buckets in the April heat might dampen your enthusiasm a tad. When I ask why people don't complain, my friends look at me blankly. There is no one to complain to, no such mechanism available for ordinary people, and there would be no point anyway, as nothing would change.

A *Thingyan* speciality, Moat Lone Yay Pawr, balls of sticky rice containing chunks of jaggery, palm sugar, is the deliciously sweet ending to our lunch.

While the rest of the team head back into the fray for another testing bout of water fights, Mallu and I decide an afternoon relaxing might be preferable. As we drive up my little street, the children are still outside, soaked and mischievous, not tired of 'shooting' at passers-by, especially not at Ma Joanna and I'm treated to one last drenching.

Back home, showered and in dry clothes, we sit in my garden enjoying a cool drink. I open my guidebook to check what it has to say about *Thingyan*, reading to Mallu: *Thingyan celebrates the descent to earth of Thagyamin, king of the thirty-seven Nats, to bring New Year blessings. He brings two books: one bound in gold to record the names of children who have been well behaved in the past year, the other in dog-skin to record the names of naughty children. Thagyamin rides a winged golden horse and bears a water jar, symbolic of peace and prosperity. Households greet Thagyamin with flowers and palm leaves at the front door. Guns are fired and music is played in salute to him. But there are moments of tranquillity in the midst of exuberance. Most revellers also make offerings at pagodas and the homes of their elders, and Buddha images are washed by the devout."* *

Mallu tells me that in the past only a small bowl of scented water would have been poured over passers-by to 'cleanse them', symbolising the purification of past wrongs and mistakes, allowing a fresh start in the new year. We laugh at how things have changed, but agreeing we wouldn't have missed this morning's experience for anything.

Over the course of my stay in Myanmar I learn about many other festivals, most revolving around the phases of the moon, a central theme of life here. For townspeople they're a welcome excuse to take some days off and visit relatives, sometimes in other parts of the country. For farmers they offer a well-earned rest after the harvest and for craftspeople, weavers, silversmiths, basket and lacquer-ware makers, carvers and stonemasons, they are a means to sell their wares. Musicians and artists readily perform on these days also, earning revenue and praise.

Although most of the festivals are Buddhist in spirit, many date further back revolving around the changing seasons and the country rituals of ploughing, planting and harvesting. All festivals, whether in honour of the Buddhist faith or Nat spirit worship, have features in common,

---

*Insight Guide – Burma / Myanmar, APA Publications GmbH & Co (2000)

offerings to monasteries, cleansing of nats, music and dancing, merchants and hawkers, pilgrimages to sacred sites, special food and drinks and, above all, the great enthusiasm with which they are celebrated.

The rice harvest festival in January or early February, is a joyful occasion when rice is offered to monasteries, elaborate meals are cooked and enjoyed by families and whole communities. After *Thingyan* in April, a more solemn season, *Dhammasetkya*, Buddhist Lent is observed, through June and July. This is a time for monks to go into retreat to study and meditate and for others to observe a period of sobriety, self-denial and religious contemplation. No marriages are allowed and to move house is also frowned upon.

By September the monsoon is almost over and, with sunny days ahead, romance is in the air. Knowing the marriage ban will be lifted soon, wedding plans are put in action. Lakes and rivers are running high with perfect conditions for sailing regattas and boat races. The most spectacular is on Inle Lake where three long-boats compete, each carrying as many as one hundred leg-rowers.

The full moon of *Thadingyut*, the Festival of Lights in October, officially marks the end of Lent, celebrating the anniversary of Buddha's return from the celestial abode. His descent was attended by Celestials who created a pathway of stars to light his way, and by lighting candles and oil lamps and festooning coloured lights on public buildings, monasteries, houses, and trees, the faithful can also find their spiritual path in life. This is a time for offering a mark of respect and gratitude to one's elders and teachers and gifts for those who have given invaluable guidance or help.

This November, I witness another festival, *Tazaungmone*, the Weaving Festival. Tradition calls for unmarried women to work at their looms all night under the full moon, making new robes for monks or to clothe Buddha statues at a pagoda. These must be completed within a single night and presented early the following morning. Ko Zaw has offered to take me to Botataung Pagoda where this festival is celebrated every year.

As we ride into town, he tells me the story of the Botataung Pagoda sited on the banks of the Yangon River. Its name comes from the legend that a thousand (*tataung*) officers (*Bo*) once waited here for the arrival of a group of Buddhist monks carrying valuable Buddha hair relics from India. The relics, housed in Botataung, were later enshrined in the great Shwedagon. Unfortunately, the temple on this site today dates only from after World War II, as bombing raids targeting the nearby docks destroyed the original.

Ko Zaw noses the car in between market booths selling offering baskets with green coconuts, bananas and flowers, temple souvenirs and photos, incense sticks and candles. The rich tang of frying snacks fills the air.

A large crowd has gathered in the central courtyard. Wooden foot-treadle looms have been installed on the raised walkway. The rhythmic clack-clack of the shuttles and battening reeds threading and tightening the weft into warp threads can be heard over the sounds of chanting and chatting. Teams of young women are attempting the near impossible task of producing a complete robe. When a woman tires, another takes her place, effortlessly taking over the shuttle, the reed and treadle without breaking the rhythm. Each group supports its team members, plying them with food and drinks and anxiously watching the progress of the others, the religious significance of the ritual perhaps today second to the competition it has engendered.

We watch in awe as the weavers surely but steadily make progress. Friends and relatives encourage them and we each choose a favourite team, willing them to edge ahead in the length of their cloth. After a while it becomes clear that all the teams will complete their task, though only the fastest and best will be rewarded.

Driving home, I think of the importance of this and other festivals, remembering the fun we had at *Thingyan* earlier in the year, the ready smiles, the willingness to offer advice and information, small snacks and sweets even when not asked for. In spite of their adversities the people of Myanmar, remarkably, have somehow managed to maintain their optimism and a sense of fun.

Days later, I talk to Marlar about this. She shrugs, but then more pensively replies that perhaps this is the Buddhist way, that these traditional festivals are in fact vitally important as they remind everyone to live for the moment, abandoning worldly cares and woes which cause so much anguish, and casting aside all thoughts of controlling the future. It's enough, for a short time, to just enter into the spirit of a celebration.

I sense she is right.

Chapter Seventeen
Farewell Ma Marlar

Even when her heart condition deteriorated so that she could hardly make it from the car to her office, Marlar continued to work with us. Every day she was able to come, she did. And everyday she was immaculately and beautifully dressed, her hair adorned, as always.

We knew the day would come when she would no longer have the strength to work and we worried about her. Everyone showed their care, helping with her bags, holding her elbow as she walked, bringing her cooling drinks, finding the perfect snack to offer with her morning tea or afternoon coffee. Mallu kept a nurse's eye on her, giving advice on which foods would keep her healthy without adding weight and checked her medicines, explaining to her the function of each. I tried not to burden her with too much work and sometimes suggested she leave early, take the afternoon or the next day off.

Marlar, now in her early forties, had worked with the International

Federation delegates for many years, experiencing the different styles, demands and foibles of the British, the Australian, the Malaysian and the Japanese delegates who had preceded me. She had been on assessments and handed out supplies after floods and earthquakes, written reports and prepared financial statements and had briefed visiting donors and dignitaries. She had more or less run the office and the other staff respected her and looked to her for guidance. When I arrived, she led me through the office and its history, often advising me on matters of protocol and the all-important relationships with the President, the Executive Committee and the staff of the National Society.

It was Marlar who one day reprimanded me for my behaviour. A small group of Delegation and MRCS staff had gathered around my coffee table to discuss the health information brochures we wanted to produce. Materials from other organizations and companies, everything from a paint catalogue to supermarket discount flyers, Health Ministry booklets to army recruitment leaflets, were spread out on the low table. The atmosphere was relaxed and I leant back in my chair listening, letting ideas and opinions flow. At a certain point, I lazily mentioned a particular brochure, casually pointing with my foot for emphasis. After the others had left, Marlar hovered, a bit hesitant, but obviously with something to say.

"Joanna, may I mention something a little delicate, if you don't mind?" she started. "In our culture it's very impolite to expose the sole of your foot. Some of the Myanmar staff were a little shocked at your gesture when you talked about the health brochure from the Ministry. It was even worse because it was something from the Government."

I was appalled at the apparent lack of respect that my casual action must have implied and thanked her, vowing to be more careful of how I communicated and presented myself, as my behaviour would surely be noted and commented upon, reflecting not only my own manners but on my organization.

Marlar was also the first to invite me to her house, where I met her husband, father and sisters. Growing up, she'd lived in Japan and Switzerland, and I think Egypt too. She was close to her father, a fascinating man who had been a diplomat. Since her mother had passed away, she sometimes accompanied him to official dinners. She had studied at Webster University, close to Geneva, and had many interesting stories about people she had met when traveling with her father. It was a great help to have a member of staff who could not only give me wise cultural counsel about Myanmar, but who also understood the complexities and influences of the wider world.

By June of 2004, Marlar's health had become severely compromised. One morning, at the beginning of July, she came to my office, Mallu supporting her as she made her way slowly to the sofa. Her doctors had told her that she had only months to live without a medical procedure, so she had decided to go to Malaysia for a twelve-day course of treatment, starting the following week. She knew they couldn't guarantee its success, but after discussing it thoroughly with her husband and father they had agreed it was worth the risk. Mallu reassured her she'd made a good decision. I could only listen to their medical talk, wish her a safe trip and a successful outcome of the procedure.

This week, Marlar and Thant Cyn are leaving for Kuala Lumpur. We prepare a card for her, signed by everyone with loving and supportive words and give it to her together with a small bouquet of silk flowers when she comes to the office to say goodbye, asking her to come back to us safely, assuring her we will be in touch while she is away.

Every day one of us calls and talks to her or to her husband and we are heartened to hear that all seems to be going well and Marlar is feeling stronger and optimistic. Just a few more days of the treatment and she'll be back in Yangon.

Sunday morning, I'm still in bed, dozing lightly, when the phone rings. It's Ko Zaw. From his quiet tone and the catch in his voice, I sense the solemn purpose of his call. He tells me that Marlar had died earlier that morning. She was having breakfast, laughing and chatting with her husband when she suddenly collapsed. They were unable to resuscitate her. I am immediately wide awake. I sit up, my heart racing from the shock, a deep feeling of dread and pain at losing a friend, rising concern for her family's loss of a wife, daughter, sister and for the others in our little delegation.

I share my thoughts with Ko Zaw, adding, "What should we do now? I need you to lead me through this, tell me what I can do to help the family and show my respects."

"We must go to her father's house, they'll expect us. I've already picked up Ma Sandy, Kyaw Kyaw and Zarni and we're on our way. Can you be ready in twenty minutes?"

"I'll be ready," I reply. "Mallu and Yvonne will want to come with us too. I'll call them now and tell them we'll pick them up in a half hour."

We are a subdued group on the way to Marlar's father's house. It would be usual to visit her husband, but as he is still in Kuala Lumpur, friends and relatives will meet at her father's house. I ask my team about what I should do in the next days and they tell me of the traditions and customs surrounding a person's death. As Marlar's boss, I will have to lead the Delegation at the funeral and will be called upon to speak. But right now, with her father, it's enough just to spend time with him. During the car ride, we occasionally break the silence with a memory of Marlar, some stories bringing smiles, others tears.

Leaving our shoes at the door, we quietly enter the house, are greeted by Marlar's sister and shown into the living room. Heavy wooden chairs are pushed back against one wall, but we sit on the floor, leaving them for more important family and friends. A tray of glasses is set on a low table and beside it a large photo of Marlar, taken when she was younger. Her father is on the phone for the first minutes after our arrival, pacing in an adjoining room. We see him through the doorway as he weaves his way around the furniture, his face furrowed in pain and worry.

Ma Kalyar, Marlar's younger sister, brings a jug of iced water and a pot of green tea, inviting us to drink something. Sandy gets up to pour and talks to her for a moment before she leaves to find something else to occupy her, to escape thoughts of her loss. We drink and talk quietly until U Than Tun comes into the room. I rise to meet him, offering my condolences and the others do likewise. He's dignified in his grief but it is difficult to know what to say, it is so hard for a father to lose his daughter. Others of the family arrive and, one by one, go to talk to Marlar's father or sister. We are at the house for almost an hour, and during that time, through a series of phone calls, it's clear the family have taken some decisions. The normal three-day period between the death and the funeral will be extended to allow for Marlar's body to be brought home. The funeral will be later in the week. We pay our respects again and leave quietly, turning away from the family only at the door.

Not wanting to be alone, I suggest we eat lunch together somewhere and the others readily agree. Settling ourselves at the low table in an outdoors cafe, we begin to relax a little and chat, the conversation returning to Marlar, her untimely death, her family and the funeral, our shared memories of her.

My first task on Monday is to inform colleagues in Bangkok and Geneva. I prepare the mails, giving the notification of Marlar's death, and request details regarding financial assistance and protocol on the death of a staff member.

I call a staff meeting. Gathered in my office, we talk about what has happened, of the important role Marlar played, and her friendship and warmth towards us all, Myanmar colleagues, and foreigners alike. We have a moment's silence for her, and several of the staff offer words of memory and sadness.

I ask my team whom else we should inform. Kyaw Kyaw responds that I must inform the President and he would in turn tell the MRCS Executive Committee and staff.

"Should I prepare something written for him, or just go up?"

"He most likely already knows of Marlar's death, one of his staff will have told him, but he'll expect you, as Marlar's Head of Delegation, to tell him in a formal visit to the National Society. I am sure he'll want to talk about the funeral and advise you on your role. He is wise and compassionate and a devout Buddhist and he'll explain more about the rites." Kyaw Kyaw pauses, before adding, "Then all of us, but you, me, and Ma Sandy in particular, need to clean our computers before the end of the day."

I look at him, puzzled, "But she died from heart failure, it is not contagious. There is no risk."

The Myanmar staff, turn to look at Kyaw Kyaw, wondering how he will explain the obvious to me, the outsider. Realising I don't understand, he tries again, "Not physically 'clean', but 'clear' our computers," he tells me. "The documents she worked on and her emails need to be cleared from her computer and from ours. We mustn't tie her to us by keeping her files or letters to or about her. She must be released from her responsibilities so her spirit is free to go where it wishes, where it needs to settle. That is our way."

Sandy continues, "And at the funeral you will be expected to do the same, to tell her that she can now go freely, her earthly responsibilities over. If you wish, I'll help you to prepare the letter you will read to her."

I talk about Marlar with the President, go through my documents, deleting some, renaming others and re-filing those vital for the management and archives of the delegation. Then I start my letter to her, while talking about her with various colleagues who pass by my office, to check everything is being done properly. At the end of the afternoon Snow White comes rather nervously to see me, Sandy in tow to give her confidence, to ask if she can come to the office a bit later this week. Normally she's the first to arrive, opening up and cleaning before we arrive. But this morning when she arrived she saw a shadow in Marlar's office and she is sure her spirit is still around. I tell her that it will be fine for her to come in later this week so she won't be alone and afraid. She leaves my office visibly relieved.

Before closing on Friday, Kyaw Kyaw has one last important task for us for us to perform. My office has been rearranged, the sofa and chairs pushed back against the walls, a length of carpet in front of the windows. Snow is preparing food and we're waiting for the monks to arrive. They will perform a cleansing rite for our offices. When they are shown in, I defer to my staff and sit at the back, listening to the chanting and watching the deliberate movements and calming ceremonies. After the formal rituals, three small tables are brought in, set before the monks and their food served. We leave them for some time and then Kyaw Kyaw asks me to join him, following the monks' circuit of the delegation offices. They walk to the far end of the corridor, then slowly and deliberately move from office to office, opening the doors one by one, chanting in each doorway and leaving the doors open. When they finish their task, we bow our thanks. All doors must be left open until after the funeral to allow her spirit to leave the workplace.

We drive to the Crematorium on the outskirts of Yangon for the funeral. The letter is in my bag, written and rewritten many times, and now printed in large type, some phrases underlined. When we arrive, it is very different from what I expected. There's a huge car park, full of cars and buses with a low building behind. Several funerals are being held at the same time and we are directed towards a room at the far right. It's a large hall with a concrete floor, pillars and a corrugated iron roof. Two or three hundred people are already seated in rows of red and blue plastic chairs either side of a central aisle. Entering from the back, I see the coffin set on a wheeled trestle at the front, flowers covering and surrounding it. Behind is a screen hung with photos of Marlar, some with her family, against which wreaths are arranged.

We take our places, on each seat a bottle of water, a sheet of paper and a coloured plastic fan, inscribed in gold with Marlar's name and life span and the time and place of her death. The note is an invitation to visit her father's house after seven days.

Five russet-clad monks sit to the left of the coffin, facing the congregation. A group of twenty nuns in pink robes sit on their right, in front of the side window. I cannot see Marlar's family, but Sandy, next to me, tells me they're in the front row, facing the monks, by the coffin.

"I'll tell you when it's time for you to speak," she says quietly. "You walk down the side, across the back behind the coffin, and then stand to read your letter facing the family. But the letter is addressed to Marlar, not her family, so you must look at her while you speak."

"Could you please come with me," I ask, "I need you with me." She nods her assent.

More people arrive, we drink our water and fan ourselves. It's hot and humid, not a breath of wind. Several people walk to the coffin and lay down flowers, showing their love and respect, before taking a seat. Then with a soft chanting, the nuns begin the ritual with the words of Buddha. It is soothing and lasts a long time, allowing everyone time for their own thoughts. I take out my letter and reread it silently. The monks then lead into the prayers and rituals for the departed soul while everyone remains seated.

Sandy nudges me. It's time to make our way to the front. My throat is dry and I am shaking. Sandy takes my hand and leads me forward until I stand facing Marlar's family, beside the coffin. She moves behind me but keeps her hand lightly on my shoulder, a calming presence. I bow my head and look into the eyes of Marlar's father, then her husband, acknowledging their grief. Turning toward the coffin, I realise it is not closed but has a small open door revealing just the face of my colleague and friend. She seems so close, somehow still so present.

Taking a deep breath to steady myself, I begin, "My dear friend and colleague Marlar, we are deeply saddened by your death, and want to thank you for all that you have done for the International Red Cross and for each of us personally." As I read my words, about her friendship and her professional achievements, about her love of family and her country, offering our words of comfort to her family and friends, I also am aware of myself in this ceremony, privileged but inadequate to perform this important task. I feel alien, ignorant of this religion and culture, but at the same time, blessed to be a part of these rites for her, as I have been of her life in these past years.

"Marlar, we will miss you, but we will not forget you. Know that you have been much loved and respected. Your influence and our memories of you will always remain. Your work with us is now complete and we willingly release you from your earthly duties. Go in peace."

I place my letter on the coffin, and bow to Marlar, tears welling. I turn to face the family and bow to them before turning and walking back to my seat. I am still shaking and my throat is aching with the effort of reading and holding in my tears. Sitting once more, I gulp some tepid water and wipe my eyes.

At the end of the ceremony, Marlar's husband and father each say their last words to Marlar, and place my letter inside with her, before closing the small door of the coffin. Other family members and close friends surround them, and as her husband holds Marlar's portrait in front, photos are taken of the group.

The family wheel the coffin down the aisle, many with their hands on the top, others walking behind bringing flowers and wreaths and carrying the photos. As they pass, each line of friends and colleagues walk out and follow the others to the doorway. From there, only the family will go the crematorium to bid their final farewell to Marlar.

Outside, we stand in a group, subdued and a bit lost. Sandy tells me that the family will each take a small leaf or flower from one of the wreaths. A traditional belief is that the spirit stays around the people and places it loves for seven days before departing.

I bend to take a leaf from one of the wreaths still leaning against the entranceway. Holding it by the stalk I swivel it in my fingers, then lay it on my palm, its fresh green a reminder that life goes on. I will keep this leaf at home, holding her spirit safe and mourning her loss to this life. Next week, when we visit her father's house again, I will take the leaf with me to pay my respects to her family.

Farewell, Ma Marlar.

Chapter Eighteen
One Hundred Days

I have formed a special rapport with the family who owns the smallest shop on my street, living and working from their tiny house that juts out a little from the rest, on a slight curve in the road. It has a wooden frame, woven split bamboo walls, a wire grill at the front and a door just high enough for a medium sized person. A wooden bench out front holds rattan baskets with snacks, dried garlic or flowers, whatever each day brings. Packets of food and household items hang in plastic bags from the grill. The woman, Yu Maw, runs the business, transactions conducted through the open doorway, customers standing in the street.

Inside, are a couple of yellow plastic jerry cans for water and shelves with provisions for sale or for the family's use. There's always a tin with fresh flowers on the top shelf. An old TV sits on a stool at the back of the room, the rattan table beside it piled with plates, bowls and glasses. In the afternoon sleeping mats are laid out for a siesta, just two mats side by side. A small hammock is slung from corner to corner, easy to rock gently from anywhere in the room, lulling a child to sleep. Pinned to the wall is a picture of a monk with a text in gold. A curtained doorway leads to the alley at the back.

To enter the room one must step over a flat wooden board set across the lower part of the doorway, a wooden bar above it, which keeps Yu Maw's small daughter in, also allowing her to stand, holding on, looking out. I'm a constant 'passer-by' in my Red Cross land cruiser or on foot and there's always a mutual wave and a smile from the mother and child.

Over several years, I've watched little Tin Zar Win grow up, from baby, to toddler, to friendly little girl, nearly always dressed in pink, thanakha carefully spread on her cheeks and brow, down to the tip of her nose. I've waited with anticipation to meet the new baby announced by her mother's growing belly and am happy for them when another little girl is born, healthy and feisty.

And now, Tin Zar Win's baby sister has made it to the important one hundred day mark and there will be a ceremony for her this Saturday. I am invited. Yu Maw brought an invitation to the house last Thursday morning, tentatively pushing the envelope to Malay through the struts of the gate, too timid to come to the house and give it to me herself. I saw the exchange from an upstairs window and ran down to take the card but she had already left. It's prettily decorated in gold and pastel colours with flowers and swirls, but the writing inside is, of course, in Burmese. I ask Malay to read it, and he smiles, telling me I'm invited to the naming ceremony, adding it will be an honour for the family if I wish to go.

"Of course I will," I respond, "I feel honoured to be invited, they must have discussed it a lot before inviting me." On the way to work that morning I ask Ko Zaw to stop by their shop and thank the family. He tells them I would be pleased to join them on Saturday afternoon and a huge smile spreads across Yu Maw's face. Ko Zaw explains that they will give alms to the monks in the morning, family and friends joining them later in the day with gifts for the child, to wish her a healthy and prosperous future. It's been this way since the time of the Kings, he adds. I wonder what she will be named.

A few weeks before, at dinner with the staff, we had a long discussion about names, their meaning and importance. They asked what day of the week and what time was I born and I told them, Sunday, though the day is not particularly important for most westerners. I don't know the exact time but think sometime in the early afternoon, as my mother always said it was just in time for tea, which, according to her, accounted for my sweet tooth.

Surnames are not part of this culture, each child being named after a grace period of a hundred days and after consultation with one or more fortune-tellers. Most people have three names, each usually of one syllable and with a particular meaning. The first name or syllable is chosen depending on the day of the week, each day associated with a different group of sounds.

"If you are Monday-born like me", explains Kyaw Kyaw, "your name begins with ka, kha, kya, ga or Nga. My name means 'famous'. Do you think I might be one day?"

"Undoubtedly', I reply with a smile

"I was born on a Friday. My name evokes the idea of beauty, like a classical sculpture. I wish I really was", adds Thu Za wistfully.

"I'm Tuesday-born," chimes in Zar Ni, "My name means brave, although," he adds modestly," I'm not sure about that yet."

A Sunday-born child's name begins with the sound ah or ei, like Aye Aye Than, meaning 'soft', or Ei Ei Myint meaning ' calm'. I'm fascinated and ask my staff what my name might be if I were Burmese. They talk among themselves, then decide. "We think Aye Mya Thida would suit your character," Sandy tells me. "It's difficult to explain in English. It means cool, fresh water, but as a name it means 'calm, open and refreshing'. Something good, like that." I beam proudly.

It's actually not uncommon for a person to be renamed more than once in a lifetime. A change of fortune or a wish to be fulfilled will prompt a visit to a seer, and new name. It must play havoc with registers and, these days, with email addresses as well.

It's difficult for an outsider to fathom mutual relationships as a woman does not take her husband's name when she marries, keeping her given name. I wonder if this will change with the influence from the outside world and hope not.

We also discuss the animals representing each day of the week. I recall a monk showing me the golden figures on the Shwedagon pagoda platform on my first visit, small silver bowls by their side, to pour water over them to cleanse their spirit, paying homage and gaining merit. Each animal, and thus each day of the week corresponds to a compass point. I wondered how seven days of the week could be organised into eight compass points.

"In bygone days that was a slight problem, but everything can be fixed when great minds come together." My guide explained, "It was decided by a great monk, that the mid weekday, Wednesday, should be split in two. So the animal representing Wednesday morning is an elephant with tusks, and the afternoon is an elephant with no tusks. Thus, the dilemma was solved," he added proudly.

Sunday born, I am a *Garuda*, a mythical bird, representing the sun, and my compass point is north-east. Reflecting on this, I realise my horoscope has become rather complicated, influenced as it is by my star sign in Sagittarius, my ascendant in Aries, the Earth Rat of the Chinese calendar and now *Garuda* as my Sunday protector. My path, with all its complexities, must have been set at birth, as is that of the new little girl. I wonder what her life will be like, what changes will occur during her lifetime in her country and her heritage.

During the week, I ask Sandy for ideas for a present. "Should I give some money and if so, how much? I ask. "Would a couple of little outfits be a better idea. Or both?" She suggests something pretty for the child and an envelope for the mother. The following day we go to a market and choose two little dresses, one in pink and another with small yellow flowers, a yellow trim on the sleeves and waistline.

On Saturday afternoon, I dress in my blue silk *longyi* and white lace blouse, to show my respect for the importance of the day and their invitation. Having spent the morning at the office, I ask Ko Zaw as he drives me back if he minds staying a little longer, to act as my interpreter, so I might for once share a proper discussion with the family, rather than communicating with them through mime and gestures.

A number of neighbours are gathered in front of the small shop, some sitting on wooden benches, others standing and chatting, enjoying drinks, small pastry savouries and sweet rice cakes. When they see us coming, the group gently parts to let us through and someone calls to Yu Maw, jutting her chin in my direction indicating we've arrived. Holding out her hand from inside the shop, she guides me through the doorway. Ko Zaw follows and we sit cross-legged on the floor, backs against the wall, taking up almost half the tiny room. We're honoured guests, so must sit inside out of the sun.

Yu Maw gently takes her sleeping baby daughter out of the hammock, leans down and puts her in my arms, warm and sleepy. I cradle her head, gently stroking the soft, plump little cheek, marvelling at the perfect eyelashes splayed against her golden skin. She is oblivious, and I cherish this moment, knowing that if she wakes, she may be alarmed to find herself in a stranger's arms. I tell Yu Maw that she has two beautiful daughters, gesturing that this little one looks like her mother. She understands and laughs, shakes her head and tells me, via Ko Zaw, that they are certainly more beautiful than she is.

The baby back in her slowly swinging cradle, I offer my gift, an envelope tucked under the ribbon. Yu Maw thanks me profusely then puts the packet carefully on the shelf to open later. It's not the Asian way to open a present when it is given. That would seem too eager. It will be enjoyed later, in private.

A young girl from a nearby house brings glasses of bright yellow cordial on a tin tray and we share a plate of fried bananas offered through the doorway, from the street outside. I ask Ko Zaw to thank the family for their invitation and to ask them how they celebrated this day. He translates for me. "Early this morning she prepared extra food and her husband bought packets of soap, towels and toothbrushes. They were ready for the monks on their morning alms round, giving them food and packages, making merit for their family and for their new daughter in particular. They then prepared more food and drinks for their neighbours so they too can welcome the new baby to our street. Tomorrow morning they will all go to Shwedagon pagoda to make offerings for the long life of their daughters."

When Yu Maw turns to greet other friends and relatives, I ask Ko Zaw if it would be acceptable to take our leave of the small family, not wanting to breach any protocol. He nods, and we stand. Stepping down into the street, we thank our hostess, turning to walk back to my house. Only then I realize I haven't asked what name the little sister has been given, the whole point of the ceremony.

"Ko Zaw", I say urgently. "But what is her given name?"

"She is Ei Tha Zin," he tells me, "It is the name of a flower, Thazin, cascading stems of small white flowers with bright gold stamens. In bygone days, only the queen had the right to wear it." I repeat the name, hoping that over the next months and years, I might watch the young queen's progress, following her first steps and waves, just as I have enjoyed her big sister's laughter, smiles and adventures out into the big wide world of our street.

Chapter Nineteen
Playing The Game

Checklist of contents
for
"Build your Branch"

- 1 game board
- 1 bank & 'take a chance' board
- 1 pair of dice
- 1 box of money chips (blue & red)
- 1 set of '*take a chance*' cards
- 1 set of *branch assets* cards
- 1 page – *Rules of the Game*
- 1 page – *Items for sale*

Participate - discuss - enjoy

It's been an exceptionally busy week—reports, administrative chores, meetings with MRCS, tough negotiations with donors, and new staff to brief. Late Friday afternoon, I realize I've not yet prepared my sessions for the Branch Development Workshop starting Monday.

Everyone else has left, only Kyaw Kyaw, our ever conscientious administrator, hovers discretely in the corridor, waiting for me to leave so he can lock up. I don't want to delay him so delve into my desk drawer looking for previously designed programmes I could use for inspiration, but find nothing. I pack, knowing I'll be spending the weekend preparing my introduction and the afternoon session for the first day.

Ko Zaw is waiting and I ask him to drop me at The Strand. I go there rarely, but the lure of a Friday night cocktail has been at the back of my mind since I finally managed to despatch a particularly irksome report to Geneva.

The famous old Strand bar, overhead fan lazily lifting the air, billiard balls clicking and clunking into the pockets, the crisp black and white attire of the barmen, is a haven of old world charm. Glancing around, I recognise the usual assortment of embassy staff, well-heeled tourists, NGO workers, and businessmen. I smile at the few people I know, find a tall stool by the bar, and order a Strand Sunset, sweet with bitter, yellow, orange, and clear liquids layered, the cold from the ice cubes misting the outside of the glass. I pause and take a deep breath before the first heady sip. It gives a decent kick, relaxing the shoulders. A few more sips and slowly I leave my week's work behind me. Some spring rolls Vietnamese style with chilled prawns and copious herbs taste fresh and tart.

I chat a little with the others, a joke or two, share some information with enquiring tourists on the why and wherefore of Myanmar, as if anybody has the answers. I am amused and troubled at the same time, hearing some of the simplistic explanations of the newly arrived experts and political analysts, tongues oiled with alcohol, brains in low gear. I contest some of the more asinine comments, trying to add perspective and am relieved when others who have been here longer also add context, complexity and knowledge to the discussions. Another cocktail, an avocado and smoked salmon stack, delicious. I'm relaxed, my mind drifting. I smile automatically at comments around me, but no longer participate. Time to go.

I have a Saturday morning headache. My body doesn't know how to deal with the lack of structure, having worked a tight schedule all week. After showering and making coffee, I acknowledge that last night's cocktails may be a contributing factor to my heavy head, though those Strand Sunsets were excellent.

By the afternoon, I can't put it off any longer. The Monday workshop looms large in my thoughts and anyway it's raining, limiting my choices of entertainment. I sit down at the desk, my mind a blank. I'd better start with some notes for the opening speech.

This past year we've conduced a first countrywide Branch Survey with our MRCS colleagues, a fascinating exercise. At first the MRCS paid lip service to the survey considering it a Federation idea, but as they became more involved, they claimed ownership and took the lead. Now, with the draft report, statistics, and strategic plan ready, branch development has become a priority. At this workshop, the headquarters staff will share their findings with the branch leaders to ensure their involvement. My role is to assist my colleagues in making the week-long workshop as interesting and participatory as possible.

I jot down some ideas for the introduction, examples of things that are working well, a fundraising success story from one branch, the new and evolving warehouse stocking and distribution system in another, the community-based first aid programme, the delta early warning flood system, the HIV/AIDS anti-stigma workshops. I add a few challenges and frustrations to acknowledge what most branch leaders face—a lack of resources, too few volunteers and uncooperative government officialdom, and practical issues, like the cost of uniforms, communications, training courses and manuals. A story or two from my travels around the country might raise a few laughs—my delight at the wooden cars in Chin State, my love of savoury, steaming Shan noodles, my attempts to speak Burmese and of what little use are the few words I can recall: *apio gyi* old spinster, *myan myan* hurry up, *pingu* spider; *yabe yabe* stop, l*u bio* young bachelor, and *cannale* take it easy.

I wander into the garden with a cup of tea, taking a break. The rain has stopped, but the bright bougainvillea hedge is still dripping. Although an ominously black sky announces another downpour the sun pierces the clouds for a moment and the bright arc of a rainbow appears on the horizon. The light is perfect, sharp and clear, the very air washed clean. The rainbow is still bright and birds are flitting from one bloom to the next. I pause, drinking in the vibrant purples of the iris, the dripping hedge and flowers, the beads of rain on a petal and the delicate pollen-covered stamen of a scarlet hibiscus weighed down with moisture.

Malay wanders out to see why I'm standing there transfixed. "I thought you were sleeping, you've been very quiet today," he comments. "Are you ok?"

"I'm preparing for a workshop," I answer, "Could you help me with a couple of sentences for my opening remarks in Burmese? That generally gets the audience's attention and usually a laugh at my pronunciation."

"Of course," he replies, and then offers, "Would you like me to prepare something for dinner tonight? Shall I can go and buy some fruit?"

Malay and Maung Taut must wonder at how solitary I am much of the time. I suspect they worry about me being lonely, but would never be impertinent enough to ask. Living in a very traditional and family oriented society, the idea that I travel, work and live on my own must be foreign to them, but I am used to it. Friends ask these questions sometimes, on one hand aware that I would like to have had children, on the other recognizing the interesting jobs and the fascinating places I have experienced, partly because of my life choices.

Just before I started this job a friend mentioned that now would be my opportunity to adopt a child, surprising me. Why here and now? Was it because she thought I could more easily find a child to adopt in Asia? Was it her perception, or prejudice, that I would be able to give a better life to a child because I was 'rich' or 'educated'?" It bothered me that someone might think I would just pick up a child like a new possession, for my own satisfaction. What about its own family, traditions, religion? Could I part a child from that? What have I to offer, at my age and with my roaming lifestyle?

I hear Malay clanging out the gate, off to buy fruit and I wonder what he will bring back, hoping for pomelo.

Back at my desk, I read through my notes again, taking time to consider and write out the order of the presentation. I feel a sense of achievement having accomplished something useful today. Tomorrow I'll tackle the session on branch development.

As the day fades, I walk through the house, lighting each room then go into the kitchen to prepare my meal, a simple vegetable pasta. Malay's already there, skinning and sectioning a pink pomelo.

"Chezu timbade Malay", I thank him. "That looks delicious, and it'll be even better after half an hour in the fridge. It's really hot today, isn't it?

"The power's not good tonight either, probably that storm this afternoon," he replies.

"I noticed. No TV programmes tonight," I respond. When the power is erratic, I get tired of losing the plot as the TV goes off and on. With a

DVD, I can take up at the point it went off. Maybe Marlar had been right, I should have stayed in Golden Valley where the generals and smart set live. But I'm happy in this house, with all its inadequacies.

On Sunday, it's raining again. I gaze out at the rain, while my mind toys with possible ideas for the branch development session.

Then it comes to me. Why not a game? Fewer words, more involvement. There's always too much talk at workshops, long dry presentations that leave you gasping for a cup of tea. A game could set the scene, involve decision-making, facts and fun. The participants will give it a go and colleagues can take notes, answer questions and observe. It could take about an hour, with another hour of discussions and questions, raising new ideas the branch leaders can identify with, enjoy and take home.

I'm energised, my mind racing and I get to work. What could be the objective of the game? I can call it 'Build your branch'. What are the characteristics of a 'well-functioning' branch? What resources are needed? Training, volunteers, equipment, relief supplies, communications. Which is more important? How to prioritize and plan?

How can I make this into a workable and semi-realistic game, to impact the mind-set of the participants? How many players per game? How to make the game boards?

I make a rough sketch of a board, a first draft of the rules and jot down some typical MRCS situations. I list the things I need Ko Zaw to buy. I ferret around in my desk drawer for anything useful and find sheets of small Red Cross stickers and some coloured cardboard. What else will I need? Dice for excitement and an element of chance, counters representing money, the stickers can indicate resources bought, action cards for group decision making.

Ko Zaw arrives and I brief him on what he should buy, explaining what I'm doing so he doesn't think I am about to set up an illegal gambling den. I will need ten dice, some play money for kid's games or some plastic counters, ten sheets of thick white cardboard, coloured electrician's tape, a long ruler, a cutting blade and glue.

By the end of the afternoon, I've designed and printed the games, complete with fancy lettering and visuals for the different resources and services needed to build their branch. I've written the directions and rules and prepared the 'chance' scenarios that will push the players to agree on what resources to buy and in what order.

With the supplies that Ko Zaw provides, I've measured, ruled, cut and pasted boards and marker cards, neatly edged in coloured electrician's tape. I've counted out the 'play money', Red Cross markers, dice, action cards—a set for each group of six. I've prepared a simple presentation on the objectives and rules of the game and listed points for myself to observe and comment on how the game is played and to anticipate questions that might arise. I'm hoping this session will resonate with reality for the players as well as provide some fun.

When I pack the games ready for the morning, I'm suddenly overwhelmed with a sense of trepidation. Might the branch leaders, all grown, if not elderly men and the few women, the President and HQ staff be insulted that I suggest they play games? The Red Cross is about very serious things —health issues, disaster, conflict. How could a Head of Delegation be so flippant and superficial? Did I get carried away? Too late, there's no time to prepare anything else.

The workshop is at Trader's Hotel. After stowing my boxes at the back of the room, I take my place with the MRCS leadership on the smart chairs at the front. I'm wearing traditional Myanmar dress and I politely greet the President and the Executive Committee.

"Mingalar bar, Joanna," the President shakes my hand, "You're looking very pretty and plump this morning. Ready for your presentations? I always look forward to hearing what you have to say. Unfortunately, I can only be at the meeting today, but I intend to be a willing participant." I smile, acknowledging his words. Thankfully, I know now that 'looking plump' is a compliment, but I'm a little worried he might not approve of the game.

The meeting follows protocol, welcome, introductory speeches from the President and Executive Committee members, then my introduction that seems to go well, even drawing a few laughs. The week's programme is outlined, introductions made and we break for tea and coffee. From now on, we are in work mode and less formal. During the break the participants renew or make new acquaintances with colleagues from other branches, the HQ staff and my delegation team. I watch them over the rim of my teacup wondering what they'll make of my game.

Over lunch I brief Alex, my Branch Development delegate, an intelligent and energetic young man recruited from the Philippines Red Cross. He looks surprised when I explain my plan, but is enthusiastic for this out of the ordinary session.

It's time. The participants settle back into their places, chairs grouped in sixes around the tables, no doubt expecting a dry lecture when their brains will be struggling with an after lunch need for a nap. I have the first slide up on the screen, a board laid out in front of me, the interpreter by my side.

"A national society is as strong as its weakest branch," I begin, "This afternoon I'd like us to explore that idea, and agree on just what constitutes a strong branch and your role as a leader. Over the weekend I prepared an exercise, a game actually, to kick off this discussion." As my words are interpreted, I see puzzled faces. "Will you give it a go?" I ask. Heads nod, some enthusiastic, others doubtful.

I outline the objective, the rules of the game and explain that for each purchase of a resource or service, the group must be in agreement. Alex sets a game board at each table. After everything is laid out and queries answered, they begin. I give them forty-five minutes to build the best branch they can.

At first, the groups discuss the rules, shooting looks at the others to make sure they're not left behind. Then as the dice begin to roll and the money starts coming in, voices rise, opinions differing about what to buy and why. Leaders emerge and discussions become more heated. Some players whoop and laugh as they get a double six, meaning another throw, or any double, giving a chance to turn over a card with a resource from of a donor, or alternately lose all they've already accrued when hit by a cyclone.

Alex and I and the HQ colleagues walk between the groups, watching how they work, listening to their arguments for one resource or another, interested in their priorities. The teams hover over their boards, not wanting to show their hand but trying to check on the others. They are enjoying this and I breathe a sigh of relief. If we can draw some meaning and real understanding out of this, it'll have been a good session.

Just as I'm starting to relax, something changes in the atmosphere. First one team, then another, and another realize that if they throw the dice fast enough and just buy, buy, buy with no discussion, they can build the perfect branch, no trouble at all. With all my rules, I had clearly forgotten the most important, to limit the number of throws per person. I catch Alex's eye and we laugh. It's time to bring the game to a close but I make a note to add a point for the follow-up discussion—money rarely falls from trees.

It takes a while to bring order, but when I have their attention, I know at least no one has fallen asleep. The debrief is lively, the teams presenting the branches they've built and explaining why they have chosen volunteer training over uniforms or purchased a warehouse rather than a vehicle. Some also explain major problems faced by their own branch or recount a success story they wish to share.

Discussions and teasing about who cheated, who won and how they beat the system, continue into the coffee break. When several approach to ask if they can take a copy to play with their own members I feel an overwhelming satisfaction at having managed to share new ideas and motivate the branch leaders.

In my closing remarks, I thank them for their participation, informing them that after adjusting the rules, we will produce a professional looking package to be used in other training sessions, which will also be available for the branches.*

"I knew it would be worthwhile attending your session, Joanna," the President remarks over coffee, "It was very interesting to observe, but next time would you allow me to play too?"

---

*Alex and I subsequently adjusted and produced a standard package of the game that we used in branch training sessions in Myanmar and other SE Asian RC Society trainings. I also used it to facilitate delegate training courses in Australia, Japan and Germany. When Alex took another posting in East Africa, he used it there too. It is still used as a training tool.

Chapter Twenty
The Fisherman's Son

At the end of a short but busy visit of my sister Pippa and brother-in-law John we travel together to Ngapali for a relaxing break by the sea. Dust rises from the tarmac as we taxi in, propellers whirring. Outside the small airport, we are gently shepherded with a few other tourists towards an old blue bus, a truck in its previous life, white flowers and 'Ngapali Beach Hotel' painted proudly along its side.

Through the open side of the bus, an elderly lady offers us leaf packets of rice studded with fruit. "For you. Welcome to Ngapali Beach. Special rice from Ngapali, strawberries inside. Very nice." I hand over my Kyat. The rice is delicious, sweet and sticky.

Ngapali is on the northern Rakhine coast, on the Bay of Bengal, and easily rivals other tropical beaches in its beauty. At present, there's only one smart hotel, the Sandaway, and several low-key choices, mainly rustic beach bungalows with shared dining rooms and reception areas, but several more are being built. Changes to the once pristine environment are becoming noticeable, trees chopped down and the beautiful golden sand dug up to make concrete. Cement mixers drown out all other sounds on a stretch of the beach, though too far to intrude on our idyllic setting. This is what happens when magazines start describing beautiful 'hidden gems,' exposing them to the masses.

The sand glows softly under the early morning sun, washed clean by the tide, dotted with shells and driftwood. The three of us walk towards the southern end of the bay, and I trail behind taking in the view—the sea liquid silver, touches of soft rose and gold shimmering over its surface, the clouds low and pink on the horizon, silhouetting lines of fishing boats.

The long curve of the bay is striped with shadows as the sun rises, slanting through the line of palms at the top of the beach. An ox cart, its heavy wooden yoke decorated with yellow and red braided tassels, creaks along the waterline through the foam and jetsam, wooden wheels carving parallel ruts in the firm sand, the driver relaxed, a sleepy child tucked beside him on the plank seat. Almost precisely halfway along the curve is an outcrop of jagged rocks, partly covered at high tide, but now marooned in a sea of sand. A bronze mermaid sits there, tail curled enticingly round a rock, gazing longingly out to sea and I wonder for whom she is waiting.

Locals walk along the beach gathering interesting and useful flotsam, looking for shells to sell or make into trinkets for the tourists. We smile as we pass, acknowledging a shared pursuit, and a heavily pregnant young woman, beckons, showing me her rattan basket full of shells, still wet and shining white, black, green, pink and brown. "You want?" she asks." I shake my head.

" Number one baby?" I ask, but she shakes for head, holding up two fingers.

Further down the beach, a girl in a flowered *longyi* stops to chat shyly, "Where are you from? Do you like it here? What is your name?" her questions come in a row, learned talk for the tourists, but in perfectly pronounced English.

"I live in Yangon where I work with Kyet Cheni, the Red Cross, but my home country is New Zealand. Do you know where it is?" I counter.

In response she picks up a stick and draws a pretty nifty map of Australia with two rather misshapen but rightfully elongated islands underneath. With a flourish, she thrusts her stick in the sand, and replies with a gentle but triumphant smile, "This is Myanmar up here and New Zealand is far away, even further than Australia."

I ask her to write her name for me and she does so, first in the wonderful curled and rounded Burmese characters, derivative of the ancient Pali script of India; then knowing I won't be able to read it, carefully spells out her name, Aye Aye Myint. "My name means 'calmness.' My father is a fisherman and I am his firstborn. I'm happy to practice my English with you," she tells me, "because I am going to work in a big hotel one day."

"That's my big sister over there," I tell her, pointing along the beach, "I'd better catch up with her. Maybe see you tomorrow." We part with a smile and a wave.

At the southern end of the beach is a fishing village, houses and bamboo fences straggling along the hillocks, smoke drifting over the beach, already a hive of activity. Several wooden fishing boats in blues, reds, greens sail in, sculling and nudging their way into the shallows, the sails, previously held aloft by flimsy bamboo poles, now loosely draped across the sterns. The fishermen wear plaid shirts, woollen hats for the chilly night's work pulled low over their foreheads. Most are smoking, inhaling deeply, puffing out clouds into the clear morning air. Oxen stand patiently, chest deep in the water, while the night's catch is loaded into carts. Older men and young boys wade into the water again and again, bringing back vividly coloured plastic tubs full of fish, the handles slung on bamboo poles and carried across their shoulders.

Lines of rope snake out from the rusted metal anchors thrown haphazardly onto the beach, boys darting over and under them, playing, soon joined by the youngest fishermen. Still lively after their night at sea, they jump from the boats and swim ashore, showing off and splashing each other. The girls don't have the luxury of play, but squat at the water's edge, cleaning the plastic tubs, meshed like huge colanders, or skimming the water with small triangular nets for tiddlers that got away.

We wander between the family groups crouched over the day's catch, communicating with my few words of Burmese and some English, checking out the catch of the day. Several magnificent large fish are stuffed in a green tub, heads down, tail fins with distinctive shapes and markings, painting wondrous shadows across the sand. Another bucket, bright blue, is full of smaller, squirming silver fish.

By the wide blue tarpaulins spread out at the highest point of the beach, Pippa and I squat and chat for a while with the women who wait for the smaller fish they will lay out to dry, an important source of food and revenue for the village. They wear traditional conical straw hats, a tuft or bobble on top in blue or red, their cheeks patterned with thanakha. When the buckets of tiny fish arrive, they rise as one, and begin their backbreaking and tedious work, tipping them onto wide, flat rattan baskets then spreading them evenly onto the tarpaulins—pour, lift, throw, pour, lift, scatter.

Returning back down the beach we notice a father and son crouched together by a small outcrop of rocks. The fisherman, wearing a brown balaclava, a pipe stuck firmly between his teeth, checks a circular net, repairing gaps here and there, tightening the mesh loops. His son watches intently, his hand resting lightly, possessively, on a beautifully crafted fishing creel beside him, woven rattan with leather straps, hinges and fastenings. We recall that Dad had one just like it and I remember playing with it as a child, the strap crossways over my chest, stuffing leaves into the opening, pretending they were fish.

Close to the shore, a group of young women stand huddled, chatting and giggling, watching and waiting for the return of boyfriends or prospective husbands, checking out the best catch. As if on cue, a group of six handsome young fishermen wade ashore, swaggering along the beach, chests bare and bronzed, bags slung over their shoulders, wet *longyis* plastered to their thighs, conscious of their virility. One of them, a red towel turban-like on his head has a particularly cheeky grin and he clowns it up for us, the foreigners. We laugh with him, acknowledging his bravado.

Piles of tangled nets, waiting to be unravelled, sit like whipped cream, fluffy and white in the sunlight. A very old woman, face brown and lined, eyes slightly vacant, wanders past, a black bucket sprouting fish tails on her head and another hanging from one arm. In her free hand she holds an enormous cheroot, puffing on it greedily every few minutes.

We stop to watch a beautiful little girl, sitting in the sand, seriously weaving together some rattan strips, her eyes focused on her fingers, tongue clenched between her lips, gold earrings sparkling in the sun. Her mother oversees with a keen eye, correcting her technique. They notice us looking, smile and wave us over. I attempt to mimic their movements and pattern, with pathetic results. The woman laughs, takes my mess, unravels it and with a few deft movements and a flick of the wrist, creates a small woven fish. With a smile, she holds it out to me in the upturned palm of her right hand, her left hand lightly touching her right forearm, the polite way of offering in Myanmar.

From the largest boats, the fishermen now carry in the last, huge bundles of fishing nets and call on their friends to assist in 'walking' them along the beach to untangle and unsnag them. Tethered to posts at one end, they are strung out, checked for holes and tears, and once dried, rolled up ready for the following night. At the water's edge, lines of young men, *longyis* pulled up through their legs and tucked in at the back, flick and lift the smaller nets to untangle them, exchanging shouted comments, the shared rhythm in their movements beautiful to watch.

The tide is slowly going out. Each family pulls in their boat and the lines of bright red, blue and green bows are aligned once again until the next tide rises, ready for another night of trawling the seas.

The carts return along the beach with their tubs of glistening fish, clipping fast on the packed wet sand at the waterline. Pippa and John follow them, hungry now for their breakfast after the morning walk, but I want to take my time, enjoy the beach a little longer.

As I meander back, enjoying the feel of the warming sand crumbling under my feet, I see the father and son wading in the shallows, walking in step, the son one pace behind his father. The fisherman has discarded his balaclava for a conical hat set absolutely straight on his head, cotton chinstrap holding it in place, his pipe still clenched, unlit, between his teeth, jutting out beneath. His mustard *longyi* is tucked up between his muscled, vein-knotted legs. He holds the weighted end of the net in his right hand, the rest loosely caught in his left. The son, clad in red football shorts, creel thrown over his shoulder, carries a short stick.

They walk together in their unmatched flip-flops, stopping, stooping, looking, checking the water patterns, wading further in at a likely spot, often crouching right down, the son mirroring his father's actions. From time to time, the man flings out his net, arcing it high in the air and letting it settle in a wide circle over and into the water, before drawing it slowly in. Again and again he flings the net, his back muscles straining, his leg lifting with the effort, his son following the swoop of it with his eyes. Time after time he throws his net, then gathers it back into his left hand, dripping, but fishless. His son never wavers, never shows boredom, but stalks his father's every move, a perfect student in the art of fishing.

I'm mesmerized by the slow and steady path of the father and son and keep pace with them from the shadow at the top of the beach, willing them to catch something and for the boy to be able to stun the fish with his stick and place it proudly in his creel. At one point they notice me and I wave, but they turn back to their task unsmiling. Not once does the fisherman take the pipe out of his mouth, nor does the son turn to glance at me again—they are totally immersed in their world of elusive shoals of fish.

Walking back towards the hotel, I wonder how many generations have followed these morning routines, traditions handed down from father to son, mother to daughter, and how much longer this traditional lifestyle will continue as the hotels and the tourists creep ever closer, with their seductive glimpses of another way of life.

Chapter Twenty-One
Cardboard Box Stories

This week I'm in Kengtung to run a workshop for doctors, nurses and health workers, together with our Health Delegate Yvonne, Dr Phone Thant from the MRCS and Aaron, an Australian working for the United Nations Global Fund for AIDS, TB and Malaria.

Kengtung, where we have a good local team and a health project already underway, is a good place to start the HIV & AIDS programme. The Australian Red Cross, our donor, wanted an anti-AIDS programme from the outset, but when we explained that in some remote areas villagers still believe malaria comes from eating green bananas and drinking cold spring water, they accepted that basic health and hygiene were clearly a priority.

Prior to 2002, the authorities had denied the existence of HIV and AIDS in Myanmar, but more recently, allowing the work and advice of WHO officials, have finally cited a small number of cases in Myanmar and have agreed to begin an education programme. The MRCS has subsequently also decided to take some initiatives in this sphere.

I feel strongly about the stigma faced by people who have AIDS or are HIV positive. My last assignment involved the design and implementation of a global anti-stigma campaign for the Red Cross and Red Crescent, launched in Mozambique. The slogan of the campaign was "The Truth about AIDS, pass it on". We intend to do just that in Kengtung.

On Monday morning some forty doctors and nurses sit in rows on the hospital's broad enclosed veranda, fans circling lazily, while the routine continues inside, occasional flurries of activity punctuating the slow pace and gentle voices of the staff. At the opening, local health authorities and the Global Fund representative voice their support for our work, and MRCS Health Director, Dr Phone Thant, gives an introductory lecture.

Session over, there's a rustle of movement. It's time for coffee. Before anyone can move, one of the local Red Cross team walks slowly to the front, carrying a chair and, putting it down, stands behind it, in silence. A second member of the team arrives, places a chair to the left of the first, and stands behind it, mute, followed by a third member with another chair. The audience is attentive, but baffled. The RC team leader enters, leading three young volunteers. The first, blindfolded, is assisted to a chair where he sits straight and quiet. The second, a bandage covering her ears, sits in the centre chair. A third seats himself in the last chair, his mouth covered with criss-crossed tape.

"Throughout the next two days," states the team leader standing to one side, "We want you to keep in mind these three figures."

Putting her hands on the blindfolded volunteer in front to her, Yin Yin Myint starts talking very quietly, the audience craning forward to hear her words, "We've known for some time that people in our communities are dying from AIDS, but many of us have chosen not to look. Maybe we're frightened or don't know how to help. It's time to take these blinkers off. As doctors and nurses, we need to acknowledge this illness affecting our communities." She pauses and gazes around the room, before untying the blindfold, saying, "We need to face reality and have others follow our lead."

Zaw Min takes up the narrative, hands on the shoulders of the young woman with bandaged ears. "How many of us haven't listened to parents and elders in our communities worried about their sick children? How many have been unsympathetic to friends or colleagues who confide they're concerned for themselves?" Looking from person to person, he pulls the bandage off the young volunteer's ears, "Isn't it time we set an example, and listen to our families and friends? As health workers we have a responsibility to fight this illness just as we treat malaria, tuberculosis and other diseases. Let us start to listen."

On the third chair is the young man with his mouth covered. Sai Lon, standing behind him continues, "It's time to speak out, tell people the facts, fight the stigma, urge people to look after their family members who are sick and teach them how to protect themselves and their communities. Let's not remain silent as this young man is forced to do, but speak out and tell the truth." Taking hold of the tape, she pulls it from his mouth.

"Oi, that hurt!" the young volunteer winces as the tape is ripped off.

"So does the truth sometimes," the team leader interjects, his words unrehearsed, but effective. "We must learn the truth about AIDS and pass that truth on. Thank you for your attention." The group is applauded. Everyone rises to queue for coffee or tea, all talking.

After the break Aaron from the Global Fund presents a well-prepared, informative lecture merging facts, figures, diagrams with data on appropriate treatment from within Myanmar and other countries. It's clear from the questions that, for many, this is the first time they've been able to discuss the issue in detail.

My session on the subject of 'Stigma' is scheduled for the afternoon. Once everyone is settled, I outline the topic and then ask, "Would anyone like to tell me about how people with HIV and AIDS are treated in this community, or mistreated, perhaps through ignorance?" No one speaks or raises a hand. There's complete silence. The subject is still very much taboo. This will not be an easy session.

"So let me start with a story", I say. "There's a first time for everything, some we remember from our childhood—our first day at school, our first adventure without our parents. As we get older, there are other 'firsts'—

our first crush, a first big disappointment." Now, for all of us, there's another first, I want to discuss today—the first time we met someone who is HIV positive or with AIDS. I'm not proud of my reaction the first time this happened to me, although perhaps you will understand."

I have their attention so continue, "In 1984, when this 'new' disease was still not well understood, I was at a Red Cross meeting. Two HIV positive young men who had spoken about their health challenges joined our table at lunch. For dessert there was a choice, lemon meringue pie or fruit salad. I chose the fruit as I was trying to lose weight, while my neighbour, one of the young men, chose the lemon meringue. Guessing I really wanted it too, he took a spoonful from his plate, offering it to me."

I pause and wait, "I admit, I hesitated for a second or two before taking his spoon. I was shocked at my own reaction. Despite having just learned I couldn't be infected by a casual encounter, by sharing bowls and spoons, my reaction was there. It was fear."

As I see heads nodding and comments flowing, I carry on. "We are all educated and can think things through for ourselves. We have access to accurate information and medical updates on HIV and AIDS and yet we too are afraid, perhaps acting in ways inconsistent with our knowledge. Imagine how it must be for villagers who've had very little education. They hear stories and are frightened by what they don't understand. They see friends and family members losing weight, becoming ill and shun them, or worse, send them away. They talk about 'those people', spreading more fear."

The room is silent. Glancing around, I see a cardboard box. Emptying out the prepared handouts and holding it up, I challenge the group to share their stories. "Without identifying yourselves, please write about your first encounter of someone with AIDS, or the practices adopted in your hospital with HIV patients, or how they are stigmatized. Then put your papers in this box." Within moments, everyone is writing, everyone has a story to tell, something to share.

Soon heads go up, people talk among themselves, hands are raised, folded papers ready. Others continue to write. I ask them to take their time, as their stories and ideas are important. One by one, the group put their papers in the box.

I ask the Red Cross leader to come forward and read the stories, first in Burmese, with a brief translation in English. Everyone is intent on the stories he recounts:

—"My only brother told me he had AIDS. I was shocked and sent him away. He brought shame on our family. Now I want to find and help him. I miss him."

—"In the hospital, we tie red string on the AIDS patients' cards that hang on the bed ends. No one wants to stay in the same room with them. Do we have to do this?"

—"At the clinic, we tell people who have AIDS or are HIV positive to come only after four o'clock. Sometimes the doctors leave early and they have to come back another day."

—"A woman in our village has AIDS. Her husband died last year. The headman told her to leave our village, but she wouldn't. No one talks to her. She and her children just get by with a small garden and a few chickens. Who'll look after the children if she dies?"

A picture slowly emerges of the way people are treated in the villages, by their families, in clinics and hospitals. With every story a new awareness of the ignorance, fear and stigma grows. I tell them, "In groups, please take half an hour to discuss and prepare suggestions on how to address this issue both immediately and over the coming months. The health professionals will work with us."

The rest of the afternoon, leaders and participants work together, debating ideas, agreeing on steps to change hospital procedures, discussing educational materials and stories that might be effective in the villages, how to link them to other health messages. Who are the key target groups? How to spread these messages? New questions are raised and answered, with Aaron in his element, having worked in many countries on just these issues. His advice is practical and the group pick methods that best suit their communities.

One of the doctors suggests periodic meetings with staff at the hospital, working with the matron and supervisors to review procedures, making sure HIV and AIDS patients are not 'labelled' or stigmatized. A group of nurses from rural clinics say they will challenge the practice of segregating patients and make sure they are treated whenever they come to the clinic. The RC team will talk with taxi drivers and motorcyclists as part of their road safety programme and give lectures, and free condoms, to men in workers' hostels. They ask if some of the doctors will help, as the workers would listen to them.

A start has been made. Discussions about different aspects of treatment and the prevention of stigma, what the medical profession and the Red Cross team can do, will continue tomorrow.

I take the floor again to thank everyone for their participation, but before I can start, Yvonne joins me at the front of the room asking if she can tell a story.

"Today you've told your stories, 'the cardboard box stories' I think we could call them," she begins, "But I have a sadder, real story about a cardboard box I'd like to share. A few weeks ago, I was with my team in a remote village, doing a health check. We were warmly welcomed by the villagers and met with the headman, a midwife and a local healer. We heard about the village's health issues and agreed to work with them in the coming months to create a clean water supply and provide treated mosquito nets for each family.

After we'd eaten, I was shown the path to a latrine at the end of the village. Walking back, I noticed a small hut behind some houses with a large broken cardboard carton under a tree. Something was moving in it, whimpering. I thought it was a puppy, but coming closer was shocked to find a thin, dirty little boy, tied to the tree by one leg. When I crouched down beside him, he shied away. He was perhaps only four but it was difficult to tell as he was so malnourished."

She pauses, "I called out to see if anyone was in the house. An old man came out and just stared at me. I tried to talk to him but we had no words in common, only my concern and his shameful look linking us over the child. I ran back to the headman's house to tell them what I had seen, asking who the old man and the boy were. Apparently both the child's parents had died of AIDS. The elders wanted to alienate him as they feared contagion. They didn't understand how the disease was spread or how to cure it. Only his grandfather looked after the child, but kept him at a distance in his fear, perhaps even hoping he would die.

We took the boy and his grandfather to the hospital. The doctors and staff nursed him back to health, taught the grandfather which foods to prepare and gave him with extra vitamins, before he came home again. Our team also returned to the village several times to help the community understand that the little boy and others like him need love and care, not fear and isolation. It was a great achievement for the whole community."

We are all shaken by the story. What has been shared today will be the catalyst for the professionals and the community to undertake wider information, education and support programmes. Tomorrow, discussions and plans will evolve.

The cardboard box stories stay with me for a long time. When Yvonne returns from a monitoring visit to Kengtung a few months later, we go for a drink together.

She reports, "The taxi driver and motorcycle campaign was a huge success. We did a two-week programme offering free helmets, first aid kits, condoms, screening for sexually transmitted diseases and health education pamphlets. Pretty much every one of the two-hundred or so taxi drivers in Kengtung, showed up at our office in the first three days! Each new village visit, we now check for 'hidden' people, and if any are found, make sure someone takes responsibility. We have organised meetings with high-risk groups and distributed educational material in high schools and workers' hostels. One of the first things we do with each new group", she finishes, "is to ask them to write their stories, concerns and ideas and put them in the cardboard box. It always works. We are reaching hundreds of new people who are learning the truth about AIDS and passing it on to their families and friends. Hopefully, in time, the fear and the stigma will lessen."

Later in the year, on World AIDS Day, an international radio correspondent in Bangkok phones asking if I'll talk about the issue of HIV and AIDS in Myanmar. I tell him I'll be glad to talk about the MRCS programmes in Yangon and in Kengtung, suggesting the Global Fund would be better placed to discuss the broader situation within the country. He agrees and tells me he'll call back at five for a live interview. Before ending the call, I specify again that I will only talk about what we are doing.

I am ready with my notes when his call comes through. I'm introduced then asked to outline my organization's position and programmes with regard to AIDS. I begin with the actions already taken, the seminar on stigma, the taxi drivers' campaign, our work in remote villages, elaborating the more interesting points, describing the excellent work the Red Cross team and the hospital staff are doing.

Mid flow, the interviewer interrupts me, "So, we understand Myanmar is exporting HIV and AIDS to neighbouring countries, particularly Thailand. What do you say about this?"

I am appalled at his choice of words, at his ugly insinuation that the country is knowingly, systematically spreading HIV and AIDS, shocked that he would stoop to such tactics to discredit the people of Myanmar. I rebut, "The Red Cross is running an important programme in Myanmar with the full knowledge of the Health Ministry and other groups are also doing excellent work in this respect. I find your line of questioning extremely subversive and offensive. I am sorry, but I do not wish to continue this interview," I conclude, hanging up. It's quite some time before my anger subsides.

Chapter Twenty-Two
Golden Rock

I have friends from England, Nick and Suze, staying. They're great company and their two-year old daughter Eva, all big blue eyes, wide smile and dimples charms everyone. When I offer them a weekend trip and ask my team to join us, everyone jumps at the idea.

After much discussion and deliberation, we decide on the Kyaik-Htiyo Pagoda, the Golden Rock, one of Myanmar's most sacred sites. It's in Mon State, east of Yangon, about a three-hour drive.

Legends state that the Golden Rock is balanced on a single hair of Buddha, so delicately, that if several men were to push the rock, it would move. I check the guidebooks for more information and learn that 'King Tissa, who lived in the 11th Century, the son of a Zawgyi and a Naga Princess, was given the Buddha's hair by an old hermit who had preserved it in his own hair-knot from centuries before. In giving King Tissa the hair, however, the hermit set one condition—the king had to find a rock which closely resembled the hermit's head, and on this rock he must build a pagoda to enshrine the hair relic.'*

By Friday, everything is organised and there's much excitement in the office. There will be eighteen of us—my little group of four, my deputy Patrik, his wife Ewa and their two young children, relief delegate Heikki, office administrator Kyaw Kyaw, IT whizz Zarni and his sister Shwe Zin, Sandy and her niece Bo, Ko Zaw, his wife and two sons. The pick-up circuit is decided and, if all goes according to plan, we should be on the road by seven.

At sunrise on Saturday morning, the four of us, picked up last, board the rented minibus and are seated in front, for the best view. We head out of town and Kyaw Kyaw, amid the chatter and laughter, gives us the plan for the day.

But the first stop is unplanned. We hear graunching as the minibus takes a corner a little fast and, slowing to a standstill on the gravel shoulder, the driver, joined by Ko Zaw, climbs down to check the engine. They're soon back on board.

"The bus isn't living up to its name," Ko Zaws grins at us, "but we might need Company help when we get to Bago, the gearbox needs sorting." We laugh, already having noted its name—The Angel Bus Company.

Leaving our driver and bus in a garage down a side road, we walk towards the main street. Our assorted bunch of adults and children, Myanmar and foreigners, soon gathers a little following, curious about us. Equally inquisitive, we peer into a school where young students perch on high wooden benches and admire the many beautifully painted roadside shrines, peopled by miniature dolls dressed in traditional dance costumes. A line of monks with their alms bowls in front walks solemnly by, the tallest in front, the smaller ones, no more than six or seven years old, struggling to keep up behind.

Kyaw Kyaw, a hive of information tells me, "They are in order of seniority, according to the seasons spent as monks, so the novices are always at the back. The smallest gets served the last portions by those

---

* *Insight Guide Burma (Myanmar) 2000.* APA Publications

seeking merit, and often has a heavier than usual bowl. By the time they make it back to the monastery to eat what has been offered, they are tired and hungry."

A tall clock tower, a reminder of colonial days, stands at the centre of Bago's main square surrounded by stalls selling clothes and household goods and a road, chaotic with bicycles, old buses and horse-drawn carts with blue canvas hoods. Food hawkers offer samosas, fried chicken, meat patties, fruit or savoury snacks, while families eat together at pavement cafes.

We stop for drinks and are immediately surrounded. Two small boys stare at Eva, Carl and Sophie, our trio of blond children. They stare back. One is dressed as Superman, the other as Spiderman and both clutch bags of dried shrimp their mother urges them to offer our children. They do so gallantly, but none of ours are game enough to try.

A beautiful young woman carrying on her head a large enamel dish of watermelon slices, glistening deliciously red, white and green greets us while her younger sister, urges us to buy. Both are of Indian origin and have matching thanakha designs, carefully striped patches on each cheek, a stripe down the nose, a peaked circle on the forehead and a heavy spot on the chin. Bright red lipstick augments their dramatic makeup and brown eyes plead that theirs is by far the sweetest watermelon in town. The younger sister takes a shine to Eva and carries her to a nearby shop to have her face painted with thanakha. We're posing for photos, chatting with locals when Ko Zaw calls us back to the bus, roadworthy once again.

Two hours later, we reach the foot of the mountain and stop for lunch. Kyaw Kyaw cautions us not to eat too heavily as we have a bumpy truck ride ahead of us, up to where we'll start the real climb to the pagoda. As we eat, women selling hats, walking sticks and mementos of Golden Rock accost us. I'm charmed by the hat lady who has circular swirls of thanakha on her cheeks, at least twenty wide brimmed straw hats perched on her head and others over her arm. I buy one, thinking of the long walk ahead.

Ko Zaw leads us to one of the trucks lined up at the bottom of a steep, winding road. The seats are just planks balanced on the high sides and I'm worried for the families at the rather precarious nature of this ride. Piling our luggage into a wire cage hanging off the back, we climb up, settling onto the plank seats, relieved it's only our group and joke a bit in our anxiety. Once on our way however, we realize a full truck, like those ahead, crammed with people, might have been better.

The first uphill stretches are taken at a reasonable pace, but when the road levels out, curling along a river some twenty or thirty feet below, the driver accelerates and we hurtle round corners at breakneck speed, horn blasting to announce our coming. We scream with fear and occasionally exhilaration on each bend and I daren't contemplate what might happen should a truck come the other way. I look ahead to Nick and Suze, Eva held firmly between them, each with an arm around her, their free hands holding on, white knuckled, to the rail above. All three are screaming like maniacs at every corner, laughing with relief on the straighter stretches. After a particularly sharp corner, I turn back to look at the rest of the team. Every one is hanging on for dear life, holding onto hats and children and the sides of the truck. All are open mouthed and screaming.

We stop about halfway and I learn that we wouldn't have faced oncoming traffic as the truck drivers have a system, travelling in convoys of five trucks at a time. Once the five trucks have made it to the half way point, the waiting trucks are free to drive the lower section of the road knowing it will be traffic free. Likewise, the trucks at the top will wait for our small convoy before they send another five down. In the next section we are better prepared for the drama, even excited by the reckless speed and perilous corners, strangely confident that the drivers know their business. Nick has secured Eva into her backpack, straps firmly fastened, so he and Suze can grip the bar with both hands. The rest of us are wedged tightly on the plank benches, braced against each other, the men taking the outside places, women and children between. Another fifteen minutes of shrieking and laughing and we arrive at a large open area ringed by small stalls, clusters of blue-shirted porters hefting open-weave bamboo baskets onto their backs.

Ko Zaw takes charge, commandeering porters to take our bags to the top. Seeing the first part of the trail rising steeply on the far side of the market place, Patrik decides that Carl at five, and Sophie, just three, are too small to walk the trail so they too are loaded into rattan baskets. They sit comfortably on narrow planks half way up the baskets, feet hanging, just their heads peeping over the rims, Carl in a green peaked cap, Sophie in a cute pink sunhat.

An old lady, red conical hat over a brown towel, her face equally brown with deeply etched lines, offers me a walking stick of stripped bamboo with a black design down its length.

"I think you might need that, Joanna," Kyaw Kyaw suggests politely "some parts of the trail are really steep". I buy the stick. Ewa, Sandy and Shwe Zin take one as well. The men scoff at the idea, wanting to show off their fitness. The trail is a mostly concreted path with ridges on the steepest slopes. It'll take an hour or two to reach the top.

I go at my own steady pace, struggling on the steeper slopes, stopping every so often to catch my breath and enjoy the view over the surrounding hills. Before long I'm at the back of the group with only Nick and Suze, Eva in the backpack, keeping me company. On the straighter stretches, stalls sell trinkets and handicrafts and small cafes offer an opportunity to rest, relax and refresh. We catch up with Ko Zaw and his family, joining them for a drink, delicious chilled coconut water straight from the shells. Ma Khin Than Naing, his wife, is rather plump and Ko Zaw teases her a little before calling over a group of palanquin bearers, to take her the rest of the way.

The palanquin, a bamboo chair with a coloured fabric seat on two long, stout bamboo poles is lowered. With Ma Khin and her young son sitting comfortably, the four young men hoist it onto their shoulders and set off up the trail at a smart clip.

Many are on the trail, families with children, grandparents, young couples, groups of friends, monks. Some will spend the night, others are returning, loping down the trail at a brisk pace. There are also the stall-owners, children playing at their feet or helping prepare food and drinks. A little boy of five or so, in an orange embroidered shirt solemnly sweeps the street in front of his mother's stall. When I take his photo he doesn't miss a beat or smile. Even when his family laughs, he just continues his sweeping.

Every few minutes I am reminded of my age, a mere fifty-six, by the men plying the palanquin trade, suggesting I'd be better off being carried to the top. Steadfastly declining their offers, eyes focussed on the path, I plod on, with my stick and the encouragement of my young fit friends, the mantra, 'Are we there yet? Are we there yet?' providing a rhythm for each step I take. Stopping at a corner to catch my breath, I look up across a bush-clad hillside, and there, high above us, under a huge white cloud, is the Golden Rock, tiny at this distance but shining, beckoning enticingly in the afternoon sun.

My reverie on the significance of this holiest of places is shattered at the next corner when I come upon a stall selling bamboo weapons, a veritable arsenal of replica M16s, AK47s and an assortment of rifles and handguns. Checking one for size and weight and clearly aiming to buy is an elderly monk, his robes and shaven head, warm smile and rimless glasses, totally at odds with the weapon he holds, however harmless. Further up the trail two younger monks, having already made their purchases, strut side by side, AK47s slung nonchalantly over their shoulders.

We plod on up the trail. Eva's fallen asleep, her flushed cheek resting on the padded rim of the backpack. Nick, Suze and I walk together in silence.

Finally we reach the last rest point, greeted by our colleagues and sink down gratefully at a cafe table outside our hotel. Ko Zaw calls for drinks, everyone talking at once, before we check into our rooms.

The grey stone hotel, clings to a steep slope, rooms connected by narrow paths and stone steps bordered with shells. It reminds me of somewhere I once stayed in Cornwall, but instead of the ocean, from my room I see row after row of forested hills, receding green to blue, into the distance.

Refreshed, we leave to walk the last part of the trail together, passing under a painted archway welcoming us and by a smaller but squarer version of the Golden Rock, set a little off the path.

"This," announces Kyaw Kyaw with a dramatic flourish of his hand, "is Kyaukthanban, the stone boat pagoda. King Tissa was helped by the king of the Nats to search for the perfect rock to enshrine the hair of the Buddha. They found it at the bottom of the sea and transported it to the mountain top by a ship which then turned to stone, as you can see today."

Tired but exhilarated, we finally step up onto the vast, smooth white marble pagoda platform, dotted with shrines, reaching the Golden Rock just as the last rays of the sun touch upon it, lighting it. From certain angles it appears golden, from others just a dark silhouette against the pink and orange striped sunset.

With hundreds already gathered beside the Rock, we descend by a steep flight of steps to a lower level. From here it's even more impressive, looming over us, a hairsbreadth from toppling off its perch. Many sit on the steps chatting with friends, others gaze up at the rock deep in prayer.

As the tropical sun sets, darkness falls quickly. The lights come on, first those along the pathways and steps and then, theatrically, the spotlights, which shine onto the rock, bringing it to new life, its gold leaf ablaze against the deep indigo sky.

On the upper platform, all along the golden railings and in front of the shrines, lit candles and incense sticks are mirrored on marble, floating as if on water. The murmur of voices rises and falls with the rippling cadence of a stream, an age-old scene, re-enacted and played out time after time. We join the other pilgrims to make our offerings, give thanks and send silent pleas to the guardian of the rock. Ma Khin offers me a candle, lighting it from hers. Dripping a little wax before me, I hold it until it stands straight, the flame steady. Kneeling beside Ko Zaw and his family, with my friends around me, I feel blessed to be here, to be a part of this pilgrimage.

As we wander back across the wide platform, many are settling into makeshift tents, bamboo walking sticks crossed and tied forming a frame, blankets and longyis fashioning colourful walls weighed down by bags and bundles. Some are already under blankets to ward off the chilly night air, others stir pots over small burners or ladle out steaming bowls of soup. I'm sure sleep will not come for several hours yet, the platform busy with people coming and going, gossip bandied between friends and strangers, all celebrating this shared extraordinary experience.

We walk down the village street, stalls shuttered for the night, several restaurants doing a roaring trade. We swap stories of the day, relaxing over the tasty fare, rice with savoury fish, chicken and pork, stir-fried vegetables in oyster sauce, with small china cups of refreshing hot green tea. Later, sleepy but not wanting the day to end, we stop at a small bar for a nightcap, a whisky for some, hot chocolate for others.

Just before dawn the next morning, I join Zarni, Shwe Zin, Sandy and Ko Zaw to visit the more renowned shrines. The streets are already busy as we elbow our way through, jostling and laughing, trying to keep together. Brightly lit cafes make brisk sales, people wanting hot drinks, noodle soup or fried rice to banish the chill of the night. We pass them, heading out of the village to a shrine inside a cavern. Bending down, we enter a large, dark cave, a beautiful golden Buddha lying on a raised shelf cut into the rock at one end. Above his head are circles of flashing lights, while baskets of fruit, flowers and burning incense sticks colour the floor below. On the left, pilgrims kneel making obeisance, heads bowed, hands joined before their faces, one a hermit in brown robes, others clad in traditional dress. Only when I look more closely at one of them, do I realize these are just life-like models, worshipping here for eternity.

We emerge from the cave into a beautiful sunrise, soft clouds floating in a pale sky, their undersides lit pink and orange. Standing on huge boulders we look out over the hills and valleys extending out and down beyond us and then turn our gaze up to the Golden Rock.

On the way back Zarni buys a bag of fried dough sticks and we all hungrily take one, blowing on them, taking tiny bites until they are cool enough to devour. They are deliciously rich and we lick our sugary fingers, still hungry after the bag is finished.

We pass the Fire Brigade Garage, a large shed, red trumpet shaped loud speakers jutting from the roof. A hand-painted sign, black helmet over crossed yellow axes against a blue and red striped background, announces its importance. A few years before, a cooking fire got out of control in this crowded part of town, destroying most of the houses. With only one main street and steep hills bordering the area, many were unable to get away and there was a heavy death toll. I imagine the fear and panic, the crowd pushing and shoving. It's a sobering thought as we retrace our steps.

We return to the hotel for a very welcome breakfast with our friends, then climb once more to the platform, all together. The sun, rising higher, casts long shadows of people moving across the white marble tiles.

Crowds of men are gathered by the Rock praying and adding gold to the already heavily gilded surface. Their hands reach as far as they can up and around the rock to attach the thin gold leaves. Women are not allowed to touch the rock but watch their fathers, husbands and sons place the gold leaves, then descend to the lower platform to make their own offerings of flowers and incense on the terrace below.

We visit small shrines, some containing life size figures with elaborate costumes and headwear, one topped with the raised head of a cobra. People push kyat notes between the figures' hands and pose for photos. Offerings of flowers, bananas, candles and coconuts pile up on the steps as the hours pass.

Tall columns topped by jewelled filigree spires tower over the platform, figures of animals or pilgrims around them. Golden plinths hold Buddha figures of all sizes and positions, surrounded by holy flags, paper money fans and astrology charts. We take our turn at pounding a heavy wooden striker against one of several huge metal bells. Long, low notes reverberate round the platform. The longer the peal, the longer your life. A tiny girl, her chubby face creased with the effort, helps her mother strike the side of a bell carved with golden lions and laughs with glee when it rings out their request for a long life.

Monks line the railings with their alms bowls, waiting for food and money from those wanting to gain merit, making the perfect backdrop for a family photo. Beyond, the Golden Rock glows, outshining all else in this holy place.

It's time to make our way back. Descending from the platform we meet a stooped old hermit being helped up the last hundred meters. Not for him the truck ride or the palanquin, he has walked for several days from the very bottom of the mountain, stopping at the springs on the way to refresh himself and staying in small shelters overnight. He's wearing the dark brown robes and tall leather hat that identify his calling. Kyaw Kyaw greets him, bowing deeply. He returns the greeting then turns and looks at me with such a beautiful smile that for a moment I can only stare at him, overwhelmed by the wisdom and compassion written in the lines of his face and the aura of serenity that surrounds him.

After lunch at a roadside restaurant, we begin the trek down the mountain, stopping every now and then to check out the stalls. Suze buys herself a shell bracelet and a matching one for Eva, Ko Zaw a bamboo whistle that puffs out a paper streamer for his younger son and a small carving for his eldest. Kyaw Kyaw shows me a stall selling herbs—wooden bowls with dried plants, roots, stems, wood chips and petals, limes balanced on top, with tin cans as measures, hand-written signs detailing their use. Medicines and tonics in clear or murky brown bottles stand on the shelves behind. Kyaw Kyaw advises me, "This is for a weak heart, that's for constipation, this for colic, and that for putting pep into older men."

I laugh with him then stop at a neighbouring stall, huge baskets of green and black pepper corns, some still on their stems beside hessian bags of the dried corns packed ready for sale, commenting, "This is more to my taste."

The way back seems shorter than our slow climb up and we are soon clambering up into one of the waiting trucks for the dashing ride back to the car park. This time we know to ride with others, tightly packed on the seats. We hang on tight and scream, as much for effect and pure devilish enjoyment as for fear, on the more crazy corners.

Bags safely stowed in our van, we start our journey back to Yangon. Before long, silence replaces soft chatting. I look round at my sleeping friends, limbs splayed, heads lolling, worn out with the excitement and exercise of the last two days.

Lulled by the movement of the van, my eyelids droop, my mind winding through our weekend of new experiences and ancient traditions. I think of the hundreds of families and pilgrims who have made their way there, year after year, generation after generation, each making offerings and silent pleas for their families and their beloved country.

I wonder how many more centuries the Golden Rock will remain balanced on the hair of the Buddha before it topples, under the caress of a hand or a breath of wind, and crashes down the mountainside.

I find myself fervently hoping that it be infinitely longer than the country itself will have to remain as it is, precariously balanced between its rich and vibrant past and an uncertain future, suspended in time.

Chapter Twenty-Three
I Moved the Flowers

In October 2004, the Myanmar Red Cross organizes a 'Partnership Meeting', the first in ten years, inviting Red Cross Societies interested in providing financial support. Colleagues from Geneva and Bangkok also attend. Our Delegation assists them in organizing a short field trip for participants and in preparing the meeting programme and documentation.

After checking with the authorities for permission, Kengtung, where several health projects are currently active, is agreed upon. The local Red Cross Branch and Yvonne's Health Team are proud to be chosen and launch themselves into the preparations. We sort out visas and travel permits, accommodation, the meeting venue, the opening ceremony and its protocol, documents, the farewell dinner to ensure a positive outcome and some real enjoyment.

Hectic weeks, but we are finally ready. The participants dribble into

Yangon over a few days. Booked into Traders Hotel where the later meeting will be held, all are given a fine welcome at the airport and at the hotel.

On Saturday morning, chatter echoes from seat to seat in the small Yangon Airways plane, friends reuniting and new alliances forged. As we descend into Heho, over red earth and lush green fields, everyone cranes their neck to get a first glimpse of rural Myanmar. A short stop and we are airborne again, another hour or so to our destination—Kengtung.

Red Cross volunteers holding a huge banner welcome us at the airport, directing us into the VIP room, all dark carved wood furniture and dusty net curtains. We're offered cool drinks and wait while passports are checked and luggage stowed in the waiting mini-buses. All is easy and cordial for the group, a far cry from the first time I arrived here when my passport and luggage were minutely inspected and I had to write half my family tree into a huge dog-eared ledger under the watchful eye of the airport authorities.

Driving into town the newcomers point to intriguing sights—market stalls selling sticky rice in bamboo tubes, motorbikes with whole families astride, people in traditional dress, loaded buses piled precariously with luggage, roadside restaurants boasting only a table and a few stools, a steaming pot as centrepiece.

We're staying at the New Kengtung Hotel for the two nights, a typical modern three star hotel, the best in town. Rooms are allocated, keys handed out by a slightly flustered reception team of immaculately dressed young women. Later we'll meet for dinner and an introduction to our programme.

On Sunday morning we gather in the lobby, impatient to be on our way, cameras and notebooks tucked into handbags or backpacks. Ushered into mini-buses our keen young Red Cross volunteer hosts, microphone in hand, explain the day's programme and then begin a running commentary on the scenic and cultural aspects of the surrounding countryside.

The winding road takes us through the territories and villages of different ethnic groups—Wa, Lisu, Ahka, Lahu, each recognisable by their distinctive dress. At our first stop, we leave the vans to walk up a short incline, a steep red clay bank one side, houses on the other.

Fifty or sixty villagers are lined up to greet us. The local volunteers, smart in their blue trousers and Red Cross t-shirts, hold yellow flags with the MRCS emblem and white flags with a red cross at intervals along the line. The older youths and the adults wear Kachin dress, resplendent in their black velvet jackets embroidered in red, the women's tall elaborate headdresses and necklaces ablaze with silver chains, engraved discs and coins.

Small children shyly offer wildflowers, breaking into giggles when the guests thank them. Walking into the village, the children hopping and skipping behind us, chattering excitedly, we are led to a covered hall set in a large arena of tamped earth. Protocol carefully observed, everyone is escorted to their assigned place. Villagers not invited, squat to watch us from the other side of a bamboo fence.

The first words of welcome are from a local celebrity, a beautiful young woman wearing red Kachin *longyi* with a delicately woven cream pattern. She greets us in English and Burmese then hands the microphone to the Headman, an imposing figure wearing a white jacket and the dark purple and green checked *longyi* of the Kachin men, a matching scarf wound around his head, the tasselled end hanging over his right ear. He holds the symbol of his leadership, a leather-sheathed sword with an ornately engraved silver handle, hung with red braided cord. He thanks us for our visit, speaking about the value of the Red Cross health programme for his village—a new understanding of diseases and what causes them, the importance of having clean water and latrines set away from the village, the use of bed nets. The interpreter manages to transmit his pride in encouraging young people to take advantage of the lessons and assume a leading role in the village's health care. This is radical, as normally the senior villagers would be tasked with passing on knowledge, rather than learning from their children and grandchildren.

Other speeches follow, from senior MRCS members, the Head of the Regional Delegation in Bangkok and the representative of Australian Red Cross, the key donor for this programme. The volunteers present different aspects of the health programme, also thanking the donors.

Formalities over, we are escorted into the heart of the village, breaking into smaller groups to see the sights—the latrines, the newly concreted water course, pumps and filters and the holding tank. A church on the hill confirms that missionaries have been at work and partially successful, or intrusive, depending on one's beliefs. The groups straggle, taking photos as children play around, showing off or bravely hold the hand of a stranger.

Most houses, on raised platforms, have bamboo walls and thatched roofs. People smile from windows, mothers holding up their babies to look at us or for us to admire them. A chubby tot peers from behind a carved slat of the family balcony, an eye either side, looking like a little ogre. Two sisters, hair plaited and beribboned, scoop up mouthfuls of rice and grin at us from their window seat. A grandmother leans back in a carved rocking chair in her front yard, grandson perched comfortably on her knee. Another, glasses perched on the end of her nose, weaves at a waist loom, her young grandchild sleeping in a basket alongside. Pigs, dogs and roosters roam through the village, a couple of little boys shooting at them with plastic machine guns which they then cheekily turn on us, feeling particularly courageous.

Some of our group stop for a drink at the two-storied village store and sit, talking, at a wooden table out front. Others join the chat and laughter of a group of women outside a mud brick factory taking a break, rattan baskets laid aside, coiled cloths still on their heads, padding required for the wooden plank on which they balance stacked bricks.

At midday we're escorted back to the open-sided hall, now a dining room. Vases of fresh flowers, bottles of beer and water have been set out, surrounded by plates of freshly washed salad greens, bean sprouts and platters of small fried fish with chilli sauce, as well as deep bowls of chicken, pork and vegetables in soup. The headman indicates where I should sit but I ask to go first to the kitchen to thank the women who have prepared the feast, now busy spooning out rice from huge woven rattan baskets lined with banana leaves.

Once everyone is seated, the headman makes a toast, inviting us to enjoy the lunch and, with a little smile, suggests we try one of their local delicacies. Turning to me he holds out a flowered plate heaped with the brown corrugated bodies of fried bamboo worms. As one, the group turns towards me and waits expectantly. I pick up a few, pop them into my mouth and chew, trying hard to show my appreciation to please our hosts. However, the pretence is unnecessary because I register only a crunch and a taste not unlike potato crisps. I lick my lips, take another mouthful, telling our host they're delicious, encouraging everyone to try them. Only a few brave souls do so, very tentatively.

Well fed, we turn to face the open clay courtyard for the entertainment. A drummer, splendid in wide pants, his black jacket embroidered in red leads in the group, solemnly beating a rhythm on the long drum slung over his shoulder. Six girls follow demurely, in red woven skirts and black velvet jackets, the front covered with intricate and heavy silver necklaces, all dangling a white handkerchief. Bringing up the rear are six young men, clad as the drummer but with a silver-handled sword hanging from their belt. Musicians squat in front, clanging finger cymbals, echoing the beat.

Taking tiny shuffling steps, the girls, eyes downcast, form a circle, swaying to the beat of the drum, treading slowly clockwise. The men, showing off their strength with bolder steps and jutting chins, form an outer circle around them, moving counter clockwise. They weave and dance as they pass. Sometimes, facing a particular young man, a girl flicks her handkerchief in his face and lifts her eyes up to his, in a universal gesture of courtship. As the beat of the drum becomes more insistent, the dancers move slowly towards each other and, with apparent ease, pair up. They continue to dance in couples, moving in the same direction, eyes gazing at each other. The line unfurls in front of us as they turn and bow. We clap loudly, enchanted.

It's time to leave. Another village visit is planned before our last stop at an after-school health programme demonstration in Kengtung. We drive down gravel roads, past cultivated fields, small rivers and scattered hamlets, the locals turning to wave at us. Reaching the next village, we park in the courtyard of a rough red brick monastery with a shingled roof, surrounded by a terrace and a few low buildings. The women's brightly coloured satin tops and *longyis*, and the men's grey wide pants with boxy grey jackets indicate that this is a Shan village, the majority ethnic group of this state.

Bright marigolds are hung around our necks and we are led to a cushion-covered platform. Plied with tea and snacks, the Red Cross volunteers entertain us by presenting health messages through dramatic and amusing mimes. Our local team explains that every weekend the young volunteers visit the villages in the area to teach about health and hygiene, combining local stories and mime so the messages are readily understood. We certainly find them effective as they ham it up, and laughing we applaud their audacity and style.

While the group waits for musicians and dancers to get organized, I walk across to the temple. A few novices gaze solemnly down at me from the terrace, their russet robes and shaven heads beautiful against the pattern of red bricks. Inside it's dark, and it takes a minute for my eyes to adjust. The cream walls are bare, roughly plastered, with low benches along either side, the floor covered with worn woven mats. A gold clothed Buddha, hung with paper offerings gazes down from a high ledge on the end wall. Kneeling before the image, I focus my thoughts on these villagers and our volunteers who try so hard to help them.

As I rise and turn to face the open doorway, my eyes trace a shaft of sunlight that dusts the straw broom leaning just inside the doorway with gold. Outside, the sun shines on a group of masked dancers swaying to the beat of a drum and the reverberating thrum of bronze gongs. In a fleeting moment of clarity, I imagine the worn broom symbolizes the beauty and resilience, the faith and shared values of the people of Myanmar. The young group outside, weaving their way through an age-old dance, watched by their elders, embodies the strength of each of the many cultures of this country and of the solid family bonds that bring joy and happiness in spite of the harsh political and economic conditions.

I am reminded of how vital it will be in the coming days of public and clandestine deliberations and declarations about Myanmar and those programmes needing support, that I remain concentrated and vocal. I must be firm about what can be done, focussed on how to ensure results, not dwell on what cannot yet be achieved.

As I step out into the sunlight, I feel stronger and calm, happy to just enjoy the afternoon and relax, watching the dancing which continues with noise and flair. Perhaps my serene mood is catching because it seems as though everyone is connecting. To my right a village elder with a white towelling gaung-baung grins at me, no teeth but a truly flirtatious twinkle in his eye. In front, a little girl in bright green satin, busy looking at the guests rather than the dancers, smiles at me then, taking the flower from behind her ear, stretches up to tuck it behind mine. The elderly man on my other side notices me admiring the line of intricate tattooing on his forehead. He runs his finger over it, then points to me. I shake my head, but running my finger along my forehead and pointing to him, nod in approval. He smiles back, proud that I'm impressed with his tattoo.

We're invited to join the final dance, the locals making a ring, guests circling outside in the opposite direction. As we pass, we touch hands, then bow and move on, a brief connection and perhaps new respect forged between hosts and visitors, which might enable better understanding and support in future.

Leaving, we slow at a junction where a boy of about ten stands alone, saluting our departure. He wears camouflage pants with a red Spiderman T-shirt. A pair of fake ray-ban sunglasses hangs from a plastic pearl necklace and his cap has a Nike logo. I wonder what the future holds for him, clearly a 'man with style and ambition'.

It's quiet on the way back to town, everyone deep in their thoughts after a day full of people and places. We drive through the rice fields, villagers escorting flocks of geese, we pass motorbikes laden with produce, whole families astride and observe monks sweeping bright yellow flowers outside their monastery. Buffalo are tethered for grazing, tied to a long bamboo pole, weighted at one end and angled through a pivot on a short post, allowing them to crop in a wide arc but not get caught in the rope.

Back in Kengtung, we stop at the school where young Red Cross volunteers are learning to be 'peer educators' in health, particularly for HIV/AIDS. Aware of the issues, the stigma as well as the cause and course of the infections, and the preventive measures, they will be able to teach others about how to care for their own and their families' health. In their 'educator' T-shirts, cartoons and messages on the back such as 'You can't get AIDS from shaking hands', they're keen to sing the songs and show the short play they use to get their messages across. Small steps by young people, but important in a country with such huge health issues, inadequate health facilities and resources.

The day ends with a formal dinner, complete with speeches and gifts for everyone, followed by a colourful and captivating display of dancing from the different regional ethnic groups—Akha, Kachin, Karen, Lahu, Lisu, Shan and the Wa. The costumes and jewellery, the hairstyling and make up are elaborate, the dances and each group's pride in performing them, beautiful. After many photos and heartfelt thanks, I join my Myanmar colleagues on the hotel steps waving goodbyes to the dancers as they climb onto open trucks for their journeys home, some villages more than a two-hour drive away.

A new day dawns, back to Yangon this afternoon, but not before we've had a walk in the market and visited a primary school. We meet for breakfast over mugs of steaming sweet coffee and tea and pancakes stuffed with shredded coconut. Everyone is given an hour to check out the market and a meeting place is agreed, allowing us time to get to the school. I sit for a moment longer over my coffee, enjoying the bustle and colour around me. An 'umbrella man' mends the spokes of an umbrella, hundreds already repaired or for sale hanging above his head. Two women pass me, deep in conversation, their heavy rattan baskets held by a forehead strap. Nearby, an elderly broom seller leans against a wall, his load of rattan and bamboo weighing him down, eyes closed in fatigue. A young man tries to sell me an embalmed pangolin, the killing and sale of which is outlawed in most countries but still sought after and acclaimed as an aphrodisiac in China, just over the border.

We enter the Primary School at eleven sharp, the children ready, lined up, quiet under the teachers' watchful eyes. On our right the pupils, like the teachers, are dressed in green and white, a Red Cross patch sewn on their sleeve indicating the members of the school Red Cross group. To our left are the youngest, paired boy and girl, all dressed in miniature versions of their ethnic groups' traditional costumes, clutching beribboned bunches of flowers, serious and proud. Coaxed forward they offer their flowers to the group of tall strangers, then back away quickly, eyes wide.

Entering a classroom, we're greeted by the children standing behind their wooden desks, arms folded, welcoming smiles and "Mingalar-ba" on their lips. Presenting their first aid knowledge, a couple of boys demonstrate how a head bandage should be applied, a girl, hair braided with green and white ribbons on each plait, ties a sling on her friend's injured arm, while another pair instructs us on the organs of the human body pointing at a large diagram of a partly dissected human figure.

For the performance of a song in English, the front desks are pushed back and the pupils move to the front in three tidy rows, one exactly behind the other. The teacher raises her hands and with a nod of her head, the children burst into song. After the second verse a small girl at the back catches my attention as she slowly but surely begins to edge forward.

She triggers a memory. One of my mother's family stories was about my first school concert. In New Zealand at that time, you started school on your fifth birthday, so I'd only been at school a couple of weeks before the end of year concert. Our class was fetchingly togged out in green leggings with crepe paper neck ruffs in different colours making us all little flowers. When the curtain went up we were crouched in rows across the stage, slowly unfurling and swaying, rising up to reach the sunny summer sky. As the music swelled, one little yellow flower elbowed and nudged its way forward through the perfectly serried ranks of blooms right to the front. My mother watched in amazement as her youngest, placed in the back row as a 'new girl' steadily worked her way forward until she was centre stage—taa-daa! Around her, others were chortling and asking 'who is that little girl?' When she came to collect me afterwards she asked, puzzled, "But why didn't you stay in your place?"

To me it was obvious, "I wanted you to see me." I sense this little Shan girl just wants to be seen and heard too, and I smile at her as the song ends and the children bow to us.

That afternoon we catch our flight back to Yangon. Some of our visitors are commenting on the villages, the programmes and the volunteers. Others are quieter, gazing out at the patchwork of green rice paddies, bright yellow fields of mustard seed, dark forested hills, clusters of brown houses alongside rust-red clay roads, the odd sparkle of a river caught by the sun. Many exclaim at the long evening shadows of palm trees, breathtakingly painted across the landscape, clearly seduced by this remarkable country, just as I have been.

The next day, the meeting begins with a formal Opening Ceremony at Traders Hotel. My team and I, with MRCS staff, work to ensure everything is perfectly prepared, flowers in place, red ribbons behind each white satin-covered chair pulled taut, microphones tested, VIP seats with a programme and name card. I've tipped the hotel technician to place a small box behind the podium when he sees me approach for my address. I will be the last speaker.

At nine I wait with the President and Executive Committee Members of MRCS and my immediate senior, the Head of the Regional Delegation in Bangkok, for the arrival of the Deputy Minister of Health, the most important of the invited guests. We've met several times in formal meetings and I find him easy and interesting to converse with. When his contingent arrives, we sip tea together in a side room, talking politely until the other guests and participants are seated and we are invited into the ballroom. As we take our appointed seats, I send a quick smile to my friend Ma Nilar, seated to my right.

The Opening Ceremony goes to plan. The welcome, the well-prepared speeches of the Deputy Health Minister and the MRCS President earn murmured comments and applause. However, from where I sit in the front row, looking up to the stage, the bouquet of flowers on the top of the podium, all but hides the speakers. It's my turn and, according to instructions, the box is placed behind the podium. As I step up, I quietly ask the technician to remove the flowers. He gives me a puzzled look but does as I bid.

Placing the notes on the podium and looking straight down at the row of VIPs, I begin, "Your Excellency Deputy Minister of Health, Mr President, distinguished guests, Red Cross colleagues, ladies and gentlemen..." As the previous speakers have done, I talk about the importance of the meeting, the challenges faced by the National Society, the role our delegation plays in assisting them as well as our function in liaising with partners and donors.

I add more personal comments and observations, "... the Federation

Delegation offices are within the MRCS Headquarters building and we meet on a daily basis for discussions, meetings and planning, sometimes arguing but most often agreeing. We are privileged to share the everyday life of the Red Cross—when it rains on the MRCS, it rains on us, when the power goes off in their offices, it goes off in ours, when they celebrate a special day, we celebrate together. But it is a delicate role we play. Sometimes we seek to promote the National Society, sometimes we defend and protect it, sometimes we act as catalyst, but at all times we recognize that the MRCS must lead its own direction, strategy and programmes…"

I continue, observing that, "…for many meetings, participants arrive and are whipped along the well-sealed road to a hotel for a few days in air-conditioned luxury, eating international food, discussing and agreeing on strategies, then head back to the airport, never having as much as smelt the air, felt the dust between their toes or tasted a plate of mohinga. Not so for this meeting. On this trip everyone has been touched by the motivation of the volunteers and the commitment of the villagers. They are impressed by the beauty of the country and moved by the friendliness and cultural diversity of the people we've met. Links have been created these days between people of different countries and backgrounds."

Concluding, I highlight a number of significant achievements and plans of the Myanmar Red Cross, stressing the importance of this meeting and how it will give direction for the years ahead. At the end of my address, I pause, look at the front row again, fold my papers and thank the distinguished guests and colleagues for their attention.

Stepping down from the podium, I return to my seat, relieved to have it over. I glance at Ma Nilar, asking quietly, "How was it?"

Not looking me in the eye she replies, "You moved the flowers."

I am surprised at her seeming non-response, "What do you mean?"

"You shouldn't have done it."

I retort in a loud whisper, "Why ever not? I wanted people to see me. When the others spoke no one could see them. Even with the box, I could hardly see anyone."

Ma Nilar looks at me. "Nobody else moved the flowers, you shouldn't have either."

My comprehension grows, it's one of those Myanmar moments.

"You must always honour the most important, the eldest, the seniors. If the minister didn't move the flowers nor the President, who are you to move the flowers? Ma Nilar explains. I ask if I should apologize.

Ma Nilar shakes her head, "You should, but not right away, it might be misinterpreted." I nod, my mind trying to get itself around this new intricacy of protocol.

At coffee break, cup in hand, I approach the minister, saying respectfully, "I would like to congratulate you on your excellent speech this morning. Our guests and especially the volunteers appreciated your words about their work."

"Thank you, Joanna, you are too kind," he acknowledges my comments.

"Ah … and," I add hesitantly, "Please excuse me but I believe it might also be appropriate at this juncture to make a small apology to you?"

"For what, might I ask?"

"For moving the flowers."

The Minister smiles at me, "Oh, that was nothing, really. Your speech was good, I liked it and I hope the donors took it to heart."

I continue to press my point, "But I understand about the flowers now, and would like to apologize for the breach of protocol. I've been here three years, I should know better."

All charm, the Minister replies, "Frankly, Joanna, I loved that you did it. Knowing you a little, I even half expected you might. So, no hard feelings, don't worry about it. Though," he adds with a smile, "maybe next time, you might want to get a bigger box."

Three days later, at the Farewell Dinner the talk is more relaxed, wine, beer and whisky flow, there are presentations of traditional dancers, lute, violin and drummers playing Myanmar classical music and newly composed Red Cross songs.

The finale is a surprise even to me. A well-known Zawgyi, a magician, steps on stage with his assistants, two beautiful young girls in red and white satin costumes. He proceeds to pull ribbons from pockets and rabbits out of a hat, fashions flowers from a shower of confetti and makes various props disappear and reappear at will. Well fed and mellow after the week's work we are captivated by his act.

There's a pause, a drum roll. The girls set a black box on a low table after showing us that it's empty. Some wand waving by the Zawgyi, and with an impressive 'boom' the box shoots smoke into the air. He reaches in slowly, his expression expectant and pulls out a round capsule about the size of his palm. He places it on the table before reaching again, taking out a second capsule. He calls three MRCS staff on stage, standing them in a line behind him. Turning back to the audience, he opens the first capsule and with a flourish unfurls the yellow MRCS flag, giving it to the first and second helpers to hold. From the second, he pulls and dramatically flaps out the cross and crescent of the Federation, which he asks the second and third helpers to hold. We clap, recognising the emblems that unite us all.

The Zawgyi turns again, holding up his hands dramatically, black cape swirling, then plunges them back into the still smoking bowl. With a flourish, he pulls out a white dove and holds it high. We clap and nod our heads acknowledging the symbolism. With a simple, elegant gesture, he releases the dove. It circles above us twice then alights, resettling onto the Zawgyi's hand.

If only one could so magically and gracefully bring peace and prosperity to this troubled land. But perhaps even the small steps we have taken and the new resolve shown by the Myanmar Red Cross and their partners mark a beginning.

Chapter Twenty-Four
Marionettes and Collaint

Arts and crafts are synonymous with life in Myanmar. Life, in turn, is so closely intertwined with Buddhism that Buddhist devotion determines, in large part, the production of Burmese artisans and greatly influences their designs. Buddhism had become an integral part of Burmese life at least by the mid-fifth century: from then onward, objects were created which reflect not only the superb craftsmanship of artisans but also their fervent Buddhist beliefs.*

I was lucky to grow up in a family that fostered an appreciation of art, teaching us that even everyday objects can be beautiful in their simplicity. Every Sunday we visited my maternal grandparents and I still recall the smell of their house, a heady mix of roses and furniture polish, and hear the slow tick of the oak-cased grandfather clock.

**Burmese Design and Architecture*, published by Periplus Editions (HK) Ltd, 2000

Filled with treasures from round the world, we enjoyed playing with the ivory and wood mahjong tiles, sifting through boxes of strange foreign coins or placing torn rose petals on the plate of the brass kaleidoscope. I remember my grandmother showing me her intricately inlaid wooden tea-caddy and explaining its significance, a revelation that tea was once so precious.

My father had a passion for puppetry. As a child, I watched as he moulded and painted papier-mâché heads for his 'Punch and Judy' hand puppets. I sat with him behind the stage as he gave his shows at birthday parties and school fairs, proud to be the one who knew exactly when to hand him the next puppet so his performance could flow smoothly.

Later, he made marionettes—first, a graveyard setting capturing the essence of Saint-Saens' melancholy music 'Danse Macabre' with a hooded violinist, a line of ghosts and a skeleton which would come apart, each bone prancing unattached across the gravestones, until the cock crowed signalling the dawn. Then the Circus with a one-wheeled cyclist, a ringmaster, a seal flipping a ball off his nose and catching it again and, of course, a clown. Best of all though, was his line-up of four cancan girls, each with her own particular style and colouring—a brunette named Rosi, two blondes, Mimi and Lulu and black-haired Fifi. It took both of us to control them so their high kicks, one knee jointed, the other not, their turns and splits, timed to Offenbach's splendid music, were perfectly coordinated. I still have these puppets as well as several of his later carvings and bronzes, wonderful, lasting memories of him.

At university, I studied archaeology, the ancient peoples of Mesopotamia and China, the Aztecs and Polynesians, fascinated at how they all portrayed their beliefs through art, in the way they adorned themselves and their environment. Ancient languages, undecipherable but with beautiful calligraphy, drinking vessels, gem-encrusted jewellery, statues, intricate mosaics and burial chambers, all created by skilled artisans to enrich everyday life and honour status and religious beliefs.

Here in Myanmar, the wealth and great beauty of tradition is clear from the beginning, but it takes longer to understand the meaning of all I see. It is from my colleagues and friends that I gradually learn the history of its architecture and the different art forms.

Visiting pagodas in Yangon gives me an appreciation of the Buddha's *asana*, the positions. The standing, walking and cross-legged postures show the Buddha in a teaching or meditative state, while the reclining Buddha depicts his death and a celebration of his attainment of *nirvana*.

Equally significant are the *mudra*, hand poses, such as the raised right hand with the palm turned outwards signalling 'displaying no fear', while in the 'calling the earth to witness' the left hand rests in the lap and the right hand touches the ground. I also begin to recognize different styles, the historic period or the region of origin stamped on their features and comportment. The Bagan-style Buddha is usually heavy-set with broad shoulders and a large face. Images from the Mon tradition are slimmer, with fuller faces, downcast eyes and long ear-lobes while Rakhine figures have elaborate crowns. Buddha images in the most revered pagodas are so heavily coated in gold leaf that the original form is impossible to identify.

The gold leaf itself supports a trade. Packets of ten wafer thin gold leaves glued along one side between two squares of waxed brown paper are sold near pagoda complexes and pressing them onto a Buddha figure ensures that offered prayers and wishes will be heard. The leaves are made by skilled gold beaters, wielding heavy wooden mallets, who pound out a parchment wrapped 'clutch' of gold squares on a marble beating slab embedded in a block of wood. Their rhythmic thudding and rippling muscles as they repeatedly strike the leaves up to seventy times a minute, mesmerizes me.

I spend many hours exploring the busy alleyways of Bogyoke Aung San market, each section offering different merchandise—velvet slippers, gold and silver ornaments, gemstones, woodcarvings, paintings, lacquer ware, ceremonial clothing, and much more. Once the vendors recognize I am not just a passing tourist, they enjoy demonstrating the depth of their knowledge explaining the significance of the patterns on bolts of silk and cotton, the uses of different shaped bowls, the ceremonies for each elaborate costume or the different quality of their jade pieces. Many invite me to sit with them, sharing their sticky, sweet snacks or a tiny china cup of green tea.

Those not originally from Yangon describe their traditions and invariably ask me which of the longyis, with distinctive borders of flowers or coloured stripes I find the most attractive. I love the Kachin designs, a border of embroidered multi-coloured geometric shapes and buy several lengths of Kachin silk in soft green shot with bronze, sky blue with red and white embroidery and grey with a black pattern. A friend takes me to her dressmaker, an interesting, if somewhat embarrassing outing. After measuring my every curve and angle, my waist, bust and height, the seamstress hitches up my bra straps and casually remarks that if I am going to look good in my Myanmar outfit, I'd better do something about my less than perky breasts. A little shocked, but amused, I tell her I certainly intend to do so.

In other postings I've not worn the country's traditional dress, considering it somehow inappropriate, maintaining my own style with a few local touches—a piece of jewellery or a shawl. In Myanmar however, my staff has frequently asked me to wear their traditional dress. At first I wear readymade *longyis* with strings slotted through to hold them up and short sleeved matching blouses, but once I have the real thing, and a securely uplifted figure, I enjoy dressing up for meetings or ceremonies. A bright cotton longyi paired with a Red Cross t-shirt is also perfect for field trips, appreciated and commented upon by locals.

After a morning at the market, I often stop just outside at 'Zawgyi's Cafe', displaying the marionette magician from whom it takes its name, to enjoy a delicious mango lassie, coupled with a samosa or two.

I'm entranced with Burmese puppet theatre, its long tradition and role in the country's cultural, social and political life. Understanding how marionettes are manipulated, I am not only captivated by the stories, but also by the way the handlers, singers and musicians manage to create a special atmosphere that makes the marionettes come alive. Unlike western tradition, puppeteers in Myanmar are an integral part of the performance, their own movements, facial expressions, and gestures, mirroring those they project through the smaller figures on the stage.

Talking with the puppet masters, I learn that although stories differ from one theatre troupe to another, the cast of characters remains the same, twenty-eight being the accepted number. There are celestial beings, a hermit or monk, royal figures, always including a prince and princess, civil ministers, court attendants—a jester and the zawgyi, astrologers and ogres, mythical animals like the naga as well as elephants, tigers, monkeys and horses. The stories are usually known to the audience being based on Jakata religious stories, folklore or nat legends and the quality is judged not so much on the story but by the way it's performed.

"Rather like life in fact," I comment to the puppet handler who tells me this, "It's not only what you do, but the way in which you do it that is even more important."

I learn that, "In the past, Burmese marionettes enjoyed a rare and powerful privilege as speakers for both Kings and subjects. Never merely for entertainment, puppetry was a high art held in much esteem by all classes. Marionettes were a means of making people aware of current events; a medium for educating the masses in literature, history, religion; a display of life styles and customs. They also functioned as mouthpieces for the people in the days of royalty, tiny hands in state and social affairs. These *yoke-thei* (small dolls) enjoyed greater freedom of speech, dress and movement that live performers."*

I decorate my house with these traditional items or gift them to friends who appreciate their beauty and meaning. I buy a set of 'opium' weights, tiny brass hinthe, mythical birds, in graded sizes encased in their wooden box, also holding the slender balancing rod and two shallow bowls slotted into the lid. Traditional sets were made with chinthe or karaweik, the mythical ducks, but more modern versions often depict elephants or other animals. The name 'opium weights' has stuck, although in fact, these weights have long been used to measure all kinds of goods, including currency, the ancient weight system translated for buyers into the more universal terminology of ounces or grams.

On a work trip to Sagaing Division I buy another boxed treasure at a morning market, a segmented hollow brass tool used for tattooing with accompanying accordion-folded parabeik, the parchment booklet

---

The Illusion of Life, Ma Thanegi, White Orchid Press, Bangkok, 1994

detailing its use and the more common designs—mythical beings with the power to conquer enemies, attract admiration or love, improve bodily beauty or increase luck. The long stylus looks lethal and conjures up images of pain and initiation rites, but it's a really good conversation starter when friends spy it in my living room.

In a pagoda complex in Mandalay I acquire several flat, double sided kyeyzi chimes, the holiest of the Burmese bells, used by monks and lay people alike when meditating or chanting, at funerals or collecting donations. Held by a cord looped through the rounded top, its flared edges give a high pitched 'ting' when flicked with a fingernail, the sound resonating until the spinning slows and stops. I hang one by my desk and if I have difficulty preparing a presentation or report, flick it gently and close my eyes, relaxing, until the sound disappears into silence. Invariably, it helps me find the phrase I am seeking.

I become friends with the delightful sisters who own the 33rd Street Lacquer Shop and they teach me about the intricate ancient techniques required to perfect a piece of lacquerware.

The making of *yun*, lacquer, is certainly among the many great artistic achievements of Myanmar, the most delicate and desirable pieces created in the dry heat of Bagan. My favourites are the simple cups, green, red or black, etched with coloured designs or decorated with gold leaf. Light and flexible, their foundation is of finely interwoven bamboo and horsehair. The inner layer of delicate forms such as bowls and trays are in split bamboo, while soft wood is used for boxes, large bowls, small folding tables or screens. The largest pieces are made of more solid wood, often teak.

Each piece is sealed by a coat of lacquer mixed with clay and put into a specially designed cellar for up to ten days. Smoothing and polishing comes next, the work mostly done by hand using a simple lathe and pumice stone, before another sealing layer is added and the still uncompleted form put back into the cellar. This procedure is repeated as many as seven or eight times before the item is deemed smooth enough. Finally, the object is given a coat of fine, glossy lacquer. The decoration follows this lengthy process—stories of the Buddha, signs of the zodiac or days of the week, patterns of leaves and flowers.

Among the objects most often bought by collectors are the 'betel boxes.' These wide cylindrical boxes have ornately decorated lids which reveal three trays—a deep bottom tray for the betel leaves, a smaller tray containing dried tobacco, and in the topmost shallow tray, tiny containers for lime, sliced areca nut, cloves and some other ingredients.

Soon after I move into my house, I discover the lively local contemporary art scene. The rainy season has ended and we're enjoying cooler temperatures and clear blue skies. I cycle to the nearest tourist hotel, the 'Nikkei', my mind set on a leisurely afternoon under a parasol by the pool. Passing through the lobby, I'm stopped in my tracks by a line of easels displaying paintings, a poster announcing the opening of an art exhibition for the following evening. Through an open door I see a hive of activity, partitions in construction, lengths of coloured silk draped, paintings hung, moved and re-positioned, spotlights installed and tested.

Approaching the man who appears in charge, I enquire about the event. I learn that he, U Myint Soe, is the organizer and one of the artists and that the small gallery on this side corridor is his. He leads me into the exhibition hall to show me one of his paintings, still not quite dry. It's a beautiful beach scene, the thick oil, partly applied with palette knife, re-creating the texture of the foaming waves and adding depth to the clouds and distant fishing boats, the figure of a lone fisherman in the foreground. I admire his talent and we talk for a while before he returns to supervising his team and I to spend my afternoon at the pool as planned. The following evening I return to make my first purchase, a trio of paintings, in bright, almost cartoon style showing the most important features of Yangon, Mandalay and Bagan. They find their place in my living room behind the sofa.

Over the next months I seek out other exhibitions and galleries. I make friends with Vicki and Peter at the Golden Valley Art Gallery, admiring the fine watercolours on display. I also love to visit Bogie's studio. He specializes in abstract paintings with a twist, using mainly oils but creating interest and texture by the introduction of crinkled tissue paper or muslin, a technique he terms 'collaint,' to describe the mix of paint and collage.

Over the following years I meet more artists and my admiration for their work grows. For many the financial rewards are few, but their passion remains steadfast. Most study in a master's atelier, sometimes joining an elite group with a common style, partly because it's the tradition but also because university courses have not been available for years. From the masters they learn the history and tradition of art but, increasingly, many experiment with new techniques and materials to express more contemporary tastes and individual styles.

The modern school of painting emerged in the thirties with the incoming influences from the west, in art as well as in literature and political thought. It is only from this time, for example, that the concept of perspective can be seen in paintings. However, the four main themes—sacred places and religious life, portraits, daily life, and landscapes—remain a constant in contemporary, as well as in traditional art.

As my passion for contemporary art grows, the idea of pursuing it after my retirement becomes more attractive. However, the transition to this as a new career occurs suddenly, events once again moving quickly, complicating my life a little.

Spending Christmas in Northern Thailand, with my friends Lasse and Sommai, they tell me they have decided to open an Art Gallery in Chiang Mai focussing on South East Asian Contemporary Art and ask me to join them in this new venture. Excited, we spend a few furious days over New Year planning and plotting. Before I return to Yangon in early January we have already signed a lease on a building along the Ping River, set a date for the opening in March and Lasse has found the name—La Luna Gallery.

During the next weeks, back in Myanmar, I spend every spare moment visiting artists and galleries, selecting and buying paintings and preparing the written 'profiles' for each of the chosen artists. In constant contact with Lasse and Sommai, I follow the progress on the renovation and discuss everything from the website to marketing plans, from our gallery colours and design to prices.

When I join them in Chiang Mai for the opening in March, I am laden with tubes of rolled paintings and boxes of lacquerware. My active role in the gallery is still limited, as I am fully committed to my job with the Red Cross. Fuller involvement will have to wait until I retire and move to Chiang Mai.

Whenever I can, over the next two years, I seek out new artists, increasing my understanding of contemporary art. In response, happy to have a new showplace for their art, many more Myanmar artists, both established and emerging, contact me to offer their artwork or ask how they can exhibit their work. Almost by accident I become an art dealer.

The concept of 'retirement' thus begins to take on a whole new meaning and I find myself well on the way to a brand new chapter in my life. The thought that gives me most pleasure, despite my love for art and sharing the work of Myanmar artists with a wider community, is that this new occupation will involve my coming back to Myanmar often, allowing me to spend time with my old friends and colleagues in this country I love.

Chapter Twenty-Five
Naga New Year

In my last year in Myanmar, I am invited by friends to participate in the New Year festival of the Naga tribes, held annually mid-January. I jump at this rare and sought after opportunity. Told it will be cold in the far north in the winter, I borrow as many warm clothes from colleagues as I am able, buy an extra battery for my camera and seek out stories and facts about the peoples and their culture.

I learn that the Naga live on the border between India and Myanmar. Recent statistics number them at three million, two hundred thousand of whom, accounting for ten of the forty-five tribes, live in Myanmar, mainly in Sagaing Division, in the Patkwai Mountains, west of the Chindwin. There is a decades-long strong revolutionary movement of the Naga peoples in India to gain their independence or at least to become an autonomous state. This struggle continues.

"Traditionally, the Naga are tribally organized, with a strong warrior tradition. Villages are sited on hilltops and until the end of the 19th Century made frequent armed raids on the plains below. Although tribes exhibit some variation, considering the diversity in their languages and traditional practices, there are many similarities, most having a similar dress code, eating habits, customs, traditional laws etc. However, one trait that sets them apart from other groups in the region is their head hunting custom, prevalent at one time in Nagaland and among the Naga tribes in Myanmar.

In what has now become an annual event, Naga groups from both sides of the Indian/Myanmar border gather in the high mountains of N.E. Myanmar in January to celebrate their Kaing-Bi or New Year Festival. In the past, festivals were a high point in the lives of the Naga, a welcome break in the monotony of a life mostly spent tending to slash-and-burn agricultural activities. After the arrival of Christianity in the late 19th Century, many festivals were banned because of their association with the old animist religion. The creation of a national festival from 1990 has proved attractive, allowing some welcome celebration, entertainment and recreation before the new agricultural season starts."*

My teeth are chattering and my feet are numb. My arms are wrapped tightly around my body, my shawl-wrapped head tucked into the collar of my jacket. I'm freezing. We left Yangon at dawn. It's now past midnight, another mountain pass ahead of us before we reach Lahe, the venue of this year's New Year Festival, held on the fourteenth and fifteenth of January.

Well after one in the morning, our truck shudders to a stop by a small wooden building, a banner 'Welcome to Lahe' over the door. We climb down stiffly, relieved to be out of the blasting cold wind, able to move our limbs again. Our luggage unloaded, the truck drives off, the sound of its engine receding until all we hear is the stamp of our feet on the gravel.

A well-wrapped woman comes out to welcome our small group—Anna and Morris, teaching friends from Yangon and myself. We're the last. She checks our names on her clipboard and hands us two keys. Pulling her blanket tightly around her, she points out the way to our rooms, wishing us good

---

* *The Naga of Burma*, J. D. Saul, Bangkok, Orchid Press, 2005

night, and steps back into her hut, firmly closing the door.

We look at each other, smiling ruefully, glad to have finally arrived. The moon shines faintly through the clouds and I'm pleased I put my torch in my pocket at the last stop before the final wild ride. We follow our directions, the moonlight outlining huts linked by paths, marked by white stones. A couple of lampposts cast circles of light around their base and near the second one a sign points to rooms 12,13, and 14—ours. Anna and Morris have the biggest room and I take the small one at the back. The bare light-bulb reveals bamboo walls reaching down to the packed earth floor, a thatched roof and a wide bamboo bed with a thin mattress, two pillows, and a Chinese padded quilt.

Taking off my shoes, I put on just about everything else I possess and climb into bed, rolling myself in a ball and pulling the quilt up over my head, still cold, but slowly beginning to thaw out. My mind wanders, back over the trip—the little plane from Mandalay bumping down onto the dirt airstrip at Hkamti, bright pink bougainvillea bushes either side. The busy riverside, boats coming and going, women washing, children playing by their side. The boat ride down the Chindwin to Sinthe, its impressive two-storey houses with thatched roofs, woven split-bamboo walls, wooden frames and porches. Our 'luck' at getting the Landrover, just the three of us perched in the back, wedged in with our luggage and assorted boxes going to Lahe. Then the breakdown an hour later. The other trucks laden with tourists chugging past us while we waited for another ride, gazing at the forest-clad mountains, the late afternoon sun turning the tall pampas grass to gold. In the half light, a boy soldier appeared out of nowhere, to sit with us, and the joy in his face as Anna, taking a couple of balloons from her bag, blowing, squeezing and twisting them under his alert gaze to fashion a dog for him. He waved, a gun in one hand and a pink balloon dog in the other, when we boarded our new truck to begin the climb up roads hacked out of the mountainside and across makeshift bridges over deep gullies. Then the second break down. A third truck finally arriving and how very, very cold it was in the back.

I knew it would be colder, but in the heat of Yangon it was hard to imagine just how much. I'd borrowed as many warm clothes as possible, a jacket here, a woollen jersey there and thick socks. Clearly not enough, are my last thoughts as I slide into sleep.

I awake with the sun in my eyes, Anna calling through the wall to ask if I'm awake. Dressed, a quick clean up, and I am ready for anything, but especially a cup of coffee.

Today we relax, finding our way around. We climb to the viewpoint, to survey circling streets and meandering river, a school with its playing fields and the arena spread out below us. Beyond, winding paths disappearing through the trees, small villages, just wisps of smoke and thatched rooftops and row upon row of forest-clad mountains. The air is fresh and invigorating, the sun burning off the morning mist, warming my back and shoulders.

Down in the arena we wander among tourists, locals and the few Naga groups already present, entering canvas and bamboo booths set up along the perimeter, displaying regional produce, posters on farming techniques, health advice and Naga traditions. Most of the locals are in artfully draped red and black blankets, the loose end thrown over their shoulder. Some are striped, others have circles of shells or seeds or beautifully embroidered warriors, crossed spears, crouching tigers, and oxen. Children, many with runny noses, gummy eyes, grimy faces and hands, dart about, excited and curious, their antics drawing smiles from the tourists or reprimands from their families. Many girls and a few boys carry younger siblings on their back but still manage to run with the others.

We watch a line of young women with waist looms deftly plying their shuttles and threads weaving colourful shawls. They all wear bright lipstick and thanakha, their hair elaborately braided, decorated with flowers. Each has a geometric tattoo on her forehead and five or seven lines etched vertically between the lips and chin.

From time to time, beating drums signal the arrival of another group into the arena. We watch in awe as first the men and then the women enter at a jog through the arched gateway. The men, holding high their dao or machete, whooping as they circle the arena, muscles rippling, red bamboo hats festooned with boar tusks and hornbill feathers, tiger claws or teeth-studded jawbones around their necks and decorated cloth panels below their waist. The women, simply dressed in long skirts, with woven hairbands and coloured necklaces follow demurely, with gliding steps and sinuous undulating movements. Their energy is impressive, considering most have travelled for several days to take part in the Kaing-Bi, stopping just outside town to don their full costumes. Each will try to outdo the others in style and ceremony, and old rivalries will be revived in athletic competitions and rituals rather than the raids and wars of the not so distant past—the last recorded headhunt still recent, in the early sixties. As the men show off their power and ferocity, I wonder how many remember and regret, those glorious days.

A constant stream of people flows through the town, selling, showing off their costumes, meeting old friends and enjoying the day away from normal chores. Most of the women have the same tattooed lozenge on their brow and chin stripes, the men sport shell earrings with human figures burnt into them, proudly showing off their finery and their heritage. Young girls gather to try out jewellery at a stall hung with strings of coloured beads, earrings and bracelets, posing and preening in front of the mirrors, choosing just the right piece to complete their costume, perhaps to catch a young warrior's eye.

In the afternoon, we take a path into the hills to visit the smaller villages. We pass women carrying huge baskets of firewood or bamboo tubes of locally brewed rice wine, the weight supported by woven straps across their forehead. In a small hamlet, several women with white and sky-blue feather earrings, black tops with strings of red beads, long black skirts striped green, pink and white, are holding hands in a circle and singing. They are beautiful to watch as they practice their intricate steps.

In a larger village, bamboo fences enclose thatched houses, some with buffalo horns above the doorway, chickens and pigs cluck and snuffle as we pass and children appear through gateways to follow our meandering path. When we stop, they surround us and Anna pulls more balloons from her backpack, blowing and twisting them into an animal shape as they watch wide-eyed. She hands it to a small boy, lines of stubble on his head, the result of a haircut with a dull razor. Soon they're all clamouring for one. Morris and I wander off to watch a man weaving a circular fishing net, laid out on the ground. He circles it, squatting on his heels, intertwining and knotting the thin cord, slowly enlarging the net loop by loop.

Back at our bungalows, the sun disappearing behind the mountains, the chill in the air forecasts a cold evening ahead. We join the queue in the public washing area, where huge vats are slung over blazing fires, to receive a bucket full of steaming, hot water. In my cubicle, I pour half into another bucket, adding dippers of cold water from a barrel to find the perfect temperature. Clean and in several layers of clothes, I'm ready for the evening.

After dinner, we walk through town to the school, where groups of people sit around fires, putting last touches to their costumes, drinking small cups of rice wine. A few are rather more lively, particularly a couple of young men, one with a wide woven hat and a sheepskin cloak, the other with a dried monkey's face on his head, high on rice wine or something stronger, their eyes glazed and dark, their wild dance uncoordinated and jerky.

The following morning I wake early. Today is the real beginning of the festival. Around mid-morning we join the throngs heading to the arena for the raising of the New Year Pole. The warriors carry in the long bamboo pole, a woven lattice thickening its lower end, some holding onto it, others simply pacing alongside. Chanting and shouting they reach the far end of the arena, and then drop it into the pre-dug hole, levering it up until it's standing straight. Its slender top is curved, a cloth bundle painted with a white skull, representing an enemy head, dangling from the end. Branches protrude from the sides, tipped with bamboo circles hung with short lengths of cane, their sweet tinkling resonating in the wind. Soft chanting fills the air as groups of women, enter in a dancing line, weaving their way across the field to join the men. Clusters of coloured balloons are released, floating away until just tiny dots in the sky.

We then head with the crowd to the morung, the drum house, on a hill overlooking the arena where a long hollowed-out log drum is housed in the open-sided thatched hut. An elder beats out a rhythm, lines of warriors standing either side with wooden dumb-bell shaped batons. They echo the beat, which rises and falls, faster then slower, soft then loud, constantly changing, challenging the drummers to follow its sequences in unison.

Outside, groups initiate circling dances on the terraced hillsides, women following the beat on wood-framed skin drums carried over their shoulder, men tapping out the rhythm with pacing feet and on brass gongs. The hillsides shimmer to the beat of the log drum, the morning sunlight glinting off the heavy brass and silver jewellery—necklaces, bracelets, arm and leg bands.

Games and competitions begin in the afternoon, the finals to be played out on the following day—racing, spear throwing, long jumping, wrestling, marching; some are good humoured matches, others more competitive, evidence of old, more blood-thirsty rivalries. In the evening the Naga youth dance in the arena, traditional mixed with modern, music blasted out through huge speakers.

On New Year's Day, we're up early to secure our place. The mist still hangs over the valley as we jockey for a good position with hundreds of other spectators, tourists and locals alike.

At first, we hear only faint chanting which slowly grows louder until the leading group appears from a corner, moving towards us at a fast pace, conical red hats, waving feathers and red tassels on the dao handles dipping and swaying in perfect unison. Despite everything we've seen over these past few days, nothing could have prepared us for the magnificent sight and sound of the thirty or so Naga groups arriving together.

As they approach, the sun glints on the gleaming curve of boar tusks above either ear, highlighting the woven leg bands and the red and black goat's hair fringes on their spears. Other warrior groups enter, hats topped with black fur, black tunics crossed with grey sashes, thick red bead necklaces, shining brass gongs hanging from their waistbands. Then blue shirts, black and red woven tunics and aprons decorated with rows of white cowrie shells, then again bamboo hats heightened by bright feather crests. The shouted chanting reverberates as the energy of the relentless stream of warriors surrounds and captivates us.

After the men, come the women, swaying to the men's stamping rhythm and picking up the chant, lighter voices sweetening the moment, their beaded costumes colourful, glances demure as they enter. Some are all in black, others in orange or white tops with darker skirts, many cloaked in tartan or striped blankets, only their woven headbands and earrings setting them apart from other groups. The men settle on the benches to the right, the women on the left, a narrow corridor separating the warriors from the maidens.

Following speeches from local Naga chiefs and government representatives, awards are handed to participating groups, elaborate trophies and sacks of rice. I circle behind the warriors, entranced by the light shining through the hundreds of black and white striped hornbill feathers adorning the men's hats. Beyond, decorating the stage of the official party, twenty flags with the red and blue colours of Myanmar are illuminated by the rising sun.

Young men and women take turns presenting Naga history and rituals, the crowd applauding loudly at the most dramatic moments. As the sun climbs and the day warms up, first the men, then the women perform their dances. The arena is bright with colour and movement, the crowd voicing its delight. Afterwards, many of the participants, standing tall and proud in their elaborate costumes, history and tradition visibly weighing on their shoulders, pose for photos.

At sunset we join groups hunkered down on blankets, eating and drinking. The arena has been cleared and at the centre is a huge stack of wood, criss-crossed logs at the base, branches intertwined above. Music blasting from the speakers, and rice wine drunk in impressive quantities, adds to the merriment and spontaneity of the crowd and many perform their own inebriated spinning dances, children clapping and laughing with them.

Suddenly, the music stops. An impressive, expectant silence falls. A Naga chief stands alone on the stage. He lights a hanging ball at the end of a long rope sending it swinging to ignite the pyramid of wood. A roar of approval rises from the crowd as the flames and sparks from the bonfire fly into the night sky.

Lights sweep the area as group after group of warriors and women begin to circle the fire, dancing, at first slowly and sedately then more and more furiously, their chanting building to a shouting crescendo. The women weave and sway, the men hold hands, stepping and jumping together, at times in a whole group, their feet several inches off the ground. As the bonfire begins to collapse into itself, the last dance is performed and the crowd flows into the arena, joining the costumed groups, a billowing, stamping, laughing mass of people.

Fireworks explode, a last blaze of colour illuminating this magical scene, marking the start of another year in the lives of the Naga of Myanmar.

Linking arms as we return to our bungalow, the tang of smoke still lingering in the air, Anna, Morris, and I all agree that we'll not easily forget the privilege of having witnessed the *Kaing-bi*, one of the few remaining festivals of the impressive Naga peoples.

Chapter Twenty-Six
Down in the Delta

26 December 2004 (CNN.com)—Earthquake Triggers Deadly Tsunami— The world's most powerful earthquake in more than 40 years struck deep under the Indian Ocean on December 26, triggering massive tsunamis that obliterated cities, seaside communities and holiday resorts, killing tens of thousands of people in a dozen countries.

I'm in Chiang Mai for Christmas, staying with Lasse and Sommai, enjoying a few days working together in La Luna. On Boxing Day morning, lazily reading in bed, I register the tremor of an earthquake, not uncommon in this region. We discuss where the epicentre could be over breakfast, but as the local news doesn't mention it, we head to the gallery as planned.

An accomplished journalist and a Red Crosser like me, Lasse is on the alert for further details and logs onto the international news channels.

As the chilling news begins to flood in, we listen and watch, horrified at the destruction spreading out from Aceh in Indonesia to Phuket and beyond, the tsunami sweeping across the Indian Ocean. The scale of the disaster is of epic proportions. My thoughts fly home to Myanmar. How badly has its coastline been hit? Are my staff and friends safe? Has Yangon been affected by surges up the river? I need to get back as soon as I can. I call, repeatedly, but can't contact the delegation or the MRCS. Imagining the worst, I book a seat on the first plane to Yangon.

I try again to get through to Heikki, in charge while I'm away. He's scheduled to spend Christmas with his partner Elena at Ngapali, and I'm worried the tsunami may have reached that far north. I know he planned to return today but am not sure when. If Ngapali has been affected, then the delta in the south with its low-lying islands and channels, will have been devastated. By evening all the news channels are broadcasting the scale of the disaster. Video links from Aceh and Phuket are shocking, but there's little news of Myanmar. Worried, I continue calling Heikki. Finally around ten, he answers.

"Heikki, is everyone ok? What's the situation in Yangon? How bad is it in the delta? And the Thaninthayi coast, near Phuket?" my questions come in a rush.

"Joanna, no worries, we are fine," he responds. "We flew in an hour ago. A Finnish colleague just called to ask if we are OK, but we knew nothing about it. Everything seems normal here. Elena is switching on the TV now." I hear the muted tones of a TV announcer, and Heikki, despite his many years of disaster response experience, exclaiming shocked, "My God, we had no idea."

I tell him I'll be there tomorrow, asking him to gather as much information as possible from the MRCS and other organizations on the ground. "I'm on it," he tells me, and I know he's the best person for the job right now.

Calmer now, I ask about his few days at Ngapali. He tells me they had noticed the tide receding farther and the stronger incoming waves that morning but hadn't thought anything of it. The previous evening, dining beachside, they had seen small bursts of fire out at sea a few kilometres off shore. As they watched, one of the locals told them, "The dragon is restless, he is angry at being disturbed." Geologists would later explain these fireballs as gas emissions from volcanic vents, activated by the movement of the tectonic plates.

In Yangon, we have our work cut out. My key role is in co-ordination and communications—chairing meetings twice daily at first, then daily, with representatives of other international organizations. We pool information, look at needs and agree on who is best placed to provide support and logistics in specific situations. UNICEF, Save the Children and Medecins du Monde who have projects in the Delta and the islands, provide additional information to that received through our MRCS channels. Time consuming, but important are the daily updates transmitted to Bangkok and Geneva, so that data for the whole devastated region is pooled and shared with sister National Societies ensuring the creation of vital global links. Information on what is required and what is donated is crucial to assess needs and how they can be met.

More time consuming but also important are the phone calls, particularly with the media requesting facts and figures, stories from the disaster area, details of our operations, all to be related with brevity, clarity, conviction and compassion. It's a challenge, as initially we are besieged by reporters claiming that the Government is hiding the real situation in Myanmar. Again and again I tell them that, based on independent surveys, our findings are of the same scope and scale as those reported by the Ministry of Relief and Resettlement, that Myanmar was spared major damage, except in the delta region, with less than one hundred killed, although many injured and between 5,000 and 10,000 were made homeless.

From day one, Heikki and his team work alongside our MRCS colleagues to manage the bids, purchases, packing, hiring of trucks and boats to move all available supplies down to the Delta, maintaining regular communication with the local RC teams. Sandy and her finance group work wonders, informing donors how best to send money and persuading the bank to allow us speedy access to our donations.

The outpouring of generosity from local individuals and companies who donate money, sacks of rice, *longyis*, blankets and other needed items, is overwhelming. We clear a corner of the lobby, put up a Red Cross flag and print 'Appreciation Certificates' so everyone has a chance to shake the hand of one of our team, receive a certificate and have their photo taken. A small, but important token of gratitude.

Heikki and I spend a long day at the airport coordinating operations for the arrival of two chartered planes, one with tents, tarpaulins and other supplies from German Red Cross, the other from the Canadian Red Cross who drop off a load of collapsible plastic jerry cans before heading on to Sri Lanka.

The days and weeks pass quickly, our team working well with the MRCS staff and volunteers. We move as fast as we're able to bring help for the affected individuals and communities, providing food and household necessities, construction materials, health care and safe drinking water for approximately 15,000 people. Later, we assist with the building of fishing boats and provision of new fishing nets, and organise community-based disaster management workshops.

Ultimately, I remember telling people that in this particular instance, Myanmar was twice lucky—firstly because the damage was less than it might have been, and secondly because they received so much assistance from the outpouring of global compassion.

By the end of March, after several hectic weeks, the emergency response phase is coming to a close, the operation moving into rehabilitation and rebuilding. We have time to focus on longer-term planning and provide reports for donors, feedback for all the help sent from across the world. The MRCS want to check on the operation and show support to their on-the-ground teams, so a mission is organized to the Ayeyarwady Delta for two of their senior staff, U Soe Thein and U Kyaw Soe. Joining them are Patrik, my deputy, myself, and two colleagues from Bangkok and Geneva. Maude is the Regional Information Delegate from Bangkok, who is reporting on the Tsunami operation across South East Asia, and Yoshi, a photographer with long Red Cross experience, to document the effects of the Tsunami and the impact of relief operations.

Few foreigners get a chance to travel to the lower reaches of the delta where numerous braided channels form islands and sandbars, discharging their waters into the sea at the 'Mouths of the Ayeyarwady'. The only way to travel there is by boat. After a long drive from Yangon we reach Laputta where the local team welcome us on board a shabby but sturdy wooden vessel. It has a large square cabin up front, a smaller cabin, doubling as a kitchen, at the back and storage and sleeping quarters for the crew on a lower level. It will be our home for three days.

The following day we set out through the channels, meandering past green islands and rice fields. Further south, the channels become wider, clay banks bordered with rough scrub, the occasional palm trees farther and farther apart. Small settlements and villages straggle along the river's edge, fishing boats go about their daily tasks.

Sitting in the prow, Patrik and I explain to Maude and Yoshi how the operation was implemented, elaborating on the more challenging aspects of working here. In return they share stories of their visits to other, more damaged countries. Maude tells of her days in Phuket right after the disaster when so many lives were lost or totally devastated. The importance of identifying bodies and listing the missing and dead, of finding shelter, clothes and food for the homeless, of organizing phone calls for stranded tourists and working with embassies to obtain their travel papers and flights home.

Aware of the many illegal workers from Myanmar in Phuket we ask how they were accounted and cared for, reports seldom mentioning them. Maude recounts how a hotel owner refused to identify a young man whose body was found caught between trees, even though his torn white waiter's jacket had the name of the hotel clearly embroidered on the chest. The death toll inside Myanmar had not been so great, but no one will ever know how many of their countrymen and women lost their lives in neighbouring Thailand. Only the families will mourn in silence, not wanting it known by the authorities that one of their own had crossed the border seeking a better life. We fall into contemplation, our silence broken only by the rhythmic splashing of waves against the hull.

After overnighting in a small fishing village we are off at the glimmer of dawn the next morning.

The sun rises over the estuary picking out small thatched houses on spindly supports, nets hung to dry over bamboo fences. We make our way past small canoes taking children to school and produce to markets and larger canoes heading out to sea for a day of fishing, catching the breeze with their sails of stitched rice sacks or faded longyis patched together.

We reach Kaing Thaung, a village built on little more than a sand spit, harbouring lines of wooden fishing boats, their high stern cabins in bright colours—blue and turquoise, green and yellow, red and blue. The boats, moored loosely on high posts, managed to ride out the waves as the mangroves and heavy vegetation along the outer banks of the sandbar took the full force of the incoming swells, saving much of the village and partly sheltering the villagers from harm.

We step off the dingy carrying us in from our boat and are saluted by a line of young Red Cross volunteers, fresh in their white and blue uniforms, behind them, rice sacks ready for distribution. Their group leader shyly tells us what they did to help after the waves had passed and what else is needed in their village. Many still recall the screams from the fishermen working offshore shouting "Run! Run! A black wall is coming". Eight people perished in the waves, three of them children.

There is really nowhere to run should there be another tsunami, but people cope in their own way. They've begun to dump broken red bricks and stones mixed with garbage along a section of the beach, so little by little a barrier is being built. Our MRCS colleagues agree to supply concrete blocks to enhance the barrier, the villagers asking when they'll arrive, concerned that it could happen again. Sixty-eight families who lost their houses will have to relocate to the mainland. They're sad to leave their village but tell us having a home is most important, life has to go on.

The school has been washed away, but teaching continues, the children sitting in rows on piles of bricks and planks under a tree. Makeshift houses are little more than a split bamboo floor and criss-crossed bamboo sticks covered in bright pink, blue, red plastic sheeting courtesy of Red Cross emergency packs. Cooking is over open fires and many ceramic water jars are overturned or broken so there is no way of storing fresh water, a real problem. The delta has brackish estuaries and it rains for only a few months each year. Most of the 'water' boats plying the delta to bring tanks of fresh water, have been damaged or destroyed in the tsunami and the monsoon is still a couple of months away. A black and white cat stands on the lip of one of the still standing water jars, its sleek body and white whiskers perfectly reflected in the still water.

A few women wait by the sagging corrugated iron and wood building that was the Red Cross office until it was swamped. In a small ceremony they are gifted a sack of rice and an envelope with twenty thousand Kyat, the equivalent of twenty US dollars. Each of us takes a turn to hand over an envelope and shake a hand, rewarded with shy smiles. The local volunteers tell us these women, most of whom have lost their husbands, are from the most needy families of the village and the extra support will make a world of difference for them. It seems so inadequate for their needs, but they are grateful.

At the headman's house, seated on a raised platform facing the sandy street, we witness the handover of foodstuffs, family packs, school supplies and new first aid and emergency packs for the Red Cross team. Sipping glasses of lukewarm soda as he gives a long speech of thanks, we gaze at the children peering at the supplies through a fence of latticed branches, a line of equally inquisitive women behind.

In the early afternoon heat we visit a building site further up the estuary, where a new village, Thit Poke, is rising from a square of flat land either side of a newly carved road. This is where the families will relocate and a hundred and forty-three houses are being built. The Myanmar government is supplying the housing material, the World Food Programme (WFP) is taking on local carpenters as part of a food for work initiative, while the MRCS is to provide the community's latrines. Women carry planks on their heads from a cargo boat anchored at the bank to the new site, others carrying them further down the road. In every house, lines of men hammer in rhythm as they lay the floorboards. The donation of building materials is enough for this community. The work, the people do for themselves.

Down another channel of the delta we visit a school, with solid concrete buildings. This is where we're to spend the night. We meet a shy young volunteer and the older woman, Daw Khin San, she escorted from a neighbouring village, the place we'll visit tomorrow, the hardest hit on this coastline. She tells how young children were brought to her after the waves had washed over the beach and through the mangroves. She had taken a Red Cross First Aid course about thirty years previously and thought she had forgotten everything, but when a young girl was brought to her unconscious and feared dead, she acted automatically.

"It all just came back," she tells us solemnly, "I remembered to tilt the head back to open the airways, put my mouth over the nose and mouth, blow quick shallow breaths and watch if the chest rose. When I saw that, I carried on breathing into the child. I was almost ready to give up, when she spluttered and took a breath. It was a miracle." Daw Kin San in fact saved three lives that day, although she was not able to resuscitate two other children. We thank her and tell her we look forward to meeting her again the next day when we visit her village.

It's a long time since I slept in a school dormitory but, after a congenial meal with the crew and school teachers we bunk down in a row of beds, our privacy as flimsy as the mosquito nets hung over each bed.

In the morning, we travel in a convoy on motorbikes, weaving our way along dusty tracks and on rice field banks. Sweat trickles down my spine, sticking my t-shirt to my back where my camera bag thuds against my body. Passing through the village, we carry on, reaching a small settlement on the beach, just behind the mangroves, seawater swishing in rhythmically. These are seasonal migrant fishermen and their families, the Rohingya, stateless for decades, pushed back and forth between Bangladesh and Myanmar, living in camps and scattered settlements along the Rakhine Coast and in the delta.

We meet fourteen-year old, Naing Lin Tun, and with him the little girl he saved—Aye Mar. This slight young man ran the race of his life to bring her to the village clinic where he believed she could be brought back to life. As the waters of the tsunami receded, he found her in a clump of sodden muddy grass by a twisting stone path, surrounded by mangroves and brown water. Breathless, he tells us his story.

"I couldn't see if she was breathing but I checked her pulse and felt it.

I knew I must act fast so just lifted her on my shoulder and went as fast as I could." Finding a motorized trolley he placed her carefully on the flatbed and took off, a chaotic three-kilometre ride through the forest to deliver her into the hands of Daw Khin San where he watched a miracle happen. He points to the blue trolley, now back by the beach. Its registration number is painted in large white numbers along the side—007. To me, he's far more of a hero than any fictional secret agent.

The fishermen ask us to join them for a meal of biscuits and bananas, rice and fish, then the group sings to us. These stoical people have weathered storms of nature and politics and yet still offer the little they have to others. I sense a renewed complicity between the fishermen and the nearby village, knowing the Tsunami did not recognize the differences in race or religion and neither did those who acted to rescue and help others.

That afternoon, in another village, we walk along the beach to see the damage wrought by the tsunami. Houses lean dangerously on their supports, coconut palms sheared off a few metres from the ground, hulls of broken boats listing drunkenly along the shoreline. But what takes our breath away, showing the full force of the waves, is the stupa. Uprooted and thrown far from its base, it now sits alone, right at the water edge, its filigree *hti* intact and its white paint still bright.

After dinner in the village, we spend the night on the boat, lulled by the rocking and slap of the waves on the hull. While we sleep, the tide turns, and we journey further out to another island, the last of the villages on our itinerary.

Awaking at our destination, we visit the monastery first. Climbing to the upper floor, we sit cross-legged on the worn linoleum to talk with the head monk. He tells us of how the villagers ran for shelter, some to the monastery, others to the other side of the island as they saw the 'Black Wall' approaching. Several were marooned on a wooden bridge some two hundred metres from the sea, the swirling, rumbling brown waters pulling at their legs.

That evening, we stroll along the seashore, the gently lapping water a picture of calm and innocence, but for many, a constant reminder of their loss and their fear.

A young volunteer shyly asks Maude if he could have a photo of her. She takes one from her wallet and gives it to him. He looks at it, then smiles his thanks. He too gets out his wallet and places it carefully in the worn brown leather, completely empty save for the photo. Perhaps he will take it with him as a talisman into other disaster operations in the coming years, offering his energy and experience to his community.

We leave as the sun is setting, warm pinks and gold rays reflected in the sea, palm trees black and stark against the silhouette of the village. Everyone follows us down to our boat to stand at the water's edge. As we release the cable, the children dive and jump in, water slick on their wet hair, clothes glued to their bodies, chasing us for the first few metres, waving and calling out their farewell.

In spite of everything the people in this vast Delta have suffered and lost, everywhere we have been, they have given what they could—a drink here, a fruit there, a cat to stroke, a child to hug. We have seen laughter and pain, real need, but also an acceptance of the reality of their lives and above all, an immense generosity.

Chapter Twenty-Seven
The Kidnap

"The most important moment in the life of a young Burmese boy is his *shin-pyu*, his initiation as a novice in the order of monks. Until a Buddhist has gone through the shin-pyu ceremony, he is regarded as being no better than an animal. To become 'human', he must for a time withdraw from secular life, following the example of the Buddha when he left his family to seek enlightenment. Unlike his illustrious predecessor, the novice will carry his alms bowl for only a short period, then return to his normal lifestyle. But this time spent studying the scriptures and strictly following the code of discipline makes him a dignified human being."*

I follow the two young princes dressed in all their finery, hoisted high on the shoulders of their father and uncles towards the steps of Shwedagon Pagoda. Once on the pagoda platform they will walk

Burma/Myanmar Insight Guide, 2000

clockwise around the dome of the stupa on the red carpet laid over the well-trodden flagstones, family and friends proudly alongside. In smaller towns princes are still led to the pagoda on horseback, but in Yangon a procession of small vans carrying relatives and friends, each with a golden parasol held out the window, indicates the importance of this voyage to adulthood.

Earlier in the day I was at Ko Zaw's house, where his sons, twelve year old Thi Ha Zaw and nine year old Thu Ta Zaw, were prepared for the ceremony. Each boy was dressed in an embroidered satin longyi—white, with red, green and gold birds for Thuta, gold with green and red spirals for Thiha. Embroidered waistcoats, with elaborate epaulettes, a sequined medallion closing the front went over their white satin shirts, red embroidery around the neck. Matching cuffs were sewn onto the shirtsleeves, stiffened with cardboard to make them stand like small fins and, as a final touch, new white socks were pulled on.

It was then time for the make up. A friend, called in to help, positioned each boy by the window to catch the light, very still, eyes closed and lips puckered. She carefully created the face of a prince on each boy, smoothing face powder over their cheeks, applying gold and pink eye shadow, outlining their eyes with mascara, darkening the eyebrows and shaping shining red lips. A new experience for the boys, eager to look in the mirror and see a new self emerge. The last part of the princely costume was the headdress, a coiled silken band with an upright embroidered peak at the back and jewelled tassels hanging over the forehead. A flower garland was finally placed around the neck of each young prince. They were ready.

A little self conscious in their ceremonial robes, the boys joined their relatives and friends in the family room. Bowing before the family shrine, with coloured lanterns, fruit, flowers and swirling incense smoke, they asked for a blessing. Everyone was in their best clothes, Ko Zaw in a dark blue silk longyi and formal white jacket and Ma Khin Than Naing in a sky blue longyi and eingyi, flowers braided in her hair. The special blessing and merit-making when sons enter a monastery is of the utmost importance. On this day, the eve of their initiation as novice monks, their sons will be celebrated as princes, the costumes a symbol of the worldly goods that each boy must renounce.

Thiha and Thuta were carried down the steep staircase into the busy street and into the waiting vans. Friends followed, holding silver offering bowls, flinging their contents—tightly folded ten and twenty kyat notes—in handfuls to people in the street. Mostly waiting neighbours but also passers-by caught unawares who clustered to benefit from the windfall, bowing their thanks and giving their blessings.

The young princes settled in the first van with their father and uncles, the rest of us squeezed in the back of the others. At the South Gate of Shwedagon, we gathered to form a loose procession, Ma Khin Than Naing at the front with the women, carrying offering bowls of beautifully displayed coconut, bananas and orchids, the men walking behind with the princes held high on their shoulders and shaded by tall golden parasols.

And now we wait with other groups, each with their young princes, at the entrance to the lift that will take us up to the pagoda platform. A small prince has a tall hat hung with white flowers, and beautifully painted circles of thanakha surrounded by dots on each cheek. Behind him are two tiny princesses in pink satin, one no more than three, each with a fitted cap on her head covered in sequins and flowers, ready to have their ears pierced in the *Na-Tha* ceremony, an important ritual for young girls, involving offerings for their future health and happiness.

On the platform, we assemble for the walk around the great shining stupa, smaller shrines surrounding us on every side. It's busy as always, families walking together, monks stepping silently, eyes downcast. Nuns sit in small groups, their pink robes fluttering in the breeze, others offer lotus flowers and incense or pour water over the statues depicting the days of the week.

We begin our walk on the red carpet, many groups before us. Ko Zaw walks in front with his elder son who is tall and graceful, proud of his place in this ceremony. His younger brother walks further back beside his mother, shy and bemused by the attention and the importance of the occasion. Ko Zaw carries the black alms bowls which will be used by his sons and Ma Khin Than Naing carries their monks' robes, tied in a bundle.

We stop for a blessing at several of the shrines, the boys solemn, anxious to act correctly, glancing at their father for his guidance, a nod of his head or a gesture showing them what to do next. Today, with so many handsome young princes and their family followers, an air of excitement stirs the usually serene pagoda compound. Behind us, curving around the platform, is a sea of angled gold parasols rising above the heads of the crowd as other groups, some with as many as a dozen young princes, begin their own circuits of the pagoda. Younger children, carried by relatives or trotting alongside, are unnaturally silent and perfectly behaved, looking in awe at their older brothers, aware of their new status and of the importance of this occasion.

Our group stops for the final part of the ceremony under a frangipani tree casting a dappled shadow over the white marble flagstones. With the men standing behind holding the parasols, the boys kneel in front facing the towering pagoda, then bow their heads, foreheads touching the stone, once, twice, thrice. They do this several times in response to the quiet cadence of words spoken by the monk who sits with them. It's quiet and cool in the shade, and I feel at peace, sheltered by the solemnity of this ancient rite of passage and in the welcoming embrace of the family and friends who have invited me to share this special day with them.

It's time for the photos. Zarni captures the group posed in front of the shining golden stupa. At first, just the family, very solemn for some photos, then a little more relaxed and laughing, one with friends, another with just the boys and their father. Zarni, hunkers down to get the right angle and make sure the full height of the pagoda and its jewelled filigree hti are captured. "Come Joanna, we want you in our photos today too," calls Ko Zaw. Ma Khin smiles and holds her hand out to me.

We pose for more photos on the stairs of the Southern Entrance, the high roof arching over us, beams of sunlight catching the coloured glass of the hanging lamps and the silver, brass and sequined souvenirs on sale in booths either side. Murmurs of approval come from others walking up the stairs and from a group of fascinated tourists.

Thiha and Thuta are carried back to the vans, now laughing and relaxed, the seriousness of the occasion forgotten for the moment. The whole group jostles for seats, wriggling along to squeeze everyone in, chatting as we go on to another of Yangon's most sacred pagodas, the Botataung in Strand Road where more offerings will be made.

Once again, the young princes are carried into the pagoda, its mirrored mosaic walls reflecting the riot of colour as we pass through the rooms and out to a smaller stupa behind. Here, they resume their demeanour and kneel to bow their heads to the ground again before posing for more photos.

Finally, we reach to the Nyaung Tone Monastery, where they'll spend the night with their father, preparing for their initiation ceremony the following morning. As we step down from the vans, I notice Ko Zaw standing by the latticed porch of the monastery, talking into his phone, hands gesticulating wildly. His wife and Thiha stand beside him, but I do not see Thuta. Sandy, watching the exchange, tells me that Ko Zaw is talking to his brother who was driving Thuta back from Botataung.

"They've kidnapped him," she tells me.

"What?" I ask, shocked.

"Ko Zaw is negotiating with them now, but they are asking too much," she adds.

I am even more concerned. "But why? His brothers are so close to Ko Zaw, they look up to him as their senior brother. Why would they do something like this and on such a day?" I'm bewildered and anxious for the whole family.

Sandy turns to smile at me, chuckling, "Oh no, Joanna, don't worry, it's part of the ritual. The family is doing it to tease their big brother. Ko Zaw will donate this money to the Monastery once they bring Thuta back. They'll comfort him and say what a brave little prince he has been."

The negotiation continues until a sum is settled on. Moments later we hear the last van arriving. A tearful Thuta climbs down and runs to his mother, sobbing, mascara smudged, headdress askew, his *longyi* barely held up by the leather belt. He hasn't understood and is confused by the strange abduction and by the fact that everyone finds it amusing. Ko Zaw takes him aside, and, squatting down, wipes the tears from his son's face, explaining and reassuring him that he is safe now, praising his courage.

Thuta calms down and soon he's laughing with his big brother and friends, standing taller, proud of having weathered another challenge in life, one not even his big brother has had to face.

The sun is setting and it's time for the young princes to relax and prepare for the morrow when they will become novice monks. The family will eat together at the monastery so I join the rest of my team at a nearby restaurant where we retell stories of the day and some recount memories of their own *Shin-pyu* ceremonies.

On Sunday I rise at dawn to go with Kyaw Kyaw to the monastery, the morning air still fresh with the smell of flowers. Apart from the family, we're the first to arrive. I am offered a chair under the trees to watch the preparations.

A monk brings two chairs into the courtyard and places them a little apart, facing me. Minutes later Thiha and Thuta emerge from the monastery, each in a plain cotton *longyi*, their hair dripping, still ruffled and white with shampoo suds, ready to have their heads shaved. Thiha is first, as the elder son. He sits, his parents and grandmother standing either side holding a white sheet in which his hair will be collected. The monk moves behind Thiha and slowly begins to shave his head with long even strokes. As the black locks fall into the sheet, some stick to Thiha's damp cheeks and he flicks them nonchalantly away with his hand, a little smile playing around his lips. He is calm and relaxed, completely prepared for this ritual. The monk splays his left hand firmly over the top of Thiha's head holding it steady until he completes his task.

Now it's Thuta's turn and a younger, bespectacled monk stands behind his chair waiting while Ko Zaw takes two corners of the sheet and hands the opposite corners to his wife, pretty and plump in pink, and his mother, slim and elegant in a flowered longyi, a shawl over her shoulders to keep out the morning chill. Thuta's feet don't quite reach the ground and he sits, shoulders hunched, as though the head-shaving might hurt. With the first stroke of the razor, he closes his eyes and scrunches up his nose, his swinging feet doing an anxious little dance of their own. Ko Zaw lays a reassuring hand on his young son's shoulder. The monk very carefully works his way across Thuta's scalp and soon all his hair is in the sheet.

Kyaw Kyaw tells me they will bury the boys' hair at the base of a tree in the compound as a symbolic end to their childhood.

Three other boys also become novices this day and once all are shorn and washed they enter the main room of the monastery and squat in a line before the head monk. He is seated on an ornate carved wooden chair, an offering bowl of coconut and bananas on a low table in front of him. Each boy holds his new monk's robes, tied with the sash. One by one, their heads bowed, they hold them out to the monk who places them in his lap. He talks quietly to them for a moment, then each, in turn, are taught how to wear their robes—the russet *longyi* first, replacing their cotton one, then the sash, then another length of cloth hanging over the left shoulder. They receive their black alms bowls, on which a fan and other necessary items are piled and return to their places in front of the monk.

Sitting behind with the family, I enjoy the quiet ritual and the gentle way the monk intones the recitation of their duties, the boys responding at the appropriate moments. Finally, the boys are given the names they will use in the monastery and again should they return for another period as a monk later in life. Thiha's given name is Shin Thu Zar Ta and Thuta will be known as Shin Thu Seik Ta. The novices bow one more time before the head monk then turn to face their parents who bow to them in recognition of their new status.

The first part of the ceremony over, the boys go outside, talking between themselves and with the other monks. They already seem older and more confident, the shaven heads, robes and dark red velvet and leather slippers adding years to their real ages. Others are arriving now, friends and relatives to share the honour of the family and to enjoy their hospitality.

In the lower courtyard the cooks are busy. Sturdy iron trivets hold wide black woks over wood fires. My guard Malay is poised over one of the woks, stirring the steaming contents with a long wooden paddle, glancing across at two others waiting for his attention. Alongside, sit large rattan baskets lined with banana leaves to keep the cooked rice warm.

We walk from the main compound, down a flowered path to the sacred hall of the monastery and enter quietly from the back. Ten monks sit, softly chanting, reading from ancient texts. It's cool in the high ceilinged hall, the polished teakwood floor reflecting the rust red monks' robes. Buddha statues, illuminated texts and photos are hung along the walls. One by one the guests shuffle in on their knees, prostrate themselves in front of the Buddha, then sit quietly for a time, each lost in their own thoughts and prayers.

Everyone will make an offering to the ten monks taking part of this ceremony and to each of the five novices. Outside the hall we line up along the path, holding our offerings—towels, soap, toothpaste, slippers, dried noodles, envelopes with money—ready to donate when the monks leave the hall. Ko Zaw, with his mother on his arm, takes his place at the head of the line. His mother seems frail in the bright sunlight, though at eighty years, she still stands straight and elegant, the sun glinting off the jade buttons of her *eingyi*.

I wonder how the monks will manage to carry the donations, but nothing is left to chance on this day, each monk receiving a black plastic bin-liner as he descends the steps. Some shake their head and make a wide sling from their shoulder robes for our donations, while others take the bags, which fill impressively, as they walk down the line. The novices come last, following in the footsteps of the older monks, each with their plastic bag to be filled.

Back in the main hall, the novices once again kneel facing the abbot, now joined by four monks, two either side of him. We sit behind, on the assorted carpets covering the worn green linoleum. The head monk begins a solemn chant, the others joining in. The novices respond with learned phrases, then bow, touching their foreheads to the floor three times. In the long monologue that follows, I understand that the novices are being told about the importance of this time they will spend as monks, how they must behave through the next days and of the daily tasks they must perform in the service of the monastery and the wider community in this district of Yangon.

Kyaw Kyaw leans over to explain the message of the talk is the importance of giving with your whole heart and that to give without full feeling and compassion means nothing.

The speech continues and my mind and eyes begin to wander. Dominating the room is a shrine with a life-size Buddha, draped with a gold cloth surrounded by flashing red lights. Bookcases hold old blue-bound tomes, gold lettering on their spines while wooden walls are covered with photos of monks, pagodas, and landscapes. Two fridges stand against the wall, one donated on the nineteenth of April 2002, the other much older, alongside a glass fronted case holding stacked blankets, reminding me of the importance of monasteries in serving their communities as havens of learning or of refuge. Electric wires connecting radio, microphone, speakers, lights and fans are strung about and loop down into view, scary looking connections and plugs in evidence, many held together with ageing tape. I love this mix of tradition, donation, and religion, practical and impractical, ancient and modern, found in most monasteries, the length and breadth of the country

The novices are a little restless as their instruction continues. I smile when Ko Zaw, sitting behind Thuta, discretely pushes an upturned offering bowl under his son's backside, offering relief for his cramped legs. Delicious smells of cooking waft in from outside, making my stomach growl and I notice the stacked round tables waiting to be set with food. It's nearly ten and our day started well before six. Some guests talk quietly and there's a continuous gentle fluttering of the plastic fans, printed with the name of the monastery, the novices and the date of this ceremony.

The monks chant again, and the novices respond bowing three more times. Another monk, standing to one side, completes the ceremony with the 'money rain,' throwing a shower of tightly folded kyat notes from a silver offering bowl into the crowd of guests. Everyone laughs, grabbing for the notes which bring good luck.

As we stretch our legs outside and congratulate the parents, inside, low tables are set with a large bowl of rice and smaller dishes of vegetables, grilled pork, steamed chicken, fish soup and salad.

Ma Khin leads me inside to join the others of our team, sitting cross-legged around a table to share the meal. As I'm served a little from each plate, I notice the smallest novice, young Thuta, showing off his bag of donations to his young cousins, counting the number of Kyat he's managed to pluck from the 'money rain'. Ko Zaw also notices and goes to his son, explaining quietly but firmly that he must be discreet, shooing him outside to eat with the other novices. A monk he may be, but he is still very much a little boy.

Afterwards, I proudly have a photo taken with the whole family and another with just the two novices. I stand a little behind them, respectful of their new status, aware I must not touch them. It feels strange not to put an arm around their shoulders as I have done so many times these past years at shared movie nights and dinners, weekend trips and fun outings. I'm happy to have been a part of their childhood but realise that now I am looking ahead, seeing them as the young men they will become.

Chapter Twenty-Eight
The Wicker Basket

The decision is taken, the date set. My mission in Myanmar ends in December, after nearly four years in this fascinating, contradictory, magical land. This decision also marks the end of my twenty-eight year career with the International Red Cross. I have very mixed feelings about leaving. On one hand, I am ready to retire while still young and energetic enough to try my hand at something new, relaxing a little and travelling for pleasure. On the other hand, I know I'm going to miss being part of this great humanitarian organization, and most particularly, I'll miss my colleagues and friends who have shared this journey with me.

Despite this radical change approaching quickly, I find it difficult to project myself into my new life and ponder on the pattern my days will take across the border in Chiang Mai with my partners in La Luna Gallery, Lasse and Sommai.

There's plenty to occupy me during the last weeks as I make sure the handover to my successor is smooth, inconveniencing neither the delegation nor the Myanmar Red Cross. We systematically check over projects, budgets, accounts, review files and make notes regarding unfinished business or outstanding issues. My replacement has already been appointed. I am pleased there won't be a gap on my departure, with a new colleague ready to take over, bringing energy and original ideas to the job.

Each day, I take a little time to work on my Final Report, attempting to summarise the achievements and progress made over the past four years, outlining key areas requiring particular attention from my replacement and her team, although, to be honest, I still struggle to think of the staff as her team, rather than my team. I retrieve and read through the original Job Description and 'Terms of Reference' for the Head of Delegation given to me in 2002 before I embarked on this voyage of discovery through Myanmar, as a 'reality check' on what I have achieved professionally.

At home, I pack the things I will take with me and fill boxes with clothes, books and belongings to share with my staff and their families. Most of the furniture and appliances belong to the delegation so the staff will pack them after I leave, ready for the incoming delegate.

My cats will be migrating to Thailand with me. They need several more inoculations, a 'place of origin' document and a health 'passport'. I can't find a carrying case in the pet shops around town but Ko Thet Oo has a friend who can make me a wicker basket. One evening I sketch what I want, like a large picnic basket, but with two separate lidded compartments, big enough for each cat to stand upright or lie full length. The floor should be solid, the lid loosely woven so the cats can see out and I can check on them. The handle must be strong and well balanced so the basket can be carried easily even if they move about. I'm told it will be ready in a few days.

In the last weeks nostalgia takes hold as the finality of the decision sinks in—I am aware that each action, conversation or visit is the last I'll make in this job and in this country. I'll miss so much. The support and friendship my staff and the MRCS team have given me, the field trips and long rides on rough roads to discover out-of-the-way places, working with local volunteers. My neighbourhood, the weekend walks and the friends in my street. My house, its calm atmosphere, early morning breakfast on the lawn and the evening sun slanting in across the living room as I relax after a day's work.

But the sadness is tempered by good memories and laughter, stories and anecdotes over coffee or lunch as we recall the more fun and crazy things which have happened over these last four years. The weekend tourist trips, the movie and karaoke nights, the staff retreats by the beach and parties to celebrate birthdays or special events or just because it seemed like a good idea.

A few weeks before I leave, the ruling party formally announces that a new capital city has been built in central Myanmar, in a place called Nay Pyi Taw. There have been rumours circulating about a new city with palatial buildings, wide boulevards, underground passages, blocks of apartments but little real information is available and questions abound. According to a friend, the area is known as the 'Snake Capital of the world'. Everyone is anxious to learn more, but most importantly, to know who will have to move there and when.

It precipitates an interesting discussion in the office, and that evening as Ko Zaw is driving me home we continue to speculate on what it will mean for the future of Yangon. Suddenly the traffic slows to walking pace. There is a problem ahead. Ko Zaw deftly manoeuvres the car into the other lane and we come alongside a large army lorry, which has broken down, being slowly pushed forwards by some twenty soldiers, all straining to make headway on the slight incline. As we pass, Ko Zaw remarks dryly, "It might take them a while get to Nay Pyi Taw", and we laugh together.

My team organise a farewell dinner, inviting our MRCS colleagues to join us. I am overwhelmed by the occasion, the speeches and presents I am offered, but manage to make an adequate thank you speech, returning compliments, assuring everyone that their welcome and acceptance of our working together on shared projects and, yes, even my mistakes over these past years have made my work here not only much easier but also truly enjoyable.

We plan a day out together with my staff and their families, a trip to a nature park and a picnic. After lunch, while the adults are dozing or chatting idly, the children burn off energy climbing trees, swinging on ropes and playing a fast and furious game of tag. It's a lovely way to spend the final weekend with my friends.

On the morning of my last day in the office, the few documents I want to take with me packed, I reread my Final Report, making a few small changes.

I leave this mission, my last for the International Federation, with very mixed feelings. It has been one of the most challenging, interesting, frustrating, and fascinating jobs I have undertaken in my 28 years with the Red Cross Movement. I believe that each and every one of my skills, learnt over the course of my professional life, has been truly tried and tested. I trust I have been able to contribute to the development and strengthening of Myanmar Red Cross, so they are better prepared to provide efficient health and care programmes across the country, provide emergency response when required, and better equipped to find funding for their development and programmes through fund-raising and income generation, and through fostering strong and supportive partnerships.

My colleagues and friends from the delegation, and from the MRCS, and the beauty and traditions of the people and country of Myanmar, will remain with me forever. As a brief final reflection, I would like to believe my contribution will have a lasting effect—that I have positively influenced a number of staff and volunteers who will now continue their important work with an added gleam of excitement in their eye, the anticipation of a fledgling idea taking shape in their mind and a new spark of motivation for finding better ways to assist the most vulnerable of their country and to be valued members of the International Red Cross and Red Crescent Movement.

I hesitate while reading the last paragraphs wondering which, if any, aspects of my work or leadership might be considered of real and lasting value. I can only hope so. Time will tell, I think; then, taking a deep breath, I send the report winging its way to Bangkok and Geneva.

Back at home the wicker basket has been delivered. My cats are circling and sniffing suspiciously, aware it has something to do with them in the overall upheaval. I open both lids so they can climb in and explore it, hoping they won't be too afraid tomorrow, housed within it for several hours.

As I finish my packing, it strikes me that what I am taking in the wicker basket is the most precious living memory of Myanmar I can have. Ma Zaw and Musi will be a constant reminder of my friends and the life I lived here. I think over the other items I have put in my 'basket of memorabilia', checking they are packed safely—my favourite blue silk *longyi* with the Kachin pattern, painted metal figures of Inle boatmen, a weaver and a line of monks, given by my staff over several birthdays, photo books, a short nub of wood and a miniature Thanakha grinding stone, tamarind candies, and gifts from my staff and colleagues, a ruby ring, a set of matched gemstones, paintings, carvings, and lacquer boxes.

My last task of the evening is to download all my photos, to take them with me. But I can't access my photo files on the computer nor open the hard-drive. I panic! It's ten pm but I call Zarni. He arrives with a friend and they crouch over the computer with me hovering nervously. I cannot countenance losing the thousands of photos taken over these past years.

He tells me that both computer and my external hard drive have crashed, in spite of rigorous surge controls, but assures me they'll do everything they can to retrieve my photos. The computer is packed into Zarni's van; I wave them off, asking them to call first thing in the morning.

I am up early, waiting for the phone call. Zarni tells me they worked all night, but managed to retrieve about eighty per cent of my photo files, eighteen DVDs in all. I thank Zarni profusely for his incredible skills, then again when he comes to deliver them. I am so relieved, at last ready to go.

But another crisis looms. The cats must be put into their basket for a trip to the vet for a sedative and then on to the airport. Musi comes when I call and, cuddling her, I pop her into the basket. But Ma Zaw is another story all together. Standoffish since the kittens were born, wary of everyone, she runs off. First just me, then Ko Zaw and Malay, and finally Maung Taut and Ko Htet Oo join in the chase as she leads us in a merry dance around the house, up and down stairs, then outside again. We are fast, but she is faster. Finally, we manage to throw a towel over her and place her, clawing and screeching, into a sack.

My bags stowed, I bid farewell to Malay and Maung Taut, setting off with Ko Zaw and Ko Thet Oo for the vet. Again, Musi is no problem. The vet injects the sedative, then, stroking her, puts her gently back into the basket. Ma Zaw is still screeching and trying to claw her way out of the sack. Not wanting to be ripped to shreds, the vet injects her through the sacking, giving her a double dose. There's not enough time for the sedative to act, so, working as a team, we hold the mouth of the sack over the basket, drop her in and quickly latch the lid then head for the airport, an indignant Ma Zaw complaining loudly and furiously. Finally the sedative begins to take effect and we all sigh with relief.

Ko Zaw comes into the airport to carry my bags and the wicker basket, which he places on the conveyer belt to send through the x-ray machine. On explaining to the security guard it contains my cats, we're asked to open the basket. We chorus, alarmed but laughing, "No way. You definitely don't want these cats loose in the airport." Fortunately, he just shrugs and, taking the basket, we place it in the capable hands of the airport staff. I will not see them again until I arrive in Chiang Mai.

I turn to say good-bye to Ko Zaw, for his patience and kindness not just today, but over all the years he has been my driver, advisor and friend. His usually warm face is solemn. I am close to tears, but we agree, with forced smiles, not to say good-bye, just farewell for now.

As the plane lifts off, circling over Yangon before heading east, I gaze down on the shining stupas, the clustered houses, the circular wheel of the infamous Insein prison, the tree-lined streets bustling with vehicles, the parks and lakes, golden light glinting off the calm water in the late afternoon. Memories whirl through my mind, most good, a few troubling. A wave of emotion washes over me, reminiscences, a degree of pride in the work accomplished, the sadness of saying goodbye to friends, the real love and concern for the country I am leaving.

But all the way to Chiang Mai, I feel, growing stronger and stronger within me, the conviction that my Myanmar story is not yet fully played out, and I know I will soon be returning to the Golden Land.

Epilogue

On the morning of 14 August 2013, I received an email from a colleague in the Federation's Bangkok office that, after a few lines of greeting and chat, read: "Would you be interested by a short term assignment in one of your previous posts, Myanmar, to support Myanmar Red Cross Society. With the opening of Myanmar, as well as in the complex and sensitive Rohingya situation, seventeen National Societies are queuing to give support, knocking at MRCS door. It is far too much for MRCS capacity to handle so many donors with so many different models of cooperation, so to avoid chaos, we would need a senior, experienced star who could help MRCS and the Federation Delegation to settle proper mechanisms.

I thought you could be the right person; you know the country and culture, you have the seniority and the right personality to handle all of these players. Can you give me a call asap and I can brief you more."

It just so happened that I was on my way to Luang Prabang in neighbouring Laos that day with a freshly printed copy of my manuscript, my intention being to spend a few quiet days in a friend's hotel, proof-reading the latest version of my book. The last sentence leapt into my mind: "But all the way to Chiang Mai, I feel growing stronger and stronger within me, the conviction that my Myanmar story is not yet fully played out and I know I will soon be returning to the Golden Land."

Thus, I hardly needed to think before picking up my phone and calling Bangkok. A week later I received a full briefing and on 9 September I was back in Yangon, with a three-month contract.

Since leaving Myanmar at the end of 2005, I have visited many times closely following the large and small changes related by friends and colleagues and watching the international news coverage of a number of momentous events. When visiting, I always spend time at the Shwedagon Pagoda, savouring its beauty, its special atmosphere and unique symbolism for the people of Myanmar. I go back to talk to my neighbours, walk through the city's markets and alleys, observing life, and chatting with people.

Spending time with my team and their families, we catch up on the latest events and happenings. It's a pleasure to hear of their professional advancements, their family stories and see the children grow, to follow their education and career choices.

I was in Yangon in August 2007, as a guest speaker on the 'Road to Mandalay', when the sudden decision of the ruling party to remove fuel subsidies causes the price of diesel and petrol to rise by more than 60% and that of natural gas to increase fivefold, in less than a week. That proverbial 'straw that breaks the camel's back', pushed the people to even more extreme levels of poverty and prompted the 'saffron revolution', the uprising led by the monks and crushed by the military within the following few weeks.

I watched the news as Cyclone Nargis struck the Ayeyarwady Delta in May 2008, causing catastrophic, widespread destruction and a death toll of more than one hundred and forty thousand. I offered my services to the International Federation's Bangkok Delegation, instrumental in getting aid workers and supplies into Myanmar, as support for the Red Cross operation being undertaken by the Delegation and the Myanmar Red Cross. Working with them for a month in Bangkok, I coaxed visas out of the Myanmar Embassy and briefed relief and health delegates, from the Red Cross and other international aid organisations, who spent weeks in Bangkok waiting for travel approval. I helped prepare daily 'Situation Reports' for the international community, using facts, figures, and stories sent to us from colleagues in Yangon and their links to the Red Cross workers in the affected region.

With the rest of the world, I have followed the encouraging and well-documented political and social changes in Myanmar over the past few years: the global headlines of November 2010 proclaiming that democracy activist Daw Aung San Suu Kyi was free, and less than two years later, in July 2012 further news stories on her election, as one of forty-three members of the National League for Democracy (NLD) in

Myanmar's parliament. Most recently, we applaud the landslide election victory of the NLD in November 2015, and the handover of power in April 2016 with U Htin Kyaw sworn in as President and Daw Aung San Suu Kyi holding several cabinet positions including Foreign Affairs.

Further news stories that the World Bank was stepping up support for reforms in Myanmar and opening a new country office with up to eighty-five million US dollars in grants to benefit men, women, and children, through community driven development programmes; that Myanmar was abolishing media censorship, and news of the highly publicized visits by both the US President, the Secretary of State, and statesmen as well as women of other countries, and of international commercial companies returning to a market closed by sanctions for years, of new job and educational opportunities, and of a booming tourist sector.

With the new assignment in 2013, back in Yangon for three months, and several more recent visits, I have the opportunity to observe the effect of the changes. Some are evident from the outset: traffic congestion, a result of some 350,000 new (or second hand from Japan) cars on the roads in a single year, and unfortunately most with left hand drive systems, not adapted to the conditions in Myanmar; jeans and short skirts replacing traditional *longyis* for both men and women; dyed and fantastically coiffed hairstyles, previously only allowed during the *Thingyan* festival; mobile phones in the hands of many rather than as prized, expensive accessories of just a few; newsstands overflowing with journals and magazines; photos of Aung San Suu Kyi everywhere—on t-shirts and posters, billboards and souvenir items; old buildings covered in scaffolding and green mesh getting a makeover; and new hotels, many of international brands, springing up in and around the city.

Yangon is jam-packed with visitors, hotel prices have trebled, or quadrupled and rented accommodation is hard to find. Serious looking businessmen, from all over Asia and further afield, deep in conversation, broker deals in hotel lobbies and restaurants. Tourists wander in droves around town, streaming from buses at tourist venues and blocking hotel entrances with impressive camera equipment and guidebooks in different languages. Development and aid workers hunch over lunches at smart restaurants to discuss their objectives and planning, and the difficulties of getting permits to travel in parts of the country they would like to target with their projects and programmes. News filters in of the increasingly violent ethnic and religious clashes particularly in the Rakhine and Kachin States, of demonstrations in Mandalay and other cities, of food shortages and horrendous conditions in jade and ruby mines, of the ineptness of government departments and the poor quality of basic education.

Over dinners with my Myanmar friends, we discuss what all this means and how they see the future for themselves and for their country. With Myanmar opening up to the outside world, new opportunities are on offer for the Myanmar people, but with these opportunities come huge challenges.

Will the revamp of the government's administrative, legal, and practical systems, and the infrastructure proceed with the speed required? How will the returning exiles be reintegrated into the country and how will the increasingly controversial and violent land issues and the ethnic and religious strife be settled? Will the system be able to keep up with the avalanche of foreign investors? Will these entrepreneurs offer some support to the country and her people? Or are they only anxious to line their own pockets and expand their own businesses, with just a passing nod to nurturing social change? Will those involved in the tourism industry accept they have a duty to protect the environment and the historical treasures of the country, or will they only rush to build more hotels, purchase bigger and better buses, and fleece the tourists for immediate profits?

I'd like to think I know what the people of Myanmar are capable of, and have seen how through all the previous, difficult years they have continued to work, read, learn, and imagine a better future. Aware that in Asia, change, community rebirth and rebuilding, move at an impressive speed, I am confident that Myanmar is capable of moving steadily forward, capitalizing on these new opportunities and challenges. I sincerely hope, that over time, the existing and re-emerging ethnic tensions can be resolved, that more equity can be forthcoming between the cities and the rural areas, and that opportunities for education and employment will be open to all the peoples of Myanmar.

And I do believe one thing: within the span of a few short years, perhaps a decade or three, this magnificent country, with its strong traditions and values, and with a new commitment to advancement, will once again become a country to be reckoned with, in Asia and in the world.

Anthropologist, teacher, photographer, writer, art gallery owner/director, **Joanna MacLean** taught in her native country New Zealand, the Solomon Islands, and England before beginning her International Red Cross career that spanned 28 years. From 2002-2005, she was Head of the International Federation of Red Cross and Red Crescent Societies' Delegation in Myanmar, and she also worked in Africa and the Caribbean/Central America. In the Geneva HQ, she held a number of Department Head posts and was a leading figure in the Movement's global events and campaigns over a period of 15 years from 1988-2002. As an independent consultant, she continues to do some training and short-term assignments for the International Red Cross, including another three-month stint in Myanmar from September to December 2013.

In 2004 she co-founded La Luna Gallery in Chiang Mai, Thailand specialising in S.E. Asian contemporary art, focussing on art from Malaysia, Myanmar, Thailand and Vietnam and since 2011 she has been joint owner/director of Colour Factory, operating shops in and around Chiang Mai. One of their main products are the painted elephants of the internationally known 'Elephant Parade'. Her company also organises events to bring attention to, and raise funds for a number of causes, including elephant welfare and pediatric heart surgery for disadvantaged children.

In her capacity as Consultant to the 'Naka Foundation,' which is dedicated to the conservation and well-being of elephants, Joanna lectures to school and university students and to service groups in Thailand on issues related to elephant conservation. She is a founding member of the ASEAN Captive Elephant Working Group (ACEWG), a group of regional elephant specialists, veterinarians, researchers and conservationists who are working to create more awareness about both the problems and the possible solutions, as well as provide recommendations to improve healthcare and management practices for captive elephants in the ASEAN countries.

She is also an Advisor to 'Skills for Life,' a foundation which provides vocational training and job opportunities for underprivileged youth from Hill Tribes around Chiang Mai.

She continues to enjoy traveling and photography in her spare time and in combining these interests and her experience has worked as a lecturer aboard cruise ships in Asia and the Americas.

Joanna has been living in Chiang Mai, Thailand since 2006.

Joanna MacLean

www.ingramcontent.com/pod-product-compliance
Lightning Source LLC
Chambersburg PA
CBHW031409290426
44110CB00011B/322